- Why did the Warren Commission ignore warnings that Russian agents might use Lee Harvey Oswald's identification papers for their own purposes?

- Why did Oswald give two different biographies to two different FBI agents?

- Why were no notes taken when Oswald was interrogated after the assassination?

These and other significant questions are answered by renowned British legal investigator Michael Eddowes in THE OSWALD FILE, a highly documented look into the crime of the century that presents new and startling information that cannot be ignored.

THE OSWALD FILE

by
Michael
Eddowes

ace books
A Division of Charter Communications Inc.
A GROSSET & DUNLAP COMPANY
360 Park Avenue South
New York, New York 10010

An Ace Book, by arrangement with
Clarkson N. Potter, Inc.

First Ace Printing: November 1978

Published simultaneously in Canada

Printed in U.S.A.

*For the American people
and seekers of the truth everywhere.*

Contents

Prologue   ix
Introduction   1

Part I: THE ASSASSINATION

1. The Marine   15
2. Birth of a New Oswald: Russia   20
3. The Impostor Enters the United States   35
4. Espionage: Dallas   48
5. Setting up the Cuban Connection   56
6. Mexico City: Prelude to the Assassination   63
7. Fixing the Assassination Site   71
8. The Assassination   87

Part II: THE AFTERMATH

 9. Dallas Police Headquarters   99
10. The Elusive 'Oswald'   116
11. Jack Ruby   120
12. The Autopsy   132
13. Fingerprints   137
14. The Authorities   146
15. George De Mohrenschildt   172
Epilogue   187

Part III: APPENDICES

A. The Historic Diary 191
B. Time Line: Oswald and 'Oswald' 206
C. Soviets Involved in the Assassination 209
D. An Analysis of Heights 211
E. The Warren Commission on Mexico City 223
F. Maps of Dallas 230

Index 234

Prologue

The reader will find, in the following pages, a story that may seem hard to believe—yet fourteen years' study of the evidence has convinced me of its truth.

The event that marked the beginning of my long investigation occurred in London on the afternoon of 24 October 1962 when the world, in deadly fear, was awaiting the outcome of the Soviet-American naval confrontation over the Cuban Missile Crisis. At 4:05 P.M. on this day, I met Captain Yevgenni Ivanov in London in the company of a 50-year-old osteopath, Stephen Ward, who numbered among his patients Winston Churchill, members of the government, the American ambassador, newspaper editors, actresses and models, as well as other professional people. At this time, I was also one of Ward's patients.

Ivanov and Ward were seated in an empty back room of a small restaurant near Ward's consulting rooms with unfinished cups of coffee before them, deep in conversation. Ward invited me to join them, introducing Ivanov as a naval attaché at the Soviet Embassy. I was surprised to find a naval attaché some two miles from his embassy during a naval crisis. The two were agitated and angry, and I noted that Ward, very much an individualist, appeared to be dominated by the younger man.

The conversation naturally centered on the naval confrontation which was expected to occur within the hour. I asked Ivanov the burning question of that day—what would happen when the Soviet merchant ships bound for Cuba with their cargoes of nuclear missiles were intercepted by the American warships? He replied, with some anger, "We will blockade Norway (the site of some American missiles) or we will drop a bomb in the sea a mile off New York (creating a tidal wave) or we will destroy England (the site of more American missiles) in seven minutes.''

Unaware of Ivanov's real status as a clandestine intelligence officer and the son-in-law of the Chairman of the Supreme Court in Moscow allegedly with direct access to Khrushchev, I attached little significance to his extravagant prophecies or to his friendship with Ward.

Eight months later, the British Minister of War, John Profumo, resigned over what came to be called the Profumo Affair and Ward was implicated. The government first considered prosecuting Ward under the Official Secrets Act but later opted for a morals charge, accusing him of being the procurer in the scandal and living on immoral earnings. It was then that I attached more significance to Ivanov's activities; I suspected that he *and* Ward had precipitated the character assassination of the minister. Within a short time Ward had committed suicide, Ivanov had left England, another person involved, Perec Rackmann *alias* Peter Rackman, had suddenly died, and the young woman in the group was imprisoned for perjury.

Around the same time, coming to New York to write a series of newspaper articles on the Profumo affair, I was approached by the FBI to help them identify individuals involved in a similar attempt at political sabotage in the United States. It was then that I discovered the connection between the London and New York groups, and recognized that it was Ivanov who had been instrumental in attempting to organize political sabotage against the newly elected President, John F. Kennedy.

Five months later, President Kennedy was not just the victim of attempted character assassination—he had been murdered.

Commencing in the fall of 1964, when the official report on the assassination, known as the *Warren Report*, and its 26 supporting volumes of Testimony and Exhibits became available, my several assistants and I began to study them. Since then, I have traveled tens of thousands of miles: in particular, I visited Dallas and on a second occasion remained there for a year. I have discussed the matter with many people who I believed could assist me, including Dallas Police Chief Curry and the mother of Lee Harvey Oswald. The basis of my study, however, has always been the contents of the volumes of Testimony and Exhibits, from which my assistants and I were able finally to assemble evidence disclosing the truth.

THE OSWALD FILE

Introduction

In this book, I will discuss the assassination of President John Fitzgerald Kennedy, in Dallas, Texas, on 22 November 1963 by a young man who had entered the country from the Soviet Union in 1962 in the name of Lee Harvey Oswald.

After being captured that day, the assassin was in turn murdered two days later in the basement of Dallas police headquarters by a 52-year-old underworld figure, Jack Ruby, who was immediately arrested and, after being convicted of murder with malice, died in prison in early 1967.

On 29 November 1963, the new President, Lyndon Baines Johnson, appointed a Commission to investigate the assassination and related matters, and to report to him. The report of the Commission, known as the Warren Report, was published in September 1964, stated that the assassin was ex-Marine Lee Harvey Oswald, who had acted alone, and that there was no available evidence of domestic or international conspiracy—conclusions that have never been free of question.

I will endeavor to prove beyond reasonable doubt:

(1) that after Kennedy was elected and subsequently opposed the aggressive moves of Soviet Premier Nikita Sergeevich Khrushchev, the latter ordered his assassination through the Soviet Secret Police (MVD);

(2) that the real ex-Marine Lee Harvey Oswald never returned to the United States but disappeared shortly after his arrival in the Soviet Union in 1959;

(1)

(3) that the man who assassinated Kennedy in 1963 was a member of Department 13, the sabotage and assassination squad of the Soviet State Security Service (KGB), and in 1962 had entered the United States in the guise of Oswald;

(4) that the Soviets intended that after the assassination the imposture would be discovered by the United States authorities;

(5) that a confusing chain of evidence had been created placing responsibility for the assassination on the Cubans or the Soviets, in that order;

(6) that because the assassin failed to escape, before 9:00 P.M. on the day of the assassination, the authorities suspected that the assassin was a Soviet impostor and a member of Department 13;

(7) that on the day after the assassination their suspicions were confirmed;

(8) that to avoid the possibility of World War III, it was at once decided that all evidence of imposture and Soviet conspiracy be withheld from the world;

(9) that the assassination was an act of war, and that the Warren Report inevitably was a declaration of peace and incidentally an admission of defeat.

The world had been riding high under the leadership of the young Kennedys, and the assassination demoralized not only the United States but the entire free world, which saw in John Fitzgerald Kennedy their only hope of peace. In my view, the assassination was to cause future Presidents to be apprehensive in opposing the Soviets, and was to disunify the free world, thus prolonging the Vietnam hostilities and enfeebling the United Nations.

It is appropriate at this juncture to state my view that during the postassassination investigation by the authorities and the creation of the official Warren Report, no individual, from President Johnson to the most junior policeman in Dallas, was guilty of malfeasance; all were acting in what were thought to be the best interests of the United States.

HISTORICAL CONTEXT

It is not the purpose of this book to dwell on motive; it may, however, be helpful to look at events in the Soviet Union and Cuba prior to the assassination.

On the death of Iosip Stalin in 1953, Georgi Malenkov became Soviet Premier and First Secretary of the Communist Party; within a week Nikita Khrushchev had taken over the position of First Secretary. The oligarchy included Molotov, Bulganin, Kaganovich, and Shepilov. In order to ensure their own physical survival, their first move was to arrest Lavrenti Beria who, next to Stalin, was possibly the most powerful man in the country as head of the gigantic State Security Service that had implemented Stalin's policy of terror and mass murder. Beria was charged as a criminal conspirator and as an agent of British intelligence, and was executed. His name was eliminated from history books and encyclopedias; he became a nonperson.

In 1955, Bulganin succeeded Malenkov as Soviet Premier, and in 1956, Khrushchev denounced Stalin, whose body was removed from its position beside the body of Lenin in a joint and public tomb, and allegedly cremated.

Moving to consolidate his power in 1957, Khrushchev deposed Molotov, Kaganovich, and Shepilov, all of whom, in one way or another, were his rivals. He also ordered the denunciation of Marshal Zhukov, the hero of World War II, the military, and the Soviet people. Zhukov was removed from his post as Minister of Defense after having been accused on Khrushchev's orders of creating a "personality cult" (an independent position that might be in opposition to Khrushchev's military strategy).

In 1958, Bulganin was toppled from power and Khrushchev became Soviet Premier, a position he was to hold for the next six years until the autumn of 1964. As undisputed leader of the Soviet people, Khrushchev was now commander in chief of the Soviet armed forces; in control of the KGB, the MVD, and Military Intelligence (GRU). He told the world that the "Stalin terror" was over and presented the Soviet Union as a modern state advancing under his policy of "peaceful coexistence." But Khrushchev's secret purpose involved a more colossal gamble than anything that the mighty Stalin had attempted. It should not, perhaps, be forgotten that Khrushchev, referring to the North American people, once said, "I will bury you."

In January 1959, Fidel Castro had overthrown the Batista dictatorship in Cuba and, by mid-1959, had accepted Khrushchev's embrace, ostensibly accepting Soviet economic and military support.

At about the time of the "Kitchen Debate" of July 1959 in Moscow between Khrushchev and Vice President Richard Nixon, the Soviet Secret Police (MVD) prepared a plan to assassinate Nixon if he was elected President in November 1960, the plan being approved by Khrushchev. This information was supplied to the CIA by Major Anatoli Golitsin of the KGB, who defected to the United States in February 1962. This information, reported in the Washington press, was only recently disclosed by the CIA.

In November 1960, Kennedy defeated Richard Nixon in a close contest for the Presidency and was inaugurated on 20 January 1961. The following June, Kennedy met Khrushchev in Vienna, where the latter reiterated Soviet demands over Berlin, giving Kennedy an ultimatum, hoping that the young President might be hectored into a posture of appeasement by threats of global war so early in his Presidency. Kennedy felt that Khrushchev could not be persuaded that the West would fight to support its rights in West Berlin.

In July 1961, Kennedy addressed the nation:

Seven weeks ago tonight I returned from Europe to report on my meeting with Premier Khrushchev and the others. His grim warnings about the future of the world, his aide-mémoire on Berlin, his subsequent speeches and threats which he and his agents have launched, and the increase in the Soviet military budget that he has announced have all prompted a series of decisions . . . We do not want to fight, but we have fought before. And others in earlier times have made the same dangerous mistake of assuming that the West was too selfish and too soft and too divided to resist invasions of freedom in other lands . . . Soviet strategy has long been aimed not merely at Berlin *but at dividing and neutralizing all of Europe, forcing us back to our own shores.* (My italics.) . . . There is peace in Berlin today. The source of world tension is Moscow, not Berlin. . . . If we do not meet our commitments to Berlin, where will we stand later? . . . And if there is one path of all others to war, it is the path of weakness and disunity . . . We shall seek peace, but we shall not surrender. That is the central meaning of this crisis and the meaning of your Government's policy . . .

By October 1961, according to published accounts, general strategic exercises had been completed in the Soviet Union on a scale hitherto unknown in the history of the Soviet Army, and Khrushchev was prepared to challenge Kennedy at a Berlin confrontation. The challenge came when Soviet tanks moved up to Checkpoint Charlie, which lay between East and West Berlin; Kennedy faced them with American tanks, forcing the Soviets to retreat.

˙THE CUBAN MISSILE CRISIS

In July and August 1962, first Raúl Castro, Cuba's Minister of Defense, then "Che" Guevara, one of the major strategists of the Cuban revolution, visited Moscow. A month later the Soviet Union and Cuba announced a security treaty. It was soon dramatically to be made known that material for missile sites had begun to arrive in Cuba several months earlier. Finally, on 14 October 1962, a CIA-operated U-2 reconnaissance plane brought back photographs of missile and bomber bases under rapid construction in Cuba.

According to Oleg Penkovsky, a GRU colonel who paid with his life for passing on military information to British and American intelligence, it was Khrushchev's intention to destroy the West in a first-strike "rainstorm of missiles . . . with the military advantage of maximum radio-active fallout . . . strike first and ask questions afterwards."

Stationed in Moscow, Penkovsky frequently traveled abroad, and had access to most Soviet military secrets as well as information about Soviet ballistic missile programs. The information he obtained appalled him, for it indicated that Khrushchev was planning to obliterate the West. He endeavored to pass his information to American intelligence officers, only to find them wary for fear of compromise. He then contacted an English businessman, Greville Wynne, who traveled frequently in eastern European countries. Wynne agreed to pass Penkovsky's information to British intelligence (SIS), which judged Penkovsky to be sincere and his information to be accurate; SIS then passed the information to the CIA. (Penkovsky's notes and memos, transmitted before his capture and execution, have been published under the title *The Penkovsky Papers*.)

From April 1961 through August 1962, using Minox cameras, Penkovsky passed to Wynne (and others) photographs of some 5,000 secret documents, including definitive data on Khrushchev's offensive missiles. The British and Americans found it difficult to believe the enormity of Khrushchev's design, and it was only when the U-2 reconnaissance flight over Cuba produced photographs of the missile sites that they were no longer skeptical of Penkovsky's information. President Kennedy's advisers apparently were able to match Penkovsky's descriptions of the offensive missiles with the U-2 photographs and when pieced together the information revealed that the missiles had a range of up to 2,800 kilometers. By using Cuban sites, the Soviets had reduced the warning time of a missile attack from 15 minutes to 30 seconds.

WASHINGTON: 22 OCTOBER 1962

On 22 October 1962, in a national address Kennedy made public the details of the missile buildup in Cuba, saying that he had received "the first hard preliminary information" of this nature on 16 October. He accused the Soviet government of making false statements to him about the presence of offensive missiles in Cuba. He said that "sudden mass destruction" faced the United States, and that this situation could not be tolerated. He called for a quarantine on arms shipments to Cuba:

. . . this secret, swift, and extraordinary build-up of Communist missiles . . . is a deliberately provocative and unjustified change in the status quo which cannot be accepted by this country if our courage and our commitments are ever to be trusted again by either friend or foe. The 1930's taught us a clear lesson: Aggressive conduct if allowed to grow unchecked and unchallenged, ultimately leads to war.

. . . I call upon Chairman Khrushchev to halt and eliminate this clandestine, reckless and provocative threat to world peace and to stable relations between our two nations. I call upon him further to abandon this course of world domination and to join in an historic effort to end the perilous arms race and transform the history of man. . . .

My fellow citizens, let no one doubt that this is a difficult and dangerous effort on which we have set out . . . But the greatest danger of all would be to do nothing. The path we have chosen for the present is full of hazards, as all paths are; but it is the one most consistent with our character and courage as a nation and our commitments around the world. The cost of freedom is always high—but Americans have always paid it. And one path we shall never choose, and that is the path of surrender or submission.

Our goal is not the victory of might but the vindication of right—not peace at the expense of freedom, but both peace and freedom, here in this hemisphere and, we hope, around the world. God willing, that goal will be achieved.

MOSCOW 22 OCTOBER 1962

On the day of the quarantine speech, 22 October, in which Kennedy identified the missiles, the Soviets arrested Penkovsky; a little more than a week later, on 2 November, Wynne was kidnapped by the KGB in Budapest. Penkovsky and Wynne were tried in Moscow in April 1963; Penkovsky was shot for treason and Wynne was sentenced to 18 years' imprisonment for espionage, but was later exchanged for Koron Melody, a Soviet spy in British hands.

Penkovsky had disclosed the direction of Soviet political thinking as interpreted through their military directives; the extent of the internal damage he inflicted is illustrated by the wholesale demotions and disappearances in Soviet military and military intelligence, including a chief marshal of the Soviet Union and the chief of the GRU, General Ivan Serov. In addition, some 300 Soviet intelligence officers were recalled to Moscow from foreign countries for briefing on the publicized Soviet version of the Cuban Missile Crisis.

THE "CUBA CRISIS" RESOLVED

After an exchange of notes between Kennedy and Khrushchev beginning on 26 October—those from Kennedy stating his absolute determination not to waver from the course that he had set and those from Khrushchev containing threats and denunciations—and culminating on 28 October, Khrushchev capitulated; a merchant fleet en route to Cuba carrying additional nuclear warheads from the Soviet Union and Soviet-controlled ports retreated, the missiles already in Cuba were withdrawn, and the missile sites were destroyed under the supervision of the United Nations.

The crisis had far-reaching international ramifications. Despite the dialectical Sino-Soviet split, around the time of the Cuban crisis the Chinese abruptly paused in their military invasion of India and, after the crisis was resolved, withdrew altogether.

The record of the days and nights at the White House during this time shows how Kennedy and his advisers finally persuaded the advocates of the bombing or invasion of Cuba—or even doing nothing—into accepting what turned out to be the successful resolution of one of the most difficult diplomatic and military problems in recent history. The assassination plot was then activated; Kennedy's decision would cost him his life.

THE PLOT TO KILL THE PRESIDENT

The MVD plot was in three parts. First, to assassinate the incumbent President (Nixon or Kennedy). Second, to let it be known after the assassination that the plot had originated in either Cuba or the Soviet Union, so that the United States authorities would be uncertain which country was responsible. Third, if the assassin failed to escape and Soviet complicity was discovered, the authorities would be forced to withhold the truth for fear of massive war.

The basics of the plot were that a young American serving in the Armed Forces of the United States would be selected (probably by the KGB) and persuaded to visit the Soviet Union at the termination of his military service. The selected American would have to be unmarried, and his immediate family would have to be somewhat disunited. He would have to be a rifleman of reasonable marksmanship and to have exhibited some Marxist or pro-Soviet sympathies which would make it credible that he might visit the Soviet Union. He would have to be of average height, of normal physique, and with a face of regular and no distinguishing features, thus making it comparatively easy for the KGB or the MVD to find a dedicated Soviet look-alike from their hundreds of thousands of members.

The entire Armed Forces of the United States would have been available to the Soviet Union from which it could select a man to suit its requirements; it seems probable that the KGB would have had a list of suitable servicemen from which it could choose the man who best fulfilled its requirements.

On visiting the Soviet Union, the American serviceman would be seized and his place taken by the look-alike already selected; the look-alike would probably already be partly trained in espionage and assassination. After two or three years and having learned the American's background, habits, gait, speech patterns, and handwriting, with the aid of deception the look-alike would enter the United States in the identity of the American serviceman and place himself in a position to take advantage of espionage opportunities, and finally to assassinate the President.

The impostor's actions leading up to the assassination were an important part of the plot. He would deliberately leave behind him a confusing trail of evidence not only concealing his Soviet identity but suggesting that there was a second man involved and that they were both operating on behalf of Fidel Castro.

There are precedents for such imposture. A young Canadian, Gordon Lonsdale, was either seized by the Soviets in 1940 during their invasion of Finland, or discovered to have previously died in Finland. Accounts are conflicting, but in any case, the boy, from a remote part of Canada, who had few relatives, disappeared. His identity was later assumed by the GRU officer believed to be Koron Melody, who successfully spied in Britain for many years before being apprehended (The Portland Spy Case). His training as a Canadian citizen was so thorough that British intelligence accepted him as Gordon Lonsdale. Five years later, when the real Gordon Lonsdale's background was finally investigated in Canada, medical records disclosed that the boy had been circumcised; Melody had not. Melody was brought to trial, imprisoned for some years, and finally exchanged for Greville Wynne.

THE WARREN COMMISSION AND THE WARREN REPORT

On 29 November 1963, being seven days after President Kennedy was killed, President Johnson appointed a Commission to investigate and report upon the assassination of his predecessor in office. He directed the Commission to evaluate all the facts and circumstances surrounding the assassination and the subsequent killing of the alleged assassin, and to report its findings and conclusions to him. The Commission was given the power to subpoena witnesses and to examine them on oath; the investigation would be held in private.

The Chairman of the seven-member Commission was Chief Justice of the United States, Earl Warren. At first he had declined the appointment but later accepted, having been told by President Johnson that it was in the national interest for him to do so. The other six members of the Commission were lawyers of distinction and experience: Richard B. Russell, John Sherman Cooper, Hale Boggs, Gerald R. Ford, Allen W. Dulles (for 8 years Director of CIA), and John J. McCloy.

J. Lee Rankin was General Counsel to the Commission and he was aided by 14 assistant Counsel and 12 staff members, the latter being lawyers, historians, and Internal Revenue officials. In addition, 37 lawyers, clerks, and secretaries were engaged.

Owing to their duties elsewhere, the Commissioners heard the testimony of fewer than one-fifth of the witnesses, and with these witnesses there was no occasion when all seven Commissioners were present. In general, there were only two or three, and even this small number was diluted by one or more of them having to leave the hearing room to attend to other business. As a result, it was left to Commission Counsel to decide who should testify and how their evidence should be evaluated; Counsel themselves had to rely upon federal and other agencies for information.

Their work completed, on 24 September 1964 the Commission submitted an 888-page Report and Appendices to President Johnson, known as the Warren Report; it purports to summarize the contents of 15 Volumes of Testimony given to the Commission by 552 people, and of 11 Volumes of Exhibits received from individuals, the FBI, the Secret Service, and other agencies, these 26 Volumes of Testimony and Exhibits amounting to some 17,000 pages. The Foreword to the Report, after setting out in detail the formation of the Commission, explains the titanic task undertaken by them and their lawyers, in which they were aided by some 200 FBI, Secret Service, and other agents, these agents conducting some 26,500 interviews and re-interviews, and submitting some 30,000 pages of reports to the Commission. Much of the material gathered by the Commission and their assistants has been placed in the National Archives of the United States, and will not be available for public inspection until the year 2039. Some of these documents have since been released either voluntarily or as a result of the Freedom of Information Act.

In reply to a reporter for the *New York Times,* on 4 February 1964, the Chief Justice was alleged to have said that a full report would be made public, "but it might not be in your lifetime. I am not referring to anything especially but there may be some things that would involve security."

The conclusions of the Commission as set out in its Report are, in brief, that the assassin was the ex-Marine, Lee Harvey Oswald; that there was no evidence that either Oswald or Ruby was part of any conspiracy, domestic or foreign; that no direct or indirect relationship between Oswald and Ruby had been discovered, nor was there any credible evidence that either knew the other; that there was no evidence that Ruby acted with any person in the killing of Oswald; and that, on the basis of the evidence before the Commission, Oswald acted alone.

The Commission could not make any definitive determination of Oswald's motives, but its Report indicates that his resentment of authority, his failure in life, an urge to find a place in history, despair over his failures, his capacity for violence, his avowed commitment to Marxism and Communism, and his other varied disappointments contributed to his capacity "to risk all in cruel and irresponsible actions."

The Report does not define Ruby's motive in killing the assassin and says only that he, too, acted alone.

The Report says that because of the difficulty in proving negatives to a certainty the possibility of others being involved with either Oswald or Ruby could not be established categorically, but if there was any such evidence it had been beyond the reach of all the investigative agencies and resources of the United States and had not come to the attention of the Commission.

The Commission signed but did not write the Report, which was compiled by their lawyers and others. It relies for its conclusions mainly upon the veracity of a historic diary alleged to be the work of the real Oswald; the testimony of Marina Oswald, wife of the impostor; George De Mohrenschildt, who was the impostor's only friend in Dallas; and Jack Ruby.

I contend that there was powerful evidence of Soviet conspiracy and that this evidence was not only within the reach of but in the possession of at least one of the investigative agencies and the Commission itself.

The material for this book, unless otherwise indicated, has been drawn from the Warren Report, the 26 volumes of supporting Testimony and Exhibits, and documents recently released from the National Archives.

References will be as follows: The Warren Report and page as (WR. 000.) and its supporting Volumes by the number of the Volume and page as (XX. 000.). Where testimony is mentioned, it will be testimony before the Commission or their lawyers between 3 February and 16 September 1964. In references to documents, CE is a Commission Exhibit contained in the Volumes of Exhibits, and CD is a document supplied to the Commission but not shown as an Exhibit and placed in the National Archives.

Where *italics* appear (apart from the names of publications) they are used to emphasize a point.

WARNINGS

3 June 1960. "Since there is a possibility that an impostor is using Oswald's birth certificate, any current information the Department of State may have concerning subject will be appreciated." J. Edgar Hoover, Director of the Federal Bureau of Investigation. Memorandum to the United States Department of State.

31 March 1961. ". . . this file contains information first, which indicates that mail from the mother of this boy is not being delivered to him and second, that it has been stated that there is an impostor using Oswald's identification data and that no doubt the Soviets would love to get hold of his valid passport, it is my opinion that the passport should be delivered to him only on a personal basis and after the Embassy is assured to its complete satisfaction that he is returning to the United States." Edward J. Hickey, Deputy Chief of the Passport Office. Memorandum to the Consular Section of the Department of State.

11 July 1961. "The Embassy's careful attention to the involved case of Mr. Oswald is appreciated. It is assumed that there is no doubt that the person who has been in communication with the Embassy is the person who was issued a passport in the name of Lee Harvey Oswald." The Honorable Dean Rusk, Secretary of State. Final paragraph of a memorandum sent by the Department of State to the United States Embassy in Moscow.

PART 1:

THE ASSASSINATION

1

The Marine

1956

On 3 October 1956, when Lee Harvey Oswald was two weeks short of 17 years of age, he wrote from his home in New Orleans to the Socialist Party of America in New York (allegedly Communist-connected), saying that he was a Marxist and had been studying socialist principles for well over 15 months, and asking for further information.

Three weeks later he enlisted in the Marines. His height on enlistment at 17 years of age was recorded at 5'8". He was rapidly growing; after completing boot camp 10 weeks later, his height measured 5'9". When he was to leave the Marines nearly three years later, he measured 5'11". Given a specialist's rating, he was assigned to a radar unit, and for most of his service he was to be employed as a radar operator in Japan, the Philippines, Taiwan, and, finally, the United States.

While in the Marines he tried to learn the Russian language, obtaining Russian language newspapers and appearing to be interested in what was happening in the Soviet Union. None of this was done in secret and he was sometimes called "comrade" by his fellow Marines, although he never expressed Communist sympathies.

As a rifleman, he was just able to qualify as a "sharpshooter," which means achieving a certain score firing an M-1 rifle at a stationary target at various distances on a given day; the designation represents someone who is not "expert" but is above "marksman."

He was an inveterate reader of books, including *Leaves of Grass*, *Das Kapital*, *Mein Kampf*, and his favorites, Orwell's *Animal Farm* and *1984*. He was regarded as having a sense of humor, as being witty, and as being at his best in company. He never displayed any sign of wishing to defect to the Soviet Union.

1957/8

After he had been in the Marines for about a year, he acquired an automatic .22 pistol which he kept in his locker. One day, it accidentally went off and wounded him about the left elbow. The slug did not exit and was later removed surgically. The wound and the surgery left Oswald with two scars.

For illegal possession of the pistol, Oswald was given an administrative court-martial. Later, in Japan, he was court-martialed for insulting a noncommissioned officer over an incident involving a spilled drink, and he was again found guilty and punished accordingly.

Apart from the two incidents, he appears to have been an average Marine Corps first-class private, performing his duties reasonably satisfactorily. The officer in command of the crew that included Oswald would testify that he found him competent in all functions during his last year of service, whether radar surveillance of aircraft or sweeping the floor. "He waited for you to tell him what to do, and he did it, no matter what you told him . . . I know that Cuba interested him more than most other situations . . . But I never heard him in any way, shape or form confess that he was a Communist, or that he ever thought about being a Communist . . . I believe he drank, sometimes to excess." (VIII. 289-303.)

MARCH 1959

On 4 March 1959, while still in the Marines but back from the Far East, Oswald, giving his height as 5'11", filled in an application form for entrance to the Albert Schweitzer College in Churwalden, Switzerland, a small college specializing in religion, ethics, science, literature, and projects for peace. On the application form Oswald said that, after a period at the college, he intended to take a summer course at the University of Turku in Finland, and would then return to America to pursue his chosen vocation of "short story writer" on contemporary American life. His application to attend the college was accepted for the 1960 third term beginning in April and he was asked to forward a deposit of $25, which he sent in June 1959 enclosed in a letter expressing his pleasure at being accepted and saying he looked forward to "a fine stay." He added that any information on the school or even the students who would attend the course would be appreciated; he wrote his mother, Marguerite Oswald, that he was happy to have been accepted.

Although he was committed to serve on active duty until 7 December 1959, on 17 August Oswald submitted a request for a dependency discharge on the grounds that his mother needed his support; he reported having heard from her in July that she had been injured in an accident at work some months previously.

SEPTEMBER 1959

Oswald's dependency discharge was approved and on 3 September 1959 he underwent a full medical examination by a Marine doctor (Vincent) when he was measured and his height recorded as 5'11". In addition, the Marine medical record states that at the age of six, Oswald had undergone a mastoidectomy which left a one-inch scar behind the left ear. (The operation necessitated the removal of part of the mastoid bone with resultant depression in the flesh.)

On 4 September, Oswald applied for a passport and stated on the application form that he intended to leave the United States on the Grace Line on about 21 September and would be away for some four months. On the form, he gave his height as 5'11" and stated that his purpose in applying for a passport was to attend the Albert Schweitzer College and the University of Turku, Finland, and to visit other countries as a tourist. He named the countries that he would visit in the following order: Cuba, Dominican Republic, England, France, Switzerland, Germany, Finland, and Russia, an ambitious itinerary for a four-month period. Moreover, this period did not even extend to the beginning of the school term for which he had applied—1 April. He was routinely issued a passport which gave his height as 5'11".

On 11 September, he was again measured and weighed by a Marine officer (Ayres) for the purpose of issuing identification cards and other material in connection with his release from the Marines and transfer to the inactive reserves. His height was again recorded as 5'11". His Marine record on this day reads: "Recommended for R (reserve) enlistment" and "Good Conduct Medal period commences 27 June 1958 (1st Award)."

Nelson Delgado, Oswald's best friend in the Marines during his last year of service in 1958/9, would testify that Oswald had been corresponding with the Cuban Consulate in Los Angeles and one night had an unidentified civilian visitor with whom he talked for one and a half to two hours outside the camp gates. Oswald and Delgado, both 19 years of age, had often talked about joining the Cuban Army and perhaps leading expeditions to free Caribbean countries, Castro's revolution being at that time popular among young Marines. Delgado was once "scared" because Oswald had actually started to make plans for them to go to Cuba, which included how they would go there, where to apply to go, and the people to contact for that purpose; Delgado had not realized that Oswald had been serious when they were having discussions about taking over, for example, the Dominican Republic.

Delgado, who used to be in the practice firing line with Oswald, said that Oswald was a poor rifleman, getting a lot of "Maggies drawers" (missing the target completely); was not interested in rifle practice, whereas the others "loved going to the range"; and did not keep his rifle in proper order. Oswald bought a Spanish-English dictionary and Delgado taught him to speak simple Spanish until Oswald could converse to a limited extent in that language. Delgado said he was surprised when he had heard Oswald had gone to the Soviet Union because he thought Oswald was going to college in Switzerland. If he had expected Oswald to go anywhere else, it would have been to Cuba. Oswald had never said anything about going to the Soviet Union, and Delgado did not think he would have had sufficient money to get there.

During his last year of service, Oswald made a voluntary allotment of part of his salary to his mother under which arrangement she received $40 in August, and he had submitted an application for a monthly "Q" allotment (dependency allowance) of $91.30 in her behalf, one payment of which was made in September.

After leaving the Marines on 11 September 1959, Oswald went to his mother's home in Fort Worth, Texas; he arrived there on 14 September. On this day he registered his dependency discharge and placed himself in the Marine Reserve at the Fort Worth Selective Service Board; his height was noted on two separate documents as 5'11". In testimony, Marguerite Oswald would say her son had told her that he intended to get a job on a ship or possibly in the export-import business, claiming that he would be able to earn more money than he could in Fort Worth—on a ship he could earn "big money" and would be able to send home "substantial" amounts.

After giving his mother $100, he left for New Orleans on 16 September and there booked passage on a Lykes Lines freighter to Le Havre, France, sailing on 20 September 1959. His mother received the following undated letter from New Orleans:

> Dear Mother,
>
> Well, I have booked passage on a ship to Europe, I would of had to sooner or later and I think it's best I go now. Just remember above all else that my values are very different from Robert's and your's (sic). It is difficult to tell you how I feel, just remember this is what I must do. I did not tell you about my plans because you could harly (sic) be expected to understand. I did not see Aunt Lillian while I was here. I will write again as soon as I land.
>
> (Signed) Lee

Oswald, who had helped to support his mother and apparently wished to continue to do so, appears to have had an unexpected change of heart in New Orleans, for this was the last she was to hear of her son—if he was the author of the letter—until about a month later when she read in the Fort Worth newspapers that he had defected to the Soviet Union.

OCTOBER 1959

The freighter carried only four passengers; besides Oswald, its passenger manifest listed a married couple and a young man with whom Oswald shared a cabin. Oswald told the other passengers that he intended to travel in Europe and possibly attend a college in Switzerland if he had sufficient funds. On arrival at Le Havre on 8 October, he left the ship and crossed by boat to England, arriving the following day at Southampton. He told immigration officials that he had $700 and that he intended to stay in England for a week before going to school in Switzerland. On the same day, he traveled, presumably by train, to London and immediately flew to Helsinki, Finland, where he applied at the Soviet Consulate for a visa to visit the Soviet Union. After two days, a six-day tourist visa was granted him, and Oswald, presumably traveling by train, arrived in the Soviet Union on 15 October 1959.

2

Birth of a New Oswald: Russia

Most of what happened to Oswald after he arrived in the Soviet Union will doubtless remain a mystery, but there are certain matters on record that throw light on subsequent events and, in particular, on the manner in which the Soviets managed to place one of their agents—an Oswald look-alike—in a position to assume the Marine Corps veteran's identity.

The sources for this period are various: Information supplied by the United States Embassy in Moscow; interviews conducted in Moscow by American journalists; and testimony that Oswald's Soviet-born wife, Marina, was to give to the Warren Commission.

Soviet Major Yuri Nosenko, who had been the deputy director of the KGB department responsible for operations against American tourists when Oswald arrived in Moscow, defected to the United States on 4 February 1964 (the day after the Warren Commission started to take testimony), bringing with him, among other things, an alleged Soviet file on Lee Harvey Oswald. Unfortunately the contents of this file, to this day, have remained a mystery; the Warren Report does not mention him.

The assassin had left behind in the rooming house in Dallas where he lived at the time of the assassination an "Historic Diary" of 12 pages reputing to record Oswald's activities while he was in the Soviet Union. Oswald's diary was probably written by the impostor and probably with the help of the KGB and American or English defectors. It is written in an ingenuous schoolboy style portraying a young and almost illiterate romantic idealist.

OCTOBER 1959

According to Soviet records used in the Warren Exhibits, the real Oswald had entered the Soviet Union on 15 October on a six-day tourist visa and went to the Hotel Berlin in Moscow on 16 October. According to his diary he was met by an Intourist representative who was responsible for him during his stay. Soviet medical reports (and Oswald's diary) claim that Oswald, on being told that he could not stay permanently, attempted suicide by slashing his left wrist. The diary records the event; the Intourist representative was probably named Rimma.

Oct. 21

Eve. 6.00 Receive word from police official. I must leave country tonight at 8.00 P.M. as visa expirs. I am shocked! My dreams! I retire to my room. I have $100. left. I have waited for 2 year to be accepted. My fondes dreams are shattered because of a petty offial; because of bad planning I planned to much!

7.00 P.M. I decide to end it. Soak rist in cold water to numb the pain. Then slash my left rist. Than plaug wrist into bathtub of hot water. I think "when Rimma comes at 8. to find me dead it will be a great shock. somewhere, a violin plays, as I

Oct 21. (con.): watch my life whirl away. I think to myself. "how easy to die" and "a sweet death, (to violins) about 8.00 Rimma finds me unconscious (bathtub water a rich red color) she screams (I remember that) and runs for help. Amulance comes, am taken to hospital where five stitches are put in my wrist. Poor Rimmea stays by my side an interrpator (my Russian is still very bad) far into the night, I tell her "go home" (my mood is bad) but she stays, she is "my friend" She has a strong will only at this moment I notice she is preety

On 21 October he was taken to the Botkin Hospital in Moscow. The hospital records state that he entered the hospital at 4:00 in the afternoon. (The diary says he tried to kill himself at 7:00 P.M. and was found by Rimma, who called an ambulance at 8:00.) The hospital records also state, "The patient does not speak Russian. One could judge only by his gestures and facial expression that he had no complaints." There are only the Soviet records to go by in determining whether or not he spoke Russian or whether any of these events actually occurred. It may be that Oswald was taken to the hospital because the man who was to assume Oswald's identity already had a scar on his wrist that needed to be justified. Whatever the circumstances of Oswald's "recovery" from the suicide attempt, he never returned to the Hotel Berlin. Instead, a man calling himself Lee Harvey Oswald went from the hospital to the Hotel Metropole on 28 October. Both the Berlin and Metropole Hotels were under extensive KGB surveillance. (XXVI. 788.)

It would seem possible that the identity of Lee Harvey Oswald was taken by the impostor at the Botkin Hospital and that the real Oswald was subsequently kept hidden. The exchange may, of course, have occurred immediately upon his arrival in the Soviet Union. In any case the swap must have been made before the end of the month when the man posing as Oswald was to make his first visit to the United States Embassy in Moscow.

(Henceforth, in order to avoid calling the impostor an impostor or "Oswald," he will be referred to simply as 'Oswald.')

On Saturday, 31 October 1959, 'Oswald' appeared at the United States Embassy in Moscow and handed over a passport with the name Lee Harvey Oswald, saying that he wished to renounce his American citizenship and that he had applied for Soviet citizenship.

'Oswald' produced a note which he had prepared in advance. Reproduced as written, it reads:

I Lee Harvey Oswald do hereby request that my present citizenship in the United States of america, be revoked.

I have entered the Soviet Union for the express purpose of appling for citizenship in the Soviet Union, through the means of naturalization.

My request for citizenship is now pending before Suprem Soviet of the U.S.S.R.

I take these steps for political reasons. My request for the revoking of my American citizenship is made only after the longest and most serious considerations.

I affirm that my allegiance is to the Union of Soviet Socialist Republics.

As a *coup de grâce* he stated his intention of disclosing to the Russians all that he had learned as a radar operator when in the Marines, flamboyantly emphasizing his allegiance to the USSR and also acting the part of the rebellious Marine.

The threat, however, was taken seriously, for a Marine officer was to testify that as a consequence, Marine aircraft call signs and codes were changed; this involved much time and effort. Other matters such as the positioning of radar sites and the details of equipment and various systems could not be changed but the Americans believed that the Soviets now knew them.

The senior consular official present was later to testify that 'Oswald' talked for about an hour and seemed to "know what his mission was. He took charge, in a sense, of the conversation right from the beginning."

In a State Department memorandum of 27 November 1963, five days after the assassination, one of the consular officials who had spoken with the young man that day stated ". . . there also seemed to be the possibility that he was following a pattern of behavior in which he had been tutored by person or persons unknown . . . In short, it seemed to me that there was a possibility that he had been in contact with others before or during his Marine Corps tour, who had guided him and encouraged him in his actions."

The Consulate officials, apparently wishing to give the young man time to think the matter over, suggested that he return the following Monday to complete the formalities. But, in fact, 'Oswald' did not return to the Embassy, thereby leaving intact his American citizenship and, thus, his ability to return to the United States should he so desire; the route to the assassination would now be unimpeded.

On reading in the newspapers in early November of Lee Harvey Oswald's defection to the Soviet Union, his mother and his brother, Robert Oswald, tried to contact him but were unable to do so. Between 8 November and 17 December, either the real Oswald or 'Oswald' wrote three letters to Robert brutally renouncing his family and denouncing the United States. He ended the last letter, "I am starting a new life and I do not wish to have anything to do with the old life. I hope you and your family will always be in good health. Lee."

About the same time, early in November, Abraham Goldberg, a free-lance American journalist in Moscow, having heard that a defector had arrived from the United States, tried to interview Oswald. Goldberg knocked at the door of 'Oswald's' room in the Hotel Metropole, and a young man wearing a white shirt and black slacks opened the door slightly. In response to Goldberg's question, he said that his name was Lee Harvey Oswald. Goldberg then told 'Oswald' that he would like to interview him, but the latter said that he did not wish to furnish any statement. Goldberg succeeded, however, in speaking to him through the slightly opened door. Goldberg asked him why he was going to remain in Russia and 'Oswald' replied only, "I've got my reasons," and would say nothing further. Goldberg tried to discourage 'Oswald' from remaining, and when he asked him if he knew the Russian language, 'Oswald' replied that he did not, but that he could learn and that he would "make out." Goldberg wanted to take a photograph, but 'Oswald' refused. (CE. 2719.) (The Warren Report states "Oswald refused to speak to him" and makes no mention of this dialogue. (WR. 694.))

On 13 November, another American journalist, Aline Mosby, interviewed a man calling himself Lee Harvey Oswald at the Hotel Metropole, the interview lasting two hours with 'Oswald' carrying on a monologue. He told her that he had saved $1,500 while in the Marines, and that for two years he had intended to divest himself of anything to do with the United States and that none of his fellow Marines knew of his plans. He did not tell her of a suicide attempt or hospitalization. She either guessed his height or asked him what it was for she recorded in her notes that he was 5'9", adding that he had brown eyes and a sallow complexion. Her story was carried by United Press International shortly afterward. She was later to report that the same little smile which she had noticed in Moscow was on his face just before he was shot, and that he looked like the same man shown in the newspaper photograph the morning after his murder.

Some years later I telephoned Miss Mosby, who had been transferred to Paris. She confirmed that her recording of his height was correct and that he certainly seemed no taller. Miss Mosby was not called to testify before the Warren Commission, although they were in possession of her notes.

On 16 November, a third journalist, Priscilla Johnson, of the North American Newspaper Alliance, conducted a five-hour interview with a man calling himself Lee Harvey Oswald at the same hotel; again 'Oswald' carried on a monologue but made no mention of a suicide attempt or hospitalization. She recorded in *her* notes that he was 5'11" in height and had blue eyes. She was to testify that his "use of (English) words struck me very much in conversation; he sometimes pronounced a particular word correctly and later pronounced it incorrectly, and that simple words he sometimes mispronounced and the hard ones he got right."

She told the Commission that his reticence and secretiveness aroused her suspicions because he seemed to have something to hide; he would not say what books he had read and would not talk about his life in the Marine Corps. He told her that he had started learning Russian the year before, along with his other preparations, and had been able to teach himself to read and write from Berlitz. When she asked him whether he just got a textbook or went to some city nearby for lessons at a school, he would not answer, and that struck her as being a strange thing about which to be evasive. She asked him again whether he practiced by himself or had a teacher, and again he would say nothing.

'Oswald' complained to her about the treatment he had received at the Embassy and said that he was not going back there "merely to get the run-around again," and that they should have allowed him "to renounce his American citizenship there and then." Although he emphasized to her his determination to renounce his American citizenship and to remain in Russia, she felt that he was leaving a loophole for himself so that he could return to the United States, and that his attempts to blame the Embassy were an excuse for not going back to renounce his citizenship formally.

To both women journalists, the man had expressed some knowledge of the real Oswald's background. Although it would appear that they were interviewing two different men, it was, of course, the same man.

In 1976, the CIA released several thousand pages of documents relating to the assassination; one of the documents contains the following:

Page 14 of the address book ('Oswald's' discovered notebook) shows the following listing:

> ZAKHAROVA
> B-14365
> 12/GORKOVA
> No. 15.

TRACES: 1. The 1960 Moscow Telephone Directory contains many ZAKHAROV'S and ZAKHAROVA'S but not for the address 12 or 15 GOR'KOGO. This directory does not list the telephone Number B-14365.

2. The Moscow Telephone Directory for Institutions, Organizations, and Enterprises lists telephone number B-14365 as the number for Vrachnobroy Kosmetiki. Min. Zdravookhraneniya (Medical Cosmetics, Ministry of Public Health) RSFSR. U1. Gor'kogo 19, Registratura (Registry).

(On p. 42 of Volume XVI of the Warren Exhibits, the reference to the ZAKHAROVA entry in 'Oswald's' notebook is limited to "Translator's Note: This is an address.")

Medical cosmetics is the professional term used for any change made to the body. "Cosmetics" is derived from the Greek, "to arrange or order," and does not necessarily signify beautification. "Medical Cosmetics" could, therefore, include operations to the nose and other parts of the body, or the implanting of scars. Why this notation should appear there cannot be imagined, unless 'Oswald' had cosmetic surgery to perfect his appearance as the real Oswald.

JANUARY 1960

On 4 January 1960, 'Oswald,' in the name of Lee Harvey Oswald, was issued a Soviet Identity Document for stateless persons, P.311479, but was not granted the Soviet citizenship that he said he desired. Had he been granted Soviet citizenship, an act of expatriation would have occurred, with consequences for subsequent events. Once he had been granted Soviet citizenship, he would never have been permitted back into the United States.

Three days later, on 7 January 1960, according to the Historic Diary and Soviet records, 'Oswald' was sent to Minsk—some 450 miles southwest of Moscow—where he was employed as an unskilled laborer at a factory manufacturing radios and where he was to continue to work until shortly before leaving the Soviet Union for the United States in May 1962. At this time, Minsk was the center for training Cuban students.

J. Edgar Hoover would testify on 14 May 1964 about 'Oswald':

But just the day before yesterday information came to me indicating that there is an espionage training school outside of Minsk—I don't know whether it is true—and that he was trained at that school to come back to this country to become what they call a "sleeper," that is, a man who will remain dormant for three to four years and in case of international hostilities rise up and be used. I don't know of any espionage school at Minsk or near Minsk, and I don't know how you could find out if there ever was one because the Russians won't tell you if you asked them. They do have espionage and sabotage schools in Russia and they do have an assassination squad that is used by them but there is no indication he had any association with anything of that kind. (V. 105.)

In reply to a question from the Warren Commission, the CIA stated that a Soviet defector had disclosed the presence of a spy school in Minsk known to be in operation in 1947. (XXVI.111.)

APRIL 1960

On 27 April, the FBI in Fort Worth interviewed Robert Oswald, who said that he had never known Lee to have any sympathy for or connection with Communism before his alleged defection. He assured the FBI that he would contact them if he received (from Soviet officials or Soviet establishments) any request to furnish any items of personal identification to Lee in Russia. (XVII.701.)

The next day, Marguerite Oswald was interviewed by the FBI in Fort Worth, and told them that Lee had never expressed any sympathy for the Soviet Union or the Communist system. She assured the FBI that she would tell them of any approach to her by Soviet officials, and that she had not been requested to furnish any items of personal identification to Lee in Russia. She told the FBI that Lee had taken *his birth certificate* with him when he left Fort Worth for New Orleans on 16 September 1959. She said that she had been very much alarmed for fear that something had happened to Lee, and as a result had corresponded with her Congressman and with the Department of State. (XVII.702-706.)

Hoover had known for six months that a man identifying himself as ex-Marine Lee Harvey Oswald had visited the United States Embassy in Moscow on 31 October 1959 in order to renounce his American citizenship, that he had handed in his passport, but that, although being asked to return in a few days to complete the formalities, he had not reappeared.

As a result of the information supplied by Marguerite Oswald, on 3 June 1960 in a memorandum to the Department of State, Hoover warned the Department that an impostor might be using Oswald's identification data in the Soviet Union or elsewhere. The memorandum ended, "Since there is a possibility that an impostor is using Oswald's birth certificate, any current information the Department of State may have concerning subject will be appreciated." (CD.294B.)

(Hoover's warning was committed to the National Archives and recently uncovered by a researcher.)

FEBRUARY 1961

On 13 February, the Embassy in Moscow received a letter from 'Oswald' which had been mailed from Minsk. He asked for the return of his passport, which he had left with the Embassy more than 15 months earlier, saying that he wanted to return to the United States, not having become a Soviet citizen. He said he could not appear personally because he could not leave Minsk without permission. The letter ended, "I hope that in recalling the responsibility I have to America that you will remember yours in doing everything you can to help me, since I am an American citizen." It is interesting to note that this and subsequent letters to the Embassy were literate as opposed to the writings in the diary.

Marguerite Oswald, who in January had visited the Department of State to inquire about her son's whereabouts, was notified of this letter.

On 17 March, 'Oswald' attended a dance at the Palace of Culture in Minsk where he met Marina Prusakova and was introduced to her by the name Alek. She would testify that Alek was only a nickname and that everyone at his place of work called him Alek because it was easier to pronounce than Lee. Marina, who had been a member of the Communist League of Youth (Komsomol), was to tell the FBI and the Commission that when she met Alek she thought he was from one of the Baltic states because, although he spoke "good Russian," he had a Baltic accent. He said that he had no mother, and forbade Marina to ask him about her. Later that evening, she learned that he was an American, Lee Harvey Oswald. Marina testified that she had not intended to go to the dance but that she was persuaded to go by her uncle, MVD Colonel Ilya Prusakov, in whose house she was then living. (XXII.745.I.90-95.)

Marina and 'Oswald' met at another dance a week later, and, after the dance, the young man walked her to her uncle's apartment; they agreed to meet again.

It is interesting to note the movements of Marina, Oswald and 'Oswald' over the two previous years. In July 1959, Oswald began his application for an early "hardship" discharge from the Marines; in August, this was being processed, and in early September 1959, he left the Marines.

In July 1959, Marina Prusakova left her work in Leningrad to live with her stepfather in that city, doing no further work for two months. She testified that she did not get on well with her stepfather and decided to leave Leningrad to go to Minsk to live with her uncle and his wife; she arrived at their house at the end of August or the beginning of September 1959. (The Warren Report states surprisingly that she did not arrive in Minsk until one year and one month later; October 1960. (WR.703.)) Shortly after arriving, she became a member of the local Komsomol.

On the same day that 'Oswald' left Botkin Hospital in Moscow on 28 October 1959, after the alleged attempt at suicide, and went to the Hotel Metropole, Marina, in Minsk, was enlisted in the military. On the day that 'Oswald' made his first visit, on 31 October 1959, to the United States Embassy in Moscow to renounce American citizenship, Marina was taken on the staff of the Third Clinical Hospital in Minsk as "analytical chemist of the pharmacy," according to testimony she would give, and supported by the hospital records submitted by the Soviets after the assassination. This was the hospital to which in due course 'Oswald' would go for ear treatment.

MARCH 1961

On 30 March, 'Oswald' in the name of Harvey, Oswald Alik (*sic*), was admitted to the Ear, Nose and Throat Division of the Clinical Hospital where Marina visited him frequently, taking advantage of her hospital uniform. 'Oswald' asked her to be his fiancée and she agreed to consider it.

One day later, Edward J. Hickey, Deputy Chief of the Passport Office, sent a memorandum to the consular section of the Department of State:

> In view of the fact that this file contains information first, which indicates that mail from the mother of this boy is not being delivered to him and second, that it has been stated that there is an impostor using Oswald's identification data and that no doubt the Soviets would love to get hold of his valid passport, it is my opinion that the passport should be delivered to him only on a personal basis and after the Embassy is assured to its complete satisfaction that he is returning to the United States. (CD.294J.)

(Hickey's warning was committed to the National Archives, and recently discovered by a researcher.)

When 'Oswald' left the hospital on 11 April, the hospital record stated that he had had a mastoidectomy between the ages of 10 and 12. Although it cannot be known when it was prepared, the record ingeniously incorporates not only the names Harvey, Oswald, and the nickname Alik (*sic*), but, in referring to the mastoidectomy, provides for a vital piece of the imposture by suggesting that Marina married the real Oswald.

On 30 April 1961, 'Oswald' and Marina were married, and later he admitted to his wife that he did have a mother in the United States.

On 5 May 1961, after 16 months' silence and after 'Oswald' and Marina were married, 'Oswald' began a long and affectionate correspondence with his mother, Marguerite, and his brother, Robert, indicating that he had changed his mind and wished to return home with Marina. The correspondence continued until 'Oswald' and Marina left for the United States. Presents were exchanged between the couple in the Soviet Union and Marguerite and Robert in the United States; included in the letters were a number of snapshots of 'Oswald,' either alone or with Marina or others, the carefully posed snapshots indicating a somewhat shorter man than the man who had left the United States in September 1959. During this time Marina became pregnant.

JULY 1961

On 11 July, the Department of State sent a communication to the United States Embassy in Moscow signed by Secretary of State Dean Rusk. The final paragraph reads, "The Embassy's careful attention to the involved case of Mr. Oswald is appreciated. It is assumed that there is no doubt that the person who has been in communication with the Embassy is the person who was issued a passport in the name of Lee Harvey Oswald." (CE.937.) The Warren Report quotes the final paragraph but deletes the last sentence. (WR.754.)

Warnings aside, on 10 July, Oswald's revalidated passport was handed to 'Oswald' so that he could "return" to the United States. Both he and Marina obtained their exit visas to leave Russia from MVD Colonel Nicholay Aksenov, who worked in the same building as her uncle, MVD Colonel Prusakov.

1962

In view of "Lee Harvey Oswald's" behavior in Russia, the Immigration and Naturalization Service (INS) was understandably resistant to admitting Marina to the United States. On the other hand, the State Department, hoping to encourage positive action by Soviet authorities in cases of relatives, suggested that Marina might avoid INS sanctions by going to Brussels and applying for an immigration visa to the United States, which could not be withheld as sanctions applied only to Communist countries. (WR.764.) The State Department, overcoming the powerful objections of INS, finally persuaded INS to grant Marina an immigration visa without her having to take these steps. INS knew nothing of Marina's membership in Komsomol; she had told the United States Embassy in Moscow that she had never been a member. (WR.767.) If INS had known that she had withheld this information, it would have been unlikely that she would have been admitted.

Komsomol is the voluntary youth organization with a center in every major town for young Communists. From its ranks the more intelligent and dedicated become members of the official Communist Party, and from the Party are drawn those who will occupy positions in the Russian hierarchy, Intelligence services, etc.

The official Komsomol code, first formulated in Stalin's time, was: "The very first task of all Komsomol education work is the necessity to seek out and recognize the enemy, who has then to be removed, purely forcibly, by methods of economic pressure, organizational-political isolation, and methods of physical destruction." Marina was probably so indoctrinated along with the other Komsomol students.

'Oswald' needed the personable Marina, and her testimony shows that she was highly intelligent and a match for her future interrogators from the Commission.

The final letter from INS to the State Department regarding her visa was sent ten months later and reads as follows:

Oswald, Marina—4
May 9, 1962 CO 243.1-P

Mr. Michel Cieplinski
Acting Administrator
Bureau of Security and Consular Affairs
Department of State
Washington, D.C.

Dear Mr. Cieplinski,

The Service file relating to the case of Mrs. Marina N. P. Oswald, subject of your letter of March 27, 1962, has been carefully reviewed by this office.

On February 28, 1962, the District Director at San Antonio wrote to the Assistant Director of the Visa Office that he declined to waive in Mrs. Oswald's case the sanctions against the issuance of immigrant visas in the Soviet Union imposed pursuant to Section 342(g) of the Immigration and Nationality Act. Your letter states that preventing Mrs. Oswald from accompanying her husband and child to the United States would weaken the attempts of the Embassy in Moscow to encourage positive action by the Soviet authorities in other cases involving Soviet relatives of United States citizens. Your letter also states that waiving of sanctions in behalf of Mrs. Oswald would be in the best interests of the United States.

In view of the strong representations made in your letter of March 27, 1962 you are hereby advised that sanctions imposed pursuant to Section 243(g) of the Immigration and Nationality Act are hereby waived in behalf of Mrs. Oswald. (Author's note: 243(g) is correct.)

Sincerely yours,
(Signed) Robert H. Robinson
Robert H. Robinson
Deputy Associate Commissioner
Travel Control

CC, REGIONAL COMMISSIONER, SAN PEDRO, CALIFORNIA

For your information.
DISTRICT DIRECTOR, SAN ANTONIO, TEXAS
For your information.

On 6 September 1964, Marina was to testify that "to the very last moment we did not believe that they would let us out of the Soviet Union." In answer to a Commissioner's question, "And none of the officials or police examined you at all about your reason for wishing to leave?" Marina replied, "It's very surprising, but nobody did." Apparently amazed that Marina had been able to leave the Soviet Union without any questioning, the Commission immediately asked the CIA for information on the practice in the Soviet Union regarding "Emigration and Travel of Soviet Nationals." The CIA replied at once:

1. Soviet Nationals seeking to emigrate from the Soviet Union or even to travel abroad are subjected to a thorough screening before receiving permission to go abroad. They are not permitted to emigrate if they are in a position to endanger the national security of the USSR.

2. In order to go abroad, a Soviet citizen must withstand a detailed investigation of his overall record and background. He must submit numerous applications, references and other supporting documents and he must undergo personal interviews conducted by government officials.

3. The KGB has the major responsibility for approving or denying requests for emigration or foreign travel. It investigates all applicants and its recommendation is given great weight by the Exit Department of the Central Committee of the Communist Party of the Soviet Union—the agency which makes the final decision.

(This important piece of Marina's testimony might go largely undiscovered in the volumes of Testimony because, of all the testimony taken from 552 persons contained in its 15 volumes, and correctly paged under "Contents" at the beginning of each volume, the page number is missing for this section (V.588) on the Table of Contents page of Volume V.)

1962

A daughter, June Lee, had been born to the 'Oswalds' in Minsk on 15 February 1962.

The Department of State, which had kept in touch with Marguerite Oswald since her son's alleged defection to the Soviet Union, now informed her that her son was about to return with wife and child.

On 1 June, 'Oswald' signed a promissory note at the United States Embassy in Moscow for a repatriation loan of $435.71. His passport was marked valid only for his return to the United States, and he and his family then boarded a train for Holland which, passing through Minsk that night, crossed the Soviet frontier on 2 June. 'Oswald' was equipped with the real Oswald's passport and Marina carried her M:1 Immigration Visa, both documents having been obtained by deception.

(Marina, according to her testimony, never again heard from her uncle.)

About three days later, Marina and 'Oswald' departed from Holland by ship. Marina would testify that she did not go on deck during the crossing because she was poorly dressed and her husband was ashamed of her.

3

The Impostor Enters
the United States

The ship on which the 'Oswalds' crossed the Atlantic docked at Hoboken, New Jersey, on 13 June, and the 'Oswalds' were met by a representative of the Travelers Aid Society which had been contacted by the Department of State. The representative received the impression that 'Oswald' was trying to avoid meeting anyone, and 'Oswald' passed through Immigration without any trouble, the representative then helping the couple through customs.

The Travelers Aid Society had referred the 'Oswalds' to the New York City Department of Welfare, which assisted them in finding a room in the Times Square Hotel. 'Oswald' told both the representatives of the Travelers Aid Society and the Department of Welfare that he had been a Marine stationed at the United States Embassy in Moscow, had married a Russian girl, had renounced his United States citizenship, and had worked in Minsk. He said that he had soon found out that Soviet propaganda was inaccurate but that he had not been able to obtain an exit visa for his wife and child for more than two years, adding that he had paid the travel expenses himself.

When 'Oswald' arrived in the United States he came well versed in the Oswald family background, having been coached to appear as an American citizen with some knowledge of American history and politics. He had been trained in espionage, and in rapid and accurate rifle and hand-gun fire, as future events were to prove.

On 14 June, the 'Oswalds' left New York by plane for Dallas, where they were met by Robert Oswald and his wife, and in whose house in Fort Worth they were to reside for six or seven weeks.

ACCEPTED RATHER THAN RECOGNIZED

A few days after the 'Oswalds' arrival, Marguerite Oswald visited Robert's house to welcome her son home. Neither she nor Robert would have been able fully to recall Oswald's appearance prior to his leaving the United States for the Soviet Union, having seen him on very few occasions since 1956 due to his having been overseas in the Pacific sector for a year of his Marine Corps career of nearly three years. They had not, of course, seen him while he was in the Soviet Union for two years and eight months. Marguerite Oswald had not been close to her son or seen him for any extended period since he was 17.

When they saw 'Oswald' on his return, they noticed considerable differences between him and the 19-year-old man who had left the United States. Assured (in all innocence) by the Department of State and the FBI that the real Oswald was returning, conditioned by their own pleasure in welcoming home the renegade, conditioned by letters and presents received from the young couple, conditioned by deceptive photographs received from the Soviet Union, and welcoming the pretty young wife and infant daughter who had both appeared in photographs and who looked and were the same, Marguerite and Robert never thought to question that the man with Marina might not be the real Oswald.

To United States counterintelligence and to everyone else, the bringing of an infant from the Soviet Union would go some way to discounting the possibility that the man they believed to be the real Oswald could be a Soviet agent.

Marguerite Oswald did say that she had noticed that Lee had lost some hair and that he had told her that it had been caused by the cold weather; she had searched her medical dictionary to find a prescription against baldness. He had also become "very, very thin." (I.132.147.)

Robert would testify that his brother Lee's complexion ". . . had changed somewhat to the extent that he had always been very fair complected—his complexion was rather ruddy at this time (1962)—you might say it appeared like an artificial suntan that you get out of a bottle, but very slight—in other words, a tint of brown to a tint of yellow." (Miss Mosby, the journalist in Moscow had also noted his complexion as sallow.) It appeared to him that Lee had picked up something of an accent, but Robert put it down to Lee's having been in Russia for over two and a half years and having spoken only the Russian language. He said that Lee's hair ". . . used to be brown and curly, a full set of hair"; he had pointed out to Lee the difference in his hair and ". . . actually had him bend his head down to where I could look at the top of it, and it was very thin on top—you could see just right down to the scalp." Lee had ". . . commented that he thought the cold weather had affected it." Robert had formed the opinion after his brother's death, ". . . due to the nature of the change in his hair and in the baldness that appeared, that he had been given something in the nature of shock treatments or something along that line had been given to him in Russia." Robert said that he was unaware of any tendency toward baldness on either his father's or mother's side of the family; he himself, his father, and half brother all had full heads of hair. Robert remembered that Lee to some extent had appeared "drawn" as compared with his appearance in 1959, and that he had lost weight. (I.329-332.)

Robert was to tell District Attorney Wade at Dallas police headquarters on the afternoon of 22 November 1963 that the family was "not too close" and "didn't have much in common."

John Pic, the older half brother of Robert and Lee, who had not seen Lee for 10 years but who had not been conditioned by the State Department, the FBI, letters, presents, and photographs, would testify that he saw Lee on only one occasion after Lee had arrived in the United States, and that this was at a Thanksgiving dinner in November 1962 at Robert's house. When asked how Lee had looked physically as compared with when he had seen him last, Pic replied, "I would have never recognized him, sir." It had struck him "quite profusely" that he was much thinner and did not have as much hair. His eyes seemed a little sunken, and because Oswald had been described to him as having a bull neck when in the Marine Corps, Pic said that, although he looked for the bull neck, he "did not notice it at all." When a visitor arrived after the dinner, Lee had introduced John Pic as his half brother, and Pic was "mad" because they had never in the past referred to the fact that they were half brothers, always calling each other "brother." (XI.55-56.59.)

It must be emphasized that Marguerite, Robert, and John Pic *accepted* rather than *recognized* the man who returned: Robert had accepted him because the Department of State, the FBI, and 'Oswald' in the Soviet Union told him that Lee was returning; Marguerite accepted him because she had been similarly conditioned and because Robert had already accepted him; the FBI accepted him because the Department of State had told them that Lee was returning and because Robert and Marguerite had already accepted him; finally, John Pic accepted him because everyone else had done so. The initial deception of Robert was all that the KGB had required; the deception of the FBI followed automatically. So far as the relatives were concerned, the focus of attention on 'Oswald' had been reduced by the presence of his pretty Russian wife and baby daughter.

Keeping Robert and Marguerite deceived required only that 'Oswald' evade or parry awkward questions about his childhood or Marine Corps days, profess loss of memory, change the subject, talk in Russian with his wife who could not speak English, and so on. To Robert, and perhaps to Marguerite, he intimated that he did not wish to talk about his alleged defection and what had prompted it. According to Marina in testimony, her husband frequently refused to talk and quarreled with Marguerite while they were living in her house for about a week after leaving Robert's house. When the 'Oswalds' left Marguerite's house to live on their own nearby, 'Oswald' tried to prevent Marina from opening the door or speaking to her. Robert testified that Marguerite and 'Oswald' "quarreled constantly."

SETTING A ZIGZAG COURSE

After joining Robert at the latter's house on 14 June, 'Oswald's' first task significantly was to employ a Fort Worth public stenographer, Pauline Bates, to type a story for him.

Miss Bates would testify that 'Oswald' came to her on 18 June with a large envelope in which he had some notes that he said he had smuggled out of the Soviet Union secreted under his clothes. He said that some of the notes had been typed on a little portable typewriter, some of them had been handwritten in ink or pencil, some of them were in Russian, and some in English. When he smuggled the notes out of the Soviet Union, "the whole time until they got over the border he was scared to death in case they would be found, and then they would not have been allowed to leave Russia." He had made the notes "surreptitiously when Marina would cover for him while he was doing this, in order to muffle the tone of the typewriter . . . so people would not know what he was doing. She would cover or watch for him so that nobody would know that he was making them—tried to steer anybody away while he was doing this because he could have got in trouble."

He said that he had taken a course in elementary Russian while in the Marine Corps, and that he had wanted to travel and had applied to the State Department for a visa. He said he did not go as an exchange student but that the State Department finally agreed to let him go, saying that they would not be responsible for him. He was "granted a visa to go over there but the State Department refused to stand behind him in case he got in trouble or anything." His notes were "very bitter" about the Soviet way of life, and he was particularly resentful about his treatment by the Soviets because he "went over there on a 2-year visa but, after marrying Marina, at the end of the two years when he wanted to leave, the Russians would not let him bring her back to America." They had said to him, "You go ahead and we'll send her to you." He told Miss Bates that he would never have seen Marina again if he had left without her; he had to stay 11 months longer until he could get her out and then only because "he raised so much 'Cain' with the Russians." (After the assassination, Marina was apparently never questioned about her husband's assertions.)

Miss Bates said that the notes were coherent, well written, and in sequence according to city and dates; the English and spelling were fairly accurate. She thought the notes were not "anything that could have been got together in just a few months. They were too detailed." She reported 'Oswald' as saying an engineer in Fort Worth wanted to publish them. (VIII.330-343.)

Miss Bates typed for 'Oswald' for three eight-hour days. He was always present while she worked for him, and when he left each day, he took what she had typed together with the carbon copy and carbon paper. He also retained all of his original notes, so that no material was ever left in her possession.

On 19 June, 'Oswald' called Peter Gregory, a petroleum engineer who was born in Siberia and who taught Russian at the Fort Worth library. 'Oswald' had obtained his name from the Fort Worth branch of the Texas Employment Commission. He asked Gregory for a letter certifying to his proficiency in Russian so that he could find employment as an interpreter or translator. Gregory asked 'Oswald' if he was Polish, saying, as had Marina, that he had a Baltic accent. 'Oswald' replied that he was not Polish but was an American. After satisfying himself that 'Oswald' could read Russian with proficiency, Gregory gave him the required letter of certification.

Afterwards, Gregory and his son, Paul, who was studying Russian, became friendly with the 'Oswalds,' and it was through Peter Gregory that they were to be introduced to the large Russian émigré group in

Fort Worth and Dallas, and to some other Russian-speaking Americans. It can only be speculation, but it would seem that 'Oswald,' armed with his notes, his typed story, and his assertion of Marina's disloyalty to her country, could then allay the suspicions, first of the Gregorys, then of the FBI, and finally of the Russian or Russian-speaking group, all of whom were somewhat suspicious of the 'Oswalds' because of the ease with which they had left the Soviet Union. Nevertheless, it was to be through the clever manipulation of these people that 'Oswald' was to be able to spy and assassinate.

ADDING TWO INCHES IN HEIGHT

On 26 June, 'Oswald' left Robert's house to be interviewed by appointment at the office of the FBI in Fort Worth. The FBI agents were Tom Carter and John Fain, senior men with long experience in security matters. The interview lasted about one and a half hours, with 'Oswald' seated at a desk facing Fain. While Carter watched and listened, Fain took notes from which he prepared a report of the interview. His report contained a physical description of "Lee Harvey Oswald" that stated his height to be 5'11" and his weight to be 150 pounds. (On arrest in Dallas 17 months later, the man the FBI interviewed was 5'9" in height and weighed 131 pounds.) When asked for Marina's height, 'Oswald' told the agents she was 5'5", two inches taller than, in fact, she is; the FBI recorded this height in its report. 'Oswald' refused to say why he went to the Soviet Union, and also refused to take a polygraph test on the question of whether he had dealings with Soviet intelligence while abroad. (XVII.730.XVI.138.)

FBI agent Fain testified:

He was tense, kind of drawn up, and rigid. He is a wiry little fellow, kind of waspy . . . He was a little insolent in his answers. He was the type of individual who apparently does not want to give out information about himself, and we asked him why he made this trip to Russia, and he looked like it got under his skin, and I noticed that he got white around the lips and tensed up, and I understood it to be a show of temper, and in a show of temper he stated that he did not care to relive the past. He didn't want to go into that at all . . . I asked him, in various ways, three or four times, trying to ascertain just what the situation was . . . He was evasive about why he went to Russia . . . He exhibited an arrogant attitude, arrogant, cold.

When asked why two agents were present at the interview, Fain said:

Fain: In internal security cases, in a case of this magnitude and this importance, we would always have two agents present.

Counsel: When you say a case of this magnitude and a case of this importance, what do you have in mind?

Fain: Well, this man has been in Russia and we want to try to find out whether he had been recruited by the Russians to do a job against the United States.

It would seem that the agents were so concerned about Oswald's intentions when they interviewed the man that it was not in their minds that he might not be Lee Harvey Oswald. Neither Carter, Fain, nor any of the other FBI agents assigned to 'Oswald's' case was ever warned that an impostor might attempt to assume Oswald's identity.

Later, this first meeting between the FBI and 'Oswald' was considered to be of such importance to the Warren Commission that six Commissioners and five of their senior Counsel were present. During his testimony Fain produced the short original FBI report of his interview with 'Oswald' upon which were typed heights for Marina and 'Oswald' which disagreed with the heights of the assassin and his living wife. Nevertheless, Fain was never asked about this discrepancy, although the evidence was there before the Commission.

That the Warren Commission was aware that the man interviewed by the FBI agents in Fort Worth might have been wearing elevated footwear to assist him in deceiving the agents is shown by the testimony of the assassin's landlady, Mrs. Mary Bledsoe, about his arrival at her rooming house on 7 October 1963, where he was to rent a room for a week. The matter of footwear was raised *by her* in testimony before the Commission:

Bledsoe: Now, I think he said he was going to get some more (luggage). He was going to get some more and he had some boots, too, in his hand. I—maybe he brought those the last time. I don't remember.

Counsel: What kind of boots?

Bledsoe: Well, they looked like they were about up to here (indicating).

Counsel: Up to the knees?

Bledsoe: No: about to there (indicating).

Counsel: Oh—

Bledsoe: There.

Counsel: Just a little above the ankle?

Bledsoe: Uh-huh.

Counsel: About three inches above the ankle?

Bledsoe: I don't know what they used them for.

Counsel: Were they cowboy boots?

Bledsoe: No: it wasn't cowboy boots.

Counsel: Were they canvas, leather, or rubber?

Bledsoe: No; just leather.

Counsel: Heavy soled?

Bledsoe: Heavy soled.

Counsel: Heavy soled. Rubber soles?

Bledsoe: Oh, no; leather.

Counsel: Any hobnails in them?

Bledsoe: No.

Counsel: Hard heel or flat heel? I mean, flat sole and heel?

Bledsoe: Oh, they had a heel, too. I remember them having that.
  (VI.420-421)

Russian boots traditionally have high heels because of the snow and slush. When 'Oswald' was in the Soviet Union, he had frequently written to Robert, and in one of his letters, asked him if he would like a pair of Russian boots sent and if so, to mark the size of his foot on a piece of paper and send it. Whether he did or not is unknown, but 'Oswald' brought back a pair of Russian boots for himself, and these were observed by Paul Gregory—shortly after 'Oswald's' interview with the FBI agents in Fort Worth. Furthermore, boots or shoes with slightly higher heels than usual but with a build-up inside the back have been on sale for many years in the Western world, advertised with the words, "Add two inches to your height."

The Exhibits contain a photograph of the assassin's possessions including sandals and shoes, but there are no photographs of boots, and presumably no boots were found. Marina was not asked by the Commission or any law enforcement agency whether her husband possessed a pair of boots and, if so, to describe them.

LOSING TWO INCHES IN HEIGHT

On 13 July, only 17 days after telling the FBI agents that his height was 5'11", 'Oswald' stated his height as 5'9" on an application form for employment at Leslie Welding in Fort Worth. On 14 August, 'Oswald' was interviewed again in Fort Worth by FBI agents Fain and Arnold Brown. The agents had waited in a car out of sight of the house where the 'Oswalds' were living, and when 'Oswald' came home from work, they drew up beside him, inviting him to sit in the back of the car. The interview again lasted for about one and a half hours.

Fain would testify that 'Oswald' again refused to answer questions about the purpose of his visit to the Soviet Union and again displayed anger.

When we asked him again why he went to the Soviet Union in the first place . . . he still declined to answer questions as to why he went to the Soviet Union in the first instance. He said he considered it nobody's business why he wanted to go to the Soviet Union. Finally, he stated he went over to Russia for his own personal reasons. He said "I went and I came back. It was something that I did." So he just bowed his neck and apparently wasn't going to do anything further at all on that point . . . He seemed to be a little bit derisive of our questions (about whether he had been recruited by Soviet intelligence) . . . He just didn't think he was that important.

He denied taking his birth certificate to Russia, and did not know where it was. He said he held no brief for the Russians or the Russian system. He refused to furnish the names of any of Marina's relatives, stating "that he 'eared some harm might come to them if he did so." He said that he was able to speak the Russian language upon his arrival in Russia. He agreed to advise the FBI if he was approached in suspicious circumstances by foreign agents, but he doubted the possibility of this happening because his employment at that time did not involve any sensitive information or manufacturing, and since the company did not have any government contracts, he could see no reason why the Soviets would desire to contact him. Fain said that the man ". . . had actually settled down. He had got a job with Leslie Machine Shop and he wasn't so tense. He seemed to talk more freely with us . . . He appeared a lot more relaxed than he was the first time."

The agents had again failed to notice that the man's height was not 5'11"; he had not chosen to correct the false heights that he had given at the first interview. (IV.403-430.)

The agents thought that the man was uncooperative about his reasons for going to the Soviet Union, but they decided that he was not a security risk, potentially dangerous, or violent. On Fain's recommendation, which was approved by the Bureau in Washington, *"Lee Harvey Oswald's" file was given a "closed status."* 'Oswald' was now free to operate clear of FBI surveillance.

FRIENDS

Two members of the Russian émigré group who demonstrated great interest in the 'Oswalds' were a middle-aged couple, George and Jeanne De Mohrenschildt. Their sophisticated life-style contrasted sharply to that of the 'Oswalds'; yet a strong relationship developed between the couples.

According to the testimony of Mr. and Mrs. George De Mohrenschildt, August 1962 was the month in which they first became acquainted with 'Oswald' and Marina. De Mohrenschildt said that he had heard about the 'Oswalds' from other members of the Russian community and, with a friend, had decided to call on Marina in August 1962 because he was curious about what kind of people 'Oswald' and his wife were. He said that he did not go to visit Marina merely because she was pretty, as suggested by Counsel, and reprimanded Counsel by saying, "We are talking about serious things." De Mohrenschildt and his wife had "hundreds of times" tried to recall exactly how they met the 'Oswalds' but the exact circumstances had "gone out of their minds" completely because so many things had happened in the meantime, "So please do not take it for sure how I first met them." (The Commission did not establish the date of their meeting; it was probably not until after the FBI gave "closed status" to 'Oswald's' file.)

When he and his friend visited Marina in Fort Worth he did not find her "particularly pretty but a lost soul, living in the slums, not knowing one single word of English with this rather unhealthy looking baby, horrible surroundings . . . A little shack, which had only two rooms, sort of clapboard-type building. Very poorly furnished, decrepit, on a dusty road."

After talking to Marina alone, 'Oswald' arrived and spoke "fluent Russian but with a foreign accent. He made mistakes, grammatical mistakes, but had remarkable fluency in Russian . . . For a fellow of his background and education, it is remarkable how fast he learned it. But he loved the language. He loved to speak it, he preferred to speak Russian than English any time. He would always switch from English to Russian." 'Oswald' told him that he lived in Minsk, and that had made De Mohrenschildt curious because he too had lived in Minsk as a child.

'Oswald' had struck him as a very sympathetic fellow, he could never get mad at him, although sometimes he was obnoxious.

> I don't know. I had a liking for him. I always had a liking for him. There was something charming about him, there was some—I don't know. I just liked the guy—that is all . . . He was very humble—with me he was very humble. If somebody expressed an interest in him, he blossomed, absolutely blossomed. If you asked him some questions about him, he was just out of this world. That was more or less the reason that I think he liked me very much.

He said that Marina's child had "kind of a big bald head, looked like Khrushchev, the child—looked like an undergrown Khrushchev. I always teased her about the fact that the baby looked like Khrushchev."

Jeanne De Mohrenschildt testified that Marina's child was fairly clean, but that Marina put the child's pacifier in her own mouth containing infected teeth before putting it in the child's mouth. This had astonished Jeanne for, although Marina was said to have been a pharmacist, she appeared to know little of hygiene. "It didn't make sense at all . . . it was just terrible, like prehistoric times she was raising that baby . . . (it) was raised on water and sugar, no food . . . She didn't know how to feed the baby."

De Mohrenschildt agreed that Marina was negligent about the child—"a poor mother, a very poor mother." He said Marina had told him it was her dream someday to live in an apartment like the one where 'Oswald' lived in Minsk, and that eventually they met and so she finally achieved her dream. "It sounds ridiculous, but that is how in Soviet Russia they dream of apartments rather than of people."

In contrast, Gary Taylor, the son-in-law of George De Mohrenschildt, had testified in answer to Counsel's question regarding his opinion of Marina, "She personally seemed to be a person of a number of fine qualities—an excellent mother, possibly even doting too much upon her child, and a clean person in her habits and, as best she could, in her dress. And she seemed very intelligent and interested in learning all that she could about her new environment."

He had noticed a strained relationship between 'Oswald' and Marina; 'Oswald' never seemed to kiss her and was more interested in talking to De Mohrenschildt than to her, although "we didn't see them very often."

About this time 'Oswald' had told George De Mohrenschildt that he was about to lose his job at Leslie Welding in Fort Worth "at least that was his version, maybe he was fired." He said that after leaving Leslie Welding, 'Oswald' got a job at some other outfit—"I forgot the name of it—a traffic outfit," and they moved from Fort Worth to Dallas about two weeks after De Mohrenschildt had met the 'Oswalds'. (The "traffic outfit" was Jaggars-Chiles-Stovall, which dealt with "highly secret" work for the Armed Forces of the United States.)

He said that he and his wife heard from others in Dallas that 'Oswald' was mistreating Marina and that she had complained to them that 'Oswald' was beating her. In testimony they claim to have forcibly removed her from the 'Oswald' apartment and taken her with the baby to stay elsewhere for a brief period.

De Mohrenschildt: Now, I do not recall what actually made me take her away from Lee.

Counsel: Now, Mr. De Mohrenschildt, there has to be something.

De Mohrenschildt: Yes, I know . . . I just don't recall how it happened. But it was because of his brutality to her . . ."

It is my belief that their conflict was a pantomime to establish that 'Oswald' and Marina were not a team. By coming to the defense of Marina, De Mohrenschildt established that his loyalty was to her and not to the impostor-assassin.

4

Espionage: Dallas

OCTOBER 1962

Marina had a friend in Dallas, Mrs. Anna Meller, who had asked her husband to telephone his friend, Mrs. Helen Cunningham, then a counselor at the Texas Employment Commission (TEC), to ask her to find a job for 'Oswald'; Mr. Meller took the precaution of warning Mrs. Cunningham that 'Oswald' had been in the Soviet Union.

Without warning and although still employed at Leslie Welding, 'Oswald' left Fort Worth for Dallas on the evening of 8 October. The next day he opened a post office box (P.O. Box 2915), and then visited TEC and was interviewed at length by Mrs. Cunningham, who noted on her counseling record cards his good appearance and considerable abilities: "Alert replies; expresses self extremely well." She also noted that she had referred him to the placement officer, Miss Louise Latham.

According to the job referral record card, E-13, on 10 October Miss Latham referred 'Oswald' to Harrell and Harrington for a job as a messenger. He was not hired as he dwelled on promotion prospects. According to John Graef, the personnel manager of Jaggars-Chiles-Stovall, Miss Latham referred 'Oswald' to him on 11 October. She did not, however, enter the referral on the card or note his acceptance as an employee. (Because it was not entered, another placement officer tried to place 'Oswald' in a job on 26 October but discovered from him that he was already working at Jaggars-Chiles-Stovall.)

In any event, on 11 October 'Oswald' secured employment as a photo-trainee at Jaggars-Chiles-Stovall, a Dallas firm that executed ex-

pert commercial photography. In a separate department, with "special-
ly cleared employees," the firm did "highly secret" work for the Department of Defense (the Army Map Service and other units of the
armed forces). The nature of the work was charting and mapping, and
the firm's task was to set words, letters, and figures on charts, maps,
and other material. The charting and mapping covered the charting of
"coastal areas, sea bottoms, and some land areas in the continental
United States and some foreign areas," but the firm had "no correla-
tion of what they (charts and maps) refer to."

Stovall and Graef of Jaggars-Chiles-Stovall were to testify (one
Counsel but no Commissioner being present) that the firm did "highly
secret" work but that Lee Harvey Oswald had no access to such work.
A fellow employee testified (one Counsel but no Commissioner being
present) that he spoke frequently to Lee and had received the impression that Lee went to the Soviet Union as an agent of the United
States, because Lee was particularly interested in talking about the military disposition of troops, tanks, and aircraft in that country, and appeared to have considerable information as to the method the Soviets
used in placing the various branches of the military in different locations. Lee told him that he had married a White Russian. None of the
three Jaggars-Chiles-Stovall staff was asked why 'Oswald' had executed work for the Army Map Service as indicated on his work sheet.
(X.167-213.)

It is vital to know how 'Oswald' was hired by a firm where he could
have access to "highly secret" material.

From the volumes of testimony it would appear (a) that someone did
not want it to be recorded that 'Oswald' had been employed by Jaggars-Chiles-Stovall through the efforts of TEC, or (b) that, in fact, he
was not employed through TEC, his application to TEC being used as
a cover for the source of the drive that, in fact, inserted him into Jaggars-Chiles-Stovall. Mrs. Cunningham was to testify at length but, although she said that she had passed 'Oswald's' name to Miss Latham
for placement, she was quite unable to explain the omission of Jaggars-
Chiles-Stovall from the referral record card (X.130-131.) (Cunningham
Exhibits No. 1-A.4.XIX.399.400.405.) 'Oswald' was to return to
TEC when he came from New Orleans to Dallas in October 1963. The
name Jaggars-Chiles-Stovall was again to be omitted from a list of
previous employers. (XIX.399.)

Graef was to testify that he had known Miss Latham for some time
and frequently telephoned her in relation to job requirements for his

firm. He said that when he needed a photo trainee in early October 1962, he had heard from Miss Latham that she had a suitable person, 'Oswald,' and that he was just out of the Marines. If Graef's memory was accurate, it would have been interesting to know who told Miss Latham that 'Oswald' was just out of the Marines, or, if nobody told her, why she had said it.

When seen by Graef, 'Oswald' told him that his name was Lee Harvey Oswald, that he was just out of the Marines with an honorable discharge, and that he had some photographic knowledge. On both the TEC records and on 'Oswald's' application for employment, his height was stated to be 5'9''.

Three other TEC personnel testified but Miss Latham, the only person who could have explained the two omissions of the name Jaggars-Chiles-Stovall, was not asked to testify and, according to the Exhibits, was not interviewed by any investigative agency.

At the time of Mrs. Cunningham's testimony, Miss Latham worked at TEC—"an off again, on again situation" according to Mrs. Cunningham—but about two days later she left Dallas for good. (Her abrupt departure from Dallas should not be interpreted as evidence of malfeasance, possibly quite the reverse.)

Three senior Counsel had come to Dallas from Washington to find out how 'Oswald' had managed to obtain work in the firm where he was to spy. In testimony, Mrs. Cunningham specifically drew their attention to Miss Latham and her imminent departure; Counsel did not invite or subpoena her to testify.

On his first working day, Friday 12 October, 'Oswald's' work sheet at Jaggars-Chiles-Stovall reads, "Training, lunch, training." On Sunday 14 October, the U-2 reconnaissance mission brought to the United States the definitive photographs of missile sites in Cuba. On Monday 15 October, 'Oswald's' work sheet reads, "Training, lunch, training." President Kennedy received "the first preliminary hard information" of Soviet-built missile sites in Cuba on Tuesday 16 October, which was the same day that 'Oswald' ceased his training and commenced work in the camera department, executing his fifth job on that morning between 9:45 A.M. and 10:10 A.M. for the Army Map Service presumably captioning photographs. Of course it was vital for the Soviets to know how much had been discovered by the U-2 flights over Cuba. Although he continued to work at the firm until 6 April 1963 when he would be dismissed, he had no further work for the Army Map Service until later in his employment, when he did a few more photographic jobs for them. (CE.1850.) The Warren Report omits all this.

THE PARAPHERNALIA OF A SPY

On the morning of the assassination, 'Oswald' had left his notebook with Marina, and on a page of the notebook he had written "Jaggars-Chiles-Stovall—microdots." (XVI.63.) On the first day of Marina's testimony before six Commissioners, including Allen Dulles, for many years the head of the CIA and known to the United States intelligence services as "the super-spy," Counsel said to Marina, "He had a reference in his notebook to the word 'Microdot.' Do you know what he meant by that?" Marina answered "No." Counsel did not mention the firm, Jaggars-Chiles-Stovall, written above the word "microdots." The subject was then dropped. No Commissioner interrupted Counsel to ask about this well-known espionage technique of transmitting photographs of plans or documents by microdot (a photograph no larger than a pinhead which can be secreted under a postage stamp or elsewhere for transmission to "headquarters"), nor did they demand to see the notebook. (I.68.)

During this time 'Oswald' accumulated a full range of spying equipment, which was found at 'Oswald's' home by the Dallas police after the assassination: a Minox camera, three other cameras, two binoculars, a new 15-power telescope, a compass and a pedometer, exposed and unexposed film, and a 4-½" blade hunting knife in sheath; the total cost of the equipment could not have been less than $500, yet the apparently penniless 'Oswald' never went hunting, nor did he ever use a camera to take a social photograph while in the United States; he did nothing that might have involved the innocent use of any of this equipment.

When Marina testified, she was shown the following items which she disclaimed having seen before:

(i) a padlock key and chain,

(ii) a new 15-power telescope,

(iii) a new 4-½" blade hunting knife in sheath,

(iv) a camera in a leather case (the word "Minox" was not used by Counsel), and

(v) an Ansco flash attachment for camera.

These Exhibits were given numbers 119, 120, 124, 137, and 138; the footnote to page xii of Volume XVI, however, states that these numbers were not used, thus avoiding the necessity of showing these items in the Exhibits. Had they been shown, espionage would have been apparent. The significance of the padlock is not known, but a spy at night usually carries a strong knife. The Minox is not mentioned in the Warren Report but appears on only one list of objects recovered by the police from the assassin's residence, and photographed by them.

'OSWALD'S' ACQUAINTANCES

After 'Oswald' joined the firm of Jaggars-Chiles-Stovall on 12 October, 38-year-old Jack Leslie Bowen, an assistant art director, was to work with him in the camera department. Bowen's real name was John Caesar Grossi, Jack Leslie Bowen being his alias. He had been an inmate at several penitentiaries. His alias, his friendship with 'Oswald,' and his criminal record would not have been discovered had there not been found in 'Oswald's' wallet after his arrest in Dallas a Dallas library card on which was typed the name Jack L. Bowen. Bowen was employed by Jaggars-Chiles-Stovall in August 1961 and left in August 1963. Although available to testify, he was never called before the Commission; neither his names nor his friendship with the assassin are mentioned in the Warren Report. (XXV.65-67.) Graef was not asked in testimony how he came to employ a man in an alias (like 'Oswald') who had a substantial criminal record, who had recommended him, and whether he had access to "highly secret" material.

'Oswald' had arrived in Dallas on 9 October. The Warren Commission was never able to account for his living arrangements for the first six days. Between 15 October and 19 October, he resided at the Dallas YMCA. He was again lost sight of until 3 November, when he took an apartment in Dallas. Even after the assassination, when 'Oswald's' name, description, and photographs were for weeks constantly before the Dallas and Fort Worth public, according to the Warren Report and the Exhibits, nobody volunteered information about where he had been living during the 20 days of his disappearance; yet somebody must have known. It would seem that 'Oswald' had used a friend who failed to tell the authorities of 'Oswald's' whereabouts.

In February 1963, a party was given in Dallas and attended by both George and Jeanne De Mohrenschildt and the 'Oswalds.' It was here that Marina first met Ruth Paine, with whom she conversed at length in the kitchen, Marina having taken along her year-old daughter and being unwilling to mingle with the other guests. Ruth liked Marina, and they arranged to meet again as soon as possible. De Mohrenschildt testified that he had noticed that there was a nice relationship developing between Mrs. Paine and Marina. When asked by Counsel whether he had assisted in arranging the party, De Mohrenschildt replied, "Yes, exactly."

Ruth unwittingly was to assist 'Oswald' in his plan to assassinate the President.

AN ATTEMPTED MURDER

On 10 April, four days after 'Oswald' had left his employment at Jaggars-Chiles-Stovall, retired Army General Edwin Walker, reputed to be a member of the John Birch Society, reported to Dallas police an attempt on his life at 9:00 P.M. A single rifle shot had been fired at him while he was sitting in his study, but the bullet, nicking a window frame, narrowly missed his head and passed through the wall behind him. The FBI was later to determine that the bullet was the same caliber as the rifle that 'Oswald' owned, an old Italian military rifle fitted with a telescopic sight. It had been purchased from a Chicago mail-order house by 'Oswald' a few days previously and had been mailed to him in the name of A. Hidell at his post office box in Dallas. Owing to mutilation, the bullet could not be identified as having been fired from 'Oswald's' rifle.

In testimony, Marina would say that early on the evening of 10 April she had seen her husband leave their apartment on Neely Street, but that she did not know where he was going and did not notice that he was carrying a rifle. After he had left the apartment, she had found a note written in Russian that alarmed her, for it set out in detail what she should do if he were killed or arrested that night. On his return, he had told her that he had tried to shoot General Walker. She further testified that he had left behind not only the note but also a notebook containing written plans for the shooting together with photographs of the general's house. Counsel asked her:

Did it seem strange to you at the time, Marina, that Lee did make these careful plans, take pictures, and write it up in a notebook, and then when he went out to shoot at General Walker he left all that incriminating evidence right in the house so that if he had ever been stopped and questioned and if that notebook had been found, it would have clearly indicated that he was the one that shot at General Walker?

She replied:

He was such a person that nothing seems peculiar to me for what he did. I had so many surprises from him that nothing surprised me. He may have wished to appear such a brave man or something.

She said that she had kept the note that he had left for her as a "hold" over him should he attempt to murder anyone else. (After the assassination of the President, the note was found between the leaves of one of her books.)

The attempted murder of Walker is peripheral to the assassination and little need be said about it except that, despite powerful evidence that two men were involved, the Warren Report asserts that Lee Harvey Oswald, without an accomplice, had fired the shot at Walker. Whatever may be the truth, there is no doubt that 'Oswald' knew of the attempt to murder the general, for he had the general's name and telephone number in his notebook. In addition, some photographs taken with one of 'Oswald's' cameras of the back and side of the general's house were found among 'Oswald's' effects after Kennedy's assassination.

General Walker was, among other things, well known as perhaps the most active opponent of Fidel Castro. The attempted murder would give color to the suspicion that both it and the assassination of Kennedy seven months later had been ordered by Castro.

On 23 April, Vice President Johnson visited Dallas; the next day the Dallas newspapers informed their readers that President Kennedy would be visiting in the fall.

That same day, 31-year-old Ruth Paine, a Russian-language tutor, who had befriended Marina since the party in February, called at the 'Oswalds' Neely Street apartment, where she was surprised to find that they were packed and proposing to leave that evening for New

Orleans. Ruth suggested that instead of the then two-months-pregnant Marina traveling with her husband and little June on a long bus journey, she would take Marina and June into her house in Irving, some 12 miles from Dallas, and when 'Oswald' had found work and an apartment in New Orleans, she would drive Marina and June south to join him. This was then agreed, and Ruth took Marina and June to Irving to await word from 'Oswald.'

5

Setting up the Cuban Connection

Arriving in New Orleans alone, 'Oswald' stayed at the home of his maternal aunt, Lillian Murret, and her family, whom Oswald last saw when he was 15 years old. They knew neither that Oswald had gone to the Soviet Union nor that he had returned.

From the Murrett's house, 'Oswald' called all the Oswalds in the telephone book and visited the cemetery where Oswald's father had been buried; he was able to locate only one elderly relative, who gave him a photograph of Oswald's father and told him that as far as she knew, the rest of the family were dead. (After the assassination, no such photograph was found among the assassin's possessions.)

MAY 1963

On 9 May, in the name of Lee Harvey Oswald, 'Oswald' found employment as a greaser of coffee machines with the Wm. B. Reily Co. He gave his height as 5'9'',and on the same day he rented an apartment at 4907 Magazine Street, also in the name of Lee Harvey Oswald. He then telephoned Marina and asked her to come to New Orleans. Ruth, Marina, and June left Irving in Ruth's car on 10 May and arrived at 'Oswald's' apartment on 11 May. Ruth remained in the apartment for three days before returning to Irving; she had been uncomfortable, sensing that her presence had caused the 'Oswalds' to quarrel.

On 26 May, 'Oswald' wrote to the Fair Play for Cuba Committee (FPCC), a group financed by the Cuban government, requesting membership. After stating his longtime interest in the organization, he suggested renting a small office for the purpose of forming an FPCC branch in New Orleans, and requested a charter. He asked for advice, and recommendations, saying that his project "might not be a roaring success but that he was willing to try," and ending, "an office, literature, and getting people to know you are the fundamentals of the FPCC as far as I can see so here's hoping to hear from you." He also requested "a picture of Fidel Castro suitable for framing," saying it would be "a welcome touch."

On 29 May, the FPCC replied, giving him a number of instructions as to the setting up of a local chapter and saying that the opening of a post office box was a "must."

JUNE 1963

Between 31 May and 5-6 June, 'Oswald' ordered certain FPCC literature and membership application forms of his own design from two different printing firms in New Orleans. To one firm he gave his name as Osborne, and to the other as Lee Osborne. The use of false names was not to hide his assumed name, for the printed matter contained the information that L. H. Oswald was the secretary of the FPCC chapter in New Orleans. The connection with the name Osborne becomes clear when it is related to 'Oswald's' secret journey to Mexico City four months later—when he shared a seat on a long-distance bus journey with 75-year-old Albert Osborne *alias* John Howard Bowen. To post-assassination investigators, it would appear that when the assassin ordered his FPCC printed material, he had not acted alone but as an agent for Osborne, and that both of them were acting and traveling to Mexico City on behalf of Castro.

On 11 June, 'Oswald' opened P.O. Box 30061 in New Orleans in the name of L. H. Oswald. Inserted in the space for names of persons entitled to receive mail through the box was written "A. J. Hidell" and "Marina Oswald." A man named Heindel, nicknamed Hidell, had served with the real Oswald in the Marines and lived in New Orleans; in no way was he involved, but 'Oswald' may have chosen New Orleans as an operational base so that the authorities would later suspect that Oswald and Heindel might conceivably have been two different people conspiring on behalf of Castro.

About this time, 'Oswald,' apparently thinking it unwise to visit a regular doctor, somehow obtained a blank form of the "International Certificate of Vaccination or Revaccination against Smallpox," which he filled out in the name of Lee Oswald, signing it Lee H. Oswald, and inserting in capitals the name DR. A. J. HIDEEL, P.O. BOX 30016, NEW ORLEANS, LA. 'Oswald' had dated the certificate 8 June and impressed a counterfeit stamp—using a cheap rubber stamping kit that he had acquired—in the space reserved for "Approved Stamp." A vaccination certificate would be required by 'Oswald' for his intended travel to and from Cuba; after the assassination it was found among his possessions, and so further involved Cuba and ex-Marine Heindel. The spelling "Hideel" and the wrong box number would again suggest to postassassination investigators that there had been two Oswalds in the United States, who made mistakes because they were not always in liaison.

On 24 June, 'Oswald' applied for a new passport which, since he had paid off his loan from the State Department some six months earlier, he received the following day. On the application form he gave his height as 5'11", and this height was recorded in the new passport. On the form he stated that he would be leaving the country by the Lykes Line during November or December, and that he planned to visit "England, France, Holland, USSR, Findland (sic), Italy and Poland." (On the application for his 1959 passport, the real Oswald had spelled Finland correctly.) Although American citizens at that time were banned by law from traveling directly to Cuba, it was possible to enter that country by way of Mexico. (XVII.666.XVIII.819.) 'Oswald' required the passport for the journey to Cuba via Mexico that he planned shortly to make.

JULY 1963

On 6 July one of Mrs. Murret's sons, Gene, who was studying to be a Jesuit priest in Mobile, Alabama, wrote to 'Oswald' asking if he would come to Mobile and speak at the Jesuit House of Studies about contemporary Russia and the practice of Communism in that country. 'Oswald' accepted and on 27 July he, Marina, and some of the Murret family traveled from New Orleans to Mobile in Mr. Murret's car, Mr. Murret paying all the expenses. 'Oswald' addressed a meeting attended by some twenty scholars and two Jesuit priests for about half an hour, and then answered questions for another half hour. He indicated that he had become disillusioned during his stay in the Soviet Union, and that in his opinion the right political system would be one which combined the best points of capitalism and communism. He did not mention Cuba; he had not yet commenced his intended FPCC street campaign in New Orleans, although he had obtained the necessary printed material a month previously. According to Gene and the two Jesuit priests who attended the meeting, all of whom were interviewed by the FBI after the assassination, 'Lee Harvey Oswald' was "neatly dressed . . . handled himself well" and gave an address of average quality.

'Oswald' had been dismissed on 19 July by his employer at the coffee company because of inefficiency and inattention to work, and obtained no further employment in New Orleans.

Though Marina professed to Ruth Paine and other acquaintances that she did not want to return to Russia, from 17 February through the end of August, Marina carried on a correspondence with Consul Reznichenko at the Soviet Embassy in Washington asking him to grant her permission to return to the Soviet Union. She also wrote several other letters to him reporting change of address as required of her as a Soviet citizen. On 5 August, Reznichenko wrote to her in New Orleans to tell her that her application for permanent residence in the USSR had been forwarded to Moscow for processing. She would testify that she had never wished to return to the Soviet Union but that her husband desired her to take this course. (On the day after the assassination she told the Secret Service that it was she who had wished to return to the Soviet Union, and that her husband had agreed to accompany her in order to preserve the marriage and on account of their children.) It would seem that if 'Oswald' had escaped after the assassination, Moscow would rapidly have processed her application, and Reznichenko would have issued the necessary reentry papers into the Soviet Union without delay; it would then appear to the American authorities that her departure for the Soviet Union soon after the assassination had not been other than the result of her earlier requests and in the normal tardy course of Soviet business of this nature. Presumably the United States authorities would have had no right to prevent her departure.

Marina was also in correspondence with Gregory Mikhaylovich Shapkin, Third Secretary at the Soviet Embassy in Washington, who had been appointed in October 1959 and withdrawn in December

1963. (C.D. 928. p. 51, Declassified, 2 February 1976.) The nature and extent of the correspondence has not been revealed. (Shapkin is not mentioned in the Warren Report; neither is Reznichenko.)

A third person with whom Marina corresponded was her good friend Ruth Paine who, 10 weeks later, was to assist 'Oswald' in obtaining employment in the Texas School Book Depository, the building from which he would shoot the President. Their letters were affectionate; in one of them Ruth writes, "I love you, Marina, and want to live with you."

AUGUST 1963

On 1 August, 'Oswald' wrote to the FPCC (the envelope is postmarked 4 August) and mentioned that there had been a "scuffle" in the street while he was handing out FPCC literature. The "scuffle" did not occur until 9 August; the letter implicated the FPCC with foreknowledge. The "scuffle" would also enable 'Oswald's' height of 5'9" to be officially recorded by the New Orleans police and the FBI, thus making the FBI believe that there must have been two 'Oswalds' operating in the United States.

On 5 August, 'Oswald' visited a store managed by a Cuban refugee who was the New Orleans delegate of the anti-Castro organization called The Cuban Student Directorate. 'Oswald,' giving his name as Lee Oswald, displayed a strong interest in joining the struggle against Castro and suggested methods of guerrilla warfare, including blowing up bridges, derailing trains, making gunpowder, and so on. The next day 'Oswald' returned to the store and left a "Guidebook for Marines" for the delegate, indicating that he had visited the headquarters of the Directorate in Miami. (After the assassination, it would be thought that it had been on Castro's instructions that he had infiltrated the opposition; the Marine Corps Guidebook confirmed that the man was an ex-Marine.)

On 9 August, the delegate and other Cuban exiles happened to hear that the young man was passing out FPCC leaflets in the street. They succeeded in finding him, and tried to tear up the leaflets and strike him, but he lowered his hands and pushed out his chin inviting a blow. When the police arrived, 'Oswald' and three Cubans were arrested for disturbing the peace. Giving the name Lee Harvey Oswald, 'Oswald' told the police that he had been born in Cuba and had married a Russian woman in Fort Worth; he omitted any mention of having lived in the Soviet Union. He was evasive about his previous places of employment, mentioning Leslie Welding but omitting Jaggars-Chiles-Stovall. The police recorded his height, taken against a scale, as 5'9" and fingerprinted him, the prints being routinely sent to the FBI fingerprint department. (XXII.820-828.)

In due course 'Oswald' and the Cubans were tried for creating a disturbance; the charges against the Cubans were dismissed, but "Lee Harvey Oswald" was convicted and fined $10. As it turned out, however, 'Oswald' was to benefit from both the melée and his arrest, suggesting that he had anticipated the results.

While in police custody, he had succeeded in directing the attention of the FBI toward the subversive FPCC. He had requested the police to telephone the New Orleans FBI and ask for an agent to interview him at the police station. Special Agent John Quigley, who had not previously heard of the young man or of the FPCC campaign in New Orleans, arrived at the police station later and interviewed 'Oswald' for some two hours, recording "from interrogation and observation" that Lee Harvey Oswald's height was 5'9". 'Oswald' talked at length about the FPCC and mentioned A. J. Hidell as the moving spirit in the New Orleans chapter, hinting that there were other members and several meeting places including his own apartment, but refusing to disclose other names or places—of which there were none. The attention of the FBI agent was thus drawn to 'Lee Harvey Oswald's' involvement with the FPCC and the name Hidell, and he submitted a five-page report of this interview dealing exclusively with the FPCC activities. (XVII.762.)

Quigley was later to testify that 'Oswald' told him that after leaving the Marines with an honorable discharge, he had lived in Fort Worth where he met and married a girl called Prossa some five months previously, and that they had come directly from Fort Worth to New Orleans. Quigley said that 'Oswald' had been reticent, evasive, and somewhat antagonistic about specific details of his FPCC chapter, and would not say why he had asked for the interview. He thought that 'Oswald's' request for this had been for the purpose of making a self-serving statement to explain why he had distributed FPCC literature, and Quigley thought 'Oswald' had lied to him about other matters. Quigley did not mention the height of 5'9", nor did the Commission ask him about it. (IV.431-440.) This interview with the FBI was 'Oswald's' last until after the assassination. Had he not been caught after the assassination the authorities would have been searching for a man who had never been to the Soviet Union.

The FBI in New Orleans and in Washington now had in their file on "Lee Harvey Oswald" two different heights and biographies; by doing nothing about it, they were further compromised.

On 17 August, William Stuckey, a local radio broadcaster who had long been looking for a member of the FPCC to appear on his program, heard through an anti-Castroite that 'Lee Harvey Oswald' was interested in the FPCC. He visited 'Oswald' by appointment at his apartment and, after noticing that 'Oswald' was wearing a pair of Marine fatigue trousers, he recorded an interview with him in which 'Oswald' talked about 'his' Marine Corps service and the FPCC. A shortened version of the interview was played back on the radio show that evening, and the contents of the playback was almost entirely about the FPCC and 'Oswald's' activities in that connection. Two days later, a debate was arranged between 'Oswald,' Stuckey, and two other men, opponents of Castro, who were experienced in Cuban and world affairs generally.

In testimony, Stuckey was to say that 'Lee Harvey Oswald' was "confident, self-assured, logical, articulate, very well able to handle the questions and very well disciplined. He seemed like somebody that took very good care of himself, very prudent, temperate, that sort of person." It was Stuckey's impression that 'Oswald' regarded himself as living in a world of intellectual inferiors. To an awkward question, 'Oswald' would say, "That is a good question" or "I am glad you asked that question, it is very good," and then would obliquely avoid answering it or else distort it for his own purposes, saying what he wanted to say while making one think he was answering the question. He was "expert at dialectics" and "his manner was sort of quasi-legal; it was almost as if he was a young attorney. He seemed very well acquainted with the legal terminology dealing with constitutional rights." It was Stuckey's impression that 'Oswald' had done a great deal of reading; 'Oswald' had said during the radio debate that "the Russians had gone soft on Communism, and that Cuba was the only real revolutionary country in the world." As customary, a copy of the radio transcripts was sent to the New Orleans FBI a few days after the broadcast, the transcripts showing that 'Oswald' admitted b:ing in the Soviet Union, thus contradicting what he had told FBI agent Quigley.

Through his street appearances where he was televised, and the two radio broadcasts, 'Oswald' had demonstrated publicly and to the FBI that he was a fervid supporter of Castro.

6

Mexico City:
Prelude to the Assassination

In mid-September, about a month after his media-aided notoriety as a Cuban expert, 'Oswald' called at the Mexican Consulate in New Orleans and applied for permission to travel through Mexico as an in-transit tourist, completing the application form for a 15-day intransit card in a curious way. He wrote his full alias, Lee Harvey Oswald, but left a gap between Lee and Harvey with the result that either the clerk who issued the card wrote "Lee, Harvey Oswald" or 'Oswald' himself inserted the comma. The issuance of the card thus inscribed enabled him (a) to travel to Mexico City under the assumed name of "Lee," (b) to register at a Mexico City hotel in the name of "Lee," (c) to return to the United States in the name of "Lee," and (d) thus to prevent the FBI from discovering his presence in Mexico until after the assassination.

'Oswald' told Marina he was going to Cuba via Mexico City but cautioned her that the trip and its purpose were to be kept strictly secret.

On 20 September, Ruth Paine had again driven to New Orleans to take Marina back to Irving. Marina was some eight months pregnant, and the plan was for Ruth to help her before and after the birth that was expected in October. Ruth, Marina, and the 'Oswald's' daughter, June, drove back to Texas on 23 September leaving 'Oswald' alone at the Magazine Street apartment.

It has never been discovered where 'Oswald' spent the next night, 24 September, but early on the next day he left New Orleans by bus for

Houston. At 2:35 A.M. on 26 September (the day the Dallas press announced Kennedy's two-day visit to Texas), traveling in the name of Harvey Oswald Lee, 'Oswald' boarded a bus in Houston and left for Laredo, Texas.

Also on this day, 26 September, in Nuevo Laredo, 75-year-old Albert Osborne, an English-born and self-styled itinerant missionary, obtained a six-month tourist card for Mexico in the name of John Howard Bowen, presenting a false birth certificate that gave his age as 60 years. His application form said untruthfully that he resided and worked in Houston.

Later in the day at Nuevo Laredo, John Howard Bowen, carrying three suitcases, joined Harvey Oswald Lee on a Mexican bus which would take them to Mexico City. Between 1:30 P.M. and 2:00 P.M. on 26 September, their bus left Nuevo Laredo, and during the whole of this last leg of the journey, from Nuevo Laredo to Mexico City, Harvey Oswald Lee sat beside and conversed with John Howard Bowen, later identified by the FBI as Albert Osborne.

Traveling on the bus were two British tourists, Dr. and Mrs. John McFarland, and in a statement to the British police in Liverpool at the request of the FBI, they said that 'Oswald' had told them that he was going to Cuba via Mexico City, that he hoped to see Fidel Castro in Havana, and that he was secretary of the New Orleans branch of the FPCC.

Also on the bus were Miss Pamela Mumford and Miss Patricia Winston, two Australian girls on a world tour. 'Oswald' made a point of talking to them, saying that he came from Fort Worth but not telling them his name. He advised them to stay at the Hotel Cuba in Mexico City where he untruthfully said he had previously stayed as it was cheap and clean. In order to show the girls that he had been in the Soviet Union, 'Oswald' took the real Oswald's 1959 passport out of a pouch on the rack above his head.

John Howard Bowen untruthfully told the McFarlands that he was writing a book on the 1777 earthquake in Lisbon, and that he was a retired school teacher who had taught in India and Arabia.

The bus carried some 35 adults together with children and small animals. There were only six English-speaking persons on the bus, 'Oswald' and Osborne on one seat, the McFarlands sitting immediately in front of them, and the two Australian girls across the aisle. The McFarlands and the girls had no difficulty in identifying from photographs

'Oswald' and Osborne as the two men they had observed sitting and conversing together.

The FBI was to conduct a vast inter-state, inter-country, and inter-continental investigation into Albert Osborne.

What the FBI discovered about his 47 years of activity in the United States, Canada, and Mexico indicates that from 1916, when he assumed the alias of John Howard Bowen on arriving in the United States from Britain, he was an espionage agent, either free-lance or Soviet, and was never a genuine missionary or itinerant preacher. In his later years, his permanent address was a native mud-walled hut in Mexico, where he carried on the pretense of missionary work, gathering small sums of money and old clothes in the United States for his Mexican "flock," although what he must have spent on his extensive travels, hotels, and YMCA residences in the United States, Canada (where he had a false address), Mexico, and elsewhere over many years would surely have exceeded anything he could have received from contributions.

Interviewed by the FBI at different and far-ranging places in the name of Albert Osborne, he maintained that he knew of the man John Howard Bowen and said that they might easily be confused with each other as they were both itinerant missionaries, and of the same age, size, and appearance. Then interviewed as John Howard Bowen, he told the FBI the same things about Osborne. When in either name shown two old photographs of himself that the FBI had discovered, he said that one was of him and the other was of the other man. Osborne also used the names Dr. Hidalgo and Alberto Osborne.

From December 1963 to March 1964, Albert Osborne made every effort to evade and mislead the FBI until finally "cornered" by them at the YMCA, Nashville, Tennessee, where he had registered as John H. Bowen of "The Old Folks Home," Grimsby, England. He finally admitted his double-identity and earlier lies, but continued to deny that he had sat beside 'Oswald' on the bus to Mexico City. He described the young man sitting beside him as "tending to be bald-headed and with a sallow complexion."

Despite the fact that he and 'Oswald' were shown on the bus manifest as traveling together, and had been positively identified, the FBI report of their last interview with Osborne ends, "He again denied that he was on a bus with any other English speaking people and that he himself spoke no English to anyone on the bus. He stated that since he had finally revealed his true identity that he would have no purpose in being further untruthful, and that if he were a passenger on the bus with **LEE HARVEY OSWALD** and other English speaking people, he would freely admit same now, but he continued to maintain that he had never seen OSWALD or been a fellow passenger with him on the bus or the above-mentioned English couple and Australian girls." (XXV.25-75.)

In referring to Albert Osborne, the Warren Report says:

The man next to Oswald was probably Albert Osborne, a native of the British Isles who has worked as an itinerant preacher in the southern United States and Mexico for many years. Osborne denied that he sat beside Oswald; but in view of his inconsistent and untrue responses to federal investigators concerning matters not directly related to Oswald, the Commission believed that his denial cannot be credited. It appeared to the other passengers on the bus that Osborne and Oswald had not previously met; extensive investigation has revealed no other contact between them.

The son of a fisherman, Albert Osborne was born in 1888 in Grimsby, England, and at an early age he enlisted in the British Army. When his regiment was ordered to India, he bought himself out of the army and emigrated to the United States.

An elderly sister, Ada Amos, who had emigrated to the United States with her husband at about the same time as Albert, when interviewed by the FBI in 1964 said that she had seen Albert only once in the last 55 years and that Albert formerly lived in New York and Washington, and had then settled in the south, mostly in areas of Tennessee. In Albert's infrequent letters he told her that he often traveled to Mexico, crossing the border at Laredo and El Paso. She believed that he had married in the United States and had a son who had been killed in action in the American Army during World War II, and that he had a daughter-in-law and a grandson in the United States. She understood that Albert's occupation was that of a preacher, but she did not know under what denomination. She believed that at some time he had been employed as an actor and also as a lecturer on India, and that in earlier years Albert had shown some talent as an artist and that he had spent some time sketching. She told the FBI that she had not heard of Albert having any scientific or technical skill, or being involved in *oceanographic or scientific projects*.

That the FBI questioned Ada about this matter indicates that they suspected espionage in Jaggars-Chiles-Stovall and were considering a possible relationship between the 75-year-old Albert Osborne *alias* John Howard Bowen and 38-year-old John Caesar Grossi *alias* Jack Leslie Bowen, the latter known to have an interest in Mexico and to have worked with 'Oswald' at Jaggars-Chiles-Stovall.

Shortly after her interview, Ada visited her sister Emily and Emily's daughter in Grimsby, and told them about the interview. She said that from the line of questioning she had concluded that the FBI suspected that Albert had been a spy. She was told by the agent that he had died but she did not know when, where or why.

ARRIVING IN MEXICO CITY

Although the real Oswald could speak a limited Spanish (cf. testimony of Delgado), while on the bus and in México City, 'Oswald' could not speak one word of Spanish and used sign language exclusively. Knowing her husband could not speak Spanish, Marina had prepared a list of 48 simple Spanish words and the numbers one through 17 with their Russian equivalents for his use while in Mexico. The list was found and intended to be found after the assassination.

After their arrival in Mexico City on 27 September, Albert Osborne's activities are unknown, but 'Oswald' booked into an hotel and signed the register as H. O. Lee. He then went to the Cuban Consulate—which shared the building with the Embassy—where, in the name of Lee Harvey Oswald, he requested a visa to visit Cuba. When asked the reason for his intended visit, 'Oswald' said that actually he was going on to the Soviet Union, but that he would like to stay in Cuba for about two weeks before proceeding, adding that he wanted to be in Cuba by 30 September. He had, in fact, no intention of going to the Soviet Union and staying there.

'Oswald's' purpose, as will be seen from his letter of 9 November 1963 to the Soviet Consulate in Washington, was to go to the Soviet Embassy in Havana to receive instructions about the assassination and escape from Dallas. The man he would probably have seen was a veteran KGB officer, Aleksandr I. Shitov, who in 1959 in the alias of Aleksandr I. Alekseev had been appointed to a cover post at the Soviet Embassy in Havana. In 1962 he had been elevated to the post of Ambassador to Cuba while still continuing his KGB activities. Had 'Oswald' gone to the Soviet Embassy in Havana as he intended to do, the name "Alek" might have been used as a code name to identify himself to Alekseev. (The name Natalie Alekseevna appears in 'Oswald's' notebook (XVI.50.); "na" is the suffix for daughter.)

In order to facilitate the processing of a Cuban visa while he was allegedly in transit to the Soviet Union, 'Oswald' supported his application by presenting the real Oswald's old 1959 passport which recorded that Oswald had lived in the Soviet Union for more than two and a half years. He also presented Oswald's work permit for that country written in Russian, and letters in the same language, proof of his being married to a Russian woman, proof of his being the secretary in New Orleans of the FPCC, newspaper cuttings relating to this arrest in New Orleans in connection with his FPCC street campaign, and the real Oswald's Marine history; all were coupled with his desire to be accepted as a "friend" of the Cuban Revolution and, therefore, someone entitled to a rapid issuance of a visa to enter Cuba.

The woman in the Cuban Consulate who interviewed 'Oswald' refused to grant him an immediate visa. 'Oswald' objected vehemently and she called Consul Eusebio Ascue, who also denied 'Oswald's' request, stating that a formal request required several weeks. Then "exceeding her duties," the woman, according to the Mexican police who later arrested and interviewed her, telephoned the Soviet Embassy to say that Lee Harvey Oswald was coming to see them about a visa for Russia.

As 'Oswald' did not wish to be seen entering the Soviet Embassy he contacted an as yet unidentified "American male" to visit the Soviet Embassy in his stead.

A CIA informant installed in the compound housing the Soviet Embassy and Consulate reported to the CIA that an "American male" appeared at the Consulate on 28 September and announced himself as Lee Oswald.

The informant described Oswald as approximately 35 years old, approximately 6' in height, of athletic build, and with a receding hairline. He spoke with Valeri Vladimirovich Kostikov, since identified as a clandestine KGB officer, and at the time suspected by the CIA and the FBI of being a member of Department 13, the sabotage and assassination squad of the KGB. The "American male" probably also talked with Paul Antonovich Yatskov, another clandestine KGB officer stationed at the Embassy, because Yatskov, Second Secretary to the Embassy, was at this time in charge of the consular section; Kostikov occupied the cover post of a consular official, having been trained in routine consular work. (In 1971, Oleg Lyalin, a member of Department 13, defected in Britain, and squad members around the world were recalled to Moscow; among the first to leave was Kostikov.)

On 1 October, the "American male" again visited the Soviet Consulate, this time to inquire about a reply to a telegram sent to Washington. This second visit was also observed and reported to the CIA by their informant. (CD.631.) The two visits of the "American male" were reported to the FBI almost immediately.

CIA surveillance cameras hidden outside the Cuban and Soviet Embassies photographed the "American male" on several occasions, and their photographs show that the informant's description of the man was accurate and that he was clearly not 'Oswald.' These photographs were not to be shown to the FBI until after the assassination.

CHANGE OF PLANS

In the meantime, between 27 September and 2 October, according to the letter of 9 November to the Soviet Consulate in Washington, 'Oswald' had "meetings" at the Soviet Embassy in Mexico City with another clandestine KGB officer, Valeri Dmitrevich Kostin. According to a CIA memorandum to the Warren Commission, Kostin was not listed as working at the Soviet Embassy in Mexico City. It would seem, therefore, that Kostin came to Mexico City either from the Soviet Embassy in Havana or direct from the Soviet Union to confer with 'Oswald' after the latter's failure to get to the Soviet Embassy in Havana. Since 'Oswald' was not observed by the CIA informant inside the Soviet Embassy nor photographed outside the Cuban or Soviet Embassies, it would seem that considerable secrecy had been maintained over the meetings between 'Oswald' and Kostin.

It is, of course, not known what occurred in Mexico City or at the Soviet Embassy between 27 September and 2 October, but the situation involved three men using aliases ('Oswald' *alias* Lee Harvey Oswald *alias* Harvey Oswald Lee. Albert Osborne *alias* John Howard Bowen. The "American male" *alias* Lee Oswald.) In addition, there were clandestine KGB officers (Kostikov, probably Yatskov, and Kostin): powerful evidence of conspiracy. There is no evidence that any attempt was made by any investigative body to ascertain the identity of the "American male." A discussion of how the Warren Commission obscured the conspiracy in Mexico City may be found in Appendix E.

On 2 October, John Howard Bowen crossed the international bridge from Nuevo Laredo into Texas and proceeded indirectly to New Orleans, where he would again become Albert Osborne. When obtaining a Canadian passport on 10 October at the Canadian Consulate in New Orleans and giving a false address in Montreal, he exhibited a birth certificate in the name of Albert Osborne, and said that he was a clergyman and a Canadian citizen having lived in Canada since 1917. He signed an affidavit claiming that no one knew him well enough in New Orleans to act as a guarantor as to his identity. Within a year, the FBI would tell his sister he was dead.

On 3 October, Harvey Oswald Lee crossed the international bridge from Nuevo Laredo into Texas and arrived in Dallas that afternoon. On arrival in Dallas, he would again become Lee Harvey Oswald. He or another person had reserved a seat—entered in the bus manifest as 'Oswld'' (*sic*)—on a bus that left Mexico City for Nuevo Laredo several hours after the bus which Harvey Oswald Lee had boarded for Dallas. It is not known when or for whom this reservation was made, but it again suggested that 'Oswald' was leaving a trail of two Oswalds.

'Oswald's' intransit tourist card entitled him to stay in Mexico for another seven days, and Albert Osborne's tourist card was good for another five months and three weeks. 'Oswald's' and Osborne's sudden departure could well have been signaled by 'Oswald's' failure to enter Cuba.

7

Fixing the Assassination Site

The visit of President Kennedy to Texas in November 1963 had been under consideration at the White House for almost a year. A one-day visit had at first been proposed for 21 November and would have required whirlwind visits to Dallas, Fort Worth, San Antonio, and Houston, with insufficient time for a motorcade through downtown Dallas. The President would have proceeded directly from Love Field airport, Dallas, along Inwood Road to speak at a luncheon arranged at the Trade Mart, and he would have returned to the airport along In-wood Road.

On 26 September 1963 (the day 'Oswald' entered Mexico), the press announced that the visit would be extended to two days, thus allowing time for a downtown motorcade in Dallas.

The traditional motorcade route was down Main Street, and when the motorcade would emerge from the built-up area of Dallas, there were only two ways for it to reach the Mart. First, the motorcade could make a right turn onto Industrial Boulevard, and then go straight to the Mart. Second, instead of using Industrial Boulevard, the motorcade could make a right turn from Main Street and then a left turn onto Elm Street, the latter leading into Stemmons Freeway which also led straight to the Mart.

On 3 October, 'Oswald' came from the Soviet Embassy in Mexico City to Dallas, and to assassinate Kennedy; he must have been told of all the possible routes that Kennedy could take. Aware of the routes, he made applications in person for employment only at firms which could

(71)

serve as possible assassination sites, thus enabling him to inspect the premises inside and out; the job taken was to be on the ideal site.

The conspirators in Mexico City had realized that the more likely route would be Main Street-Industrial Boulevard, so on 4 October 'Oswald' was to visit and make a written application to a firm on the boulevard. For security reasons, however, the organizers of the motorcade finally decided that Elm Street-Stemmons Freeway would be both quicker and safer than Main Street-Industrial Boulevard. The conspirators would have appreciated this possibility and that the Industrial Boulevard site might be useless. A site had to be found that would cover both Main Street and Elm Street before they respectively turned onto Industrial Boulevard and Stemmons Freeway. The assassination site chosen was to be the Texas School Book Depository on Elm; not only did Main Street and Elm Street run close enough to the Depository for 'Oswald' to be able to assassinate the President when passing along either street, but the site gave him a reasonable chance of unassisted escape.

On 14 October, 'Oswald' caused Ruth Paine to make an eventually successful application to the Depository for 'Oswald's' employment. If by chance 'Oswald' should fail to gain employment or, having been employed, he should for some reason—such as a last-minute cancellation of the parade or an unexpected event such as dismissal—be thwarted from using the Depository site, an alternate plan had to be developed.

On 14 October, therefore, 'Oswald' visited and made written application for employment at a firm situated on Inwood Road. If the Depository could not be used for the assassination, 'Oswald' could have taken his dismantled rifle to the Inwood Road site while Kennedy was at the luncheon. 'Oswald' could have assassinated Kennedy on Inwood Road on his way back to the airport.

The Industrial Boulevard and Inwood Road sites were less attractive topographically and geographically than the Depository because, although Kennedy would be an easy target, the escape of the assassin from the immediate vicinity would probably have needed a car and possibly an accomplice, which was not to be necessary for his escape from the Depository.

On 15 October, 'Oswald' visited and made written application for employment at the Depository, and the next day he commenced working. Having visited Industrial Boulevard, Elm Street, and Inwood Road, 'Oswald' was ready for any eventuality.

(The Warren Report discloses 'Oswald's' applications for work on Industrial Boulevard—from where 'Oswald' could not have shot Kennedy because the Elm Street-Stemmons Freeway route had been selected—and on Elm Street, but it does not mention the application for work on Inwood Road—from where 'Oswald' could have shot Kennedy. The importance of the Inwood Road site is emphasized by the facts that the personnel officers from the Industrial Boulevard and Elm Street sites were to testify, but the personnel officer at the Inwood Road site was not asked to testify. There is no report in the Exhibits of any interview with him by any investigative agency, although the FBI went to the firm and removed 'Oswald's' application form, which does not appear in the Exhibits and may never have reached the National Archives.)

When 'Oswald' had arrived in Dallas on 3 October, he stayed the night at the YMCA. In the morning he applied and was turned down for the job on Industrial Boulevard at Padgett Printing Company. The next day, he visisted Marina and June, who were now settled in Ruth Paine's small house in Irving. (Before leaving New Orleans for Mexico City, 'Oswald' had given Ruth's Texas address as his forwarding address at the New Orleans post office.) He spent the weekend there, from 4 October through the sixth, and told Marina that, if FBI agents should call at the house when he was not there, she should note and let him have the registration number of their car.

On Monday, 7 October, Ruth drove 'Oswald' to the bus station in Irving, from which 'Oswald' returned to Dallas allegedly to look for work and a place to live. He left the YMCA and inquired about a room at 1026 North Beckley Avenue in the Oak Cliff suburb of Dallas, but there was no vacancy. (The rooming house was about one mile, as the crow flies, from Jack Ruby's apartment, both being in Oak Cliff.) He next responded to a "For Rent" sign seven blocks east at Mrs. Bledsoe's rooming house at 621 Marsalis Street, obtained a room for which he paid a week's rent of $7 in advance, moved in on the same day, and registered in the name of L. H. Oswald. Marsalis was one of the two possible routes Ruby could take from his businesses in downtown Dallas to his apartment at 223 South Ewing, one and a half miles away from 621 Marsalis. Mrs. Bledsoe's son reported that each evening of his short stay 'Oswald' sat in a chair on the porch of the house overlooking the road. These possible sight contacts with Ruby could have been 'Oswald's' first encounter with the man assigned to arrange his escape. 'Oswald' then allegedly resumed his search for work, relying partially on referrals by TEC, none of which he attempted to pursue.

Marina was to testify that he telephoned her twice a day from 7 October until a few days before 22 November because he was worried about her well-being. In the light of subsequent events, it is probable that in addition to an interest in her well-being, 'Oswald' was anxious to know if the FBI was calling at Ruth's house. Unknown to him, however, the New Orleans FBI were not to find the forwarding address of Ruth's house until 25 October.

'Oswald' spent the next weekend of 12-13 October at Ruth's house and told her that he had received the last of the unemployment checks due him; Ruth was to testify that he appeared to be extremely discouraged, because Marina was expecting her second baby in a month's time, and he badly needed a job.

Early on Monday morning, 14 October, Ruth, needing to repair her Russian typewriter, drove 'Oswald' to downtown Dallas and dropped him off within two blocks of the Texas School Book Depository.

THE DECISIVE COFFEE KLATCH

Ruth, having now returned from downtown Dallas, went with the eight-months-pregnant Marina next door to the home of Mrs. Dorothy Roberts for coffee. Mrs. Linnie Randle, whose house stood on the other side of Ruth's house, was also present. Mrs. Randle's younger brother, 19-year-old Wesley Frazier, had obtained work at the Depository on 13 September, the day on which the Dallas newspapers first carried the announcement that President Kennedy would be visiting Texas on a one-day tour. Frazier had been living with Mrs. Randle only from the beginning of September, having arrived from Huntsville—200 miles away—in order to look for work in Dallas. He had been advised to seek work at the Depository by an unnamed woman at an employment agency.

At the gathering, the four women discussed the possibility of obtaining work for 'Oswald,' several places being suggested but most of them apparently unsuitable for him because it was believed that he could not drive a car. Mrs. Randle tentatively suggested that there might be a job opening at the Depository, and Ruth asked if she would telephone the personnel manager to find out. Mrs. Randle refused, saying that she did not know the manager, but when Ruth and Marina returned to Ruth's house after the party, Marina asked Ruth to telephone the Depository. Ruth told the personnel manager, Roy Truly, that she had a fine young man living in her house with his wife and baby, his wife was expecting another baby in a few days, and he wanted work desperately. In reply to Ruth's call, Truly said that he might have a temporary job and that Ruth should tell 'Oswald' to visit him at the Depository.

(Neither Mrs. Dorothy Roberts nor the woman at the employment agency—the vital witnesses—was named or interrogated by the Warren Commission. Nor, according to the Exhibits, was either of them interviewed by the FBI or any other agency.)

After the coffee party and after Ruth's call to Truly, 'Oswald' collected his belongings from Mrs. Bledsoe's rooming house and returned to 1026 North Beckley, where he was now allotted a room for $8 a week, signing the register "O. H. Lee." This bedroom was "not usually let," did not have a room number, was on the ground floor leading off the lounge, and adjoined the bedroom of the elderly housekeeper whose sister was an acquaintance of Jack Ruby. That evening, on telephoning Ruth's house, 'Oswald' was told by Marina that Ruth had made contact with Truly and that he had been asked to visit the Depository.

That same day, and probably at about 2:00 P.M., 'Oswald' applied for employment on Inwood Road at the Wiener Lumber Co., Inwood Road being the direct route between the airport and the Trade Mart. He told the personnel manager that he had a car and that he had served two terms in the Marines, finishing as Sergeant, the last term of service ending in September 1963. The personnel manager typed on the bottom of his form, "Wore Summer Shirt but with tie very neat looking. Important: although this man makes an excellent appearance & seems quite intel. he seemed unable to understand when I continually & clearly asked him for his honorable discharge card or papers for the latest (just ended) hitch—I believe he does not have & will not get such a paper or card—DO NOT CONSIDER FOR THIS REASON ONLY—."

The next day, 15 October, 'Oswald' went to the Depository from 1026 and completed an application form for employment. On the form he gave his name as Lee Harvey Oswald and his height as 5'9", stating that his last employment had been in the Marines. He was neatly dressed and called Truly "sir." He was engaged to commence work on

16 October, his duties being to fill book orders, and his hours of work being 8:00 A.M. to 4:45 P.M. at the rate of $1.25 an hour. As with previous employments—apart from his conversations with one employee at Jaggars-Chiles-Stovall (and of course with Grossi *alias* Bowen)—he kept to himself during his employment at the Depository; most of his fellow employees were to know him only by sight, while those who spoke with him knew him only by the name of Lee.

On 20 October, Marina gave birth to a second daughter in Parkland Hospital, Dallas, and named her Audrey Marina Oswald. On the day of the birth, 'Oswald' had remained at Ruth's house to look after June and Ruth's two children while Ruth was at the hospital. When 'Oswald' did go to Parkland Hospital the next day, presumably it was he who filled in two spaces on the birth certificate—reserved for the description of work and place of employment of the father—with the words "Laborer" and "School Book Depository." Another part of the certificate already filled in at the hospital gave the name of the newborn child as Audrey Marina Oswald, but 'Oswald' squeezed in the name Rachel at a slant after the name Marina. From the date of her birth, the newborn child was called and referred to as Rachel by Ruth, Marina, and 'Oswald.' In the letter that 'Oswald' was to write to the Soviet Consulate in Washington on 9 November, he omitted the name Rachel in a paragraph referring to the name of the newborn child. The birth certificate does not appear in the Exhibits but is on record in the Texas state capital of Austin.

On 1 November, 'Oswald' rented P.O. Box 6225 at the Terminal Annex Post Office and gave the names of persons allowed to receive mail as Lee Harvey Oswald, the American Civil Liberties Union, and FPCC. The post office was some five minutes on foot from the Depository and some 10 minutes on foot from Ruby's nightclub, the Carousel, where Ruby maintained a daytime office. That same day, Dallas FBI agent Hosty, who by then had heard from the New Orleans FBI that Marina was living at Ruth's address in Irving, called at Ruth's house, where he spoke to Ruth and Marina, Ruth acting as interpreter.

Hosty was to testify that he had understood from Ruth that Marina and her little daughters were living with her, that 'Oswald' was living at a rooming house somewhere in Dallas, that the address was unknown to either of the women, that he was employed as a laborer in the Texas School Book Depository and, in response to Hosty's specific inquiry, that he was no longer actively engaged in FPCC activities.

Hosty said that Marina was "alarmed and upset" when he arrived but that he calmed her by saying that he was not there to harm or harass her and that it was the task of the FBI to protect people. When he came to leave, Marina was "smiling and happy, and shook hands"; Marina knew that her husband had visited the Soviet Embassy in Mexico City but Hosty had not questioned her about it.

He testified that Ruth had hesitated before telling him that 'Oswald' was employed at the Depository as 'Oswald' had told her that the FBI was the cause of his losing his jobs. In reply to Hosty's request, Ruth said that she would try to obtain the address of the rooming house, but she did not tell Hosty that she had the telephone number of the rooming house, 1026 North Beckley, in her private book of phone numbers, nor did she tender the number to Hosty so that he could then and there ascertain the address. She was to testify, and Hosty confirmed, that she had told him that 'Oswald' visited her house on weekends. As Hosty was leaving, he wrote down on a piece of paper his name and business telephone number, and Ruth passed this information to 'Oswald' later that day, Friday, when he came from the Depository to Irving for the weekend.

While Hosty was in or leaving Ruth's house, Marina noted the license number of his car, which was parked some distance away, but she misread one of the digits. When her husband came to Irving that evening, she told him the number that she had recorded.

Shortly thereafter, 'Oswald' called at the office of the Dallas FBI where he left a letter for Hosty. (In 1975 the *Dallas Times Herald* discovered that the letter was destroyed by Hosty shortly after Ruby shot the assassin; Hosty now says that the letter was destroyed on orders from his superiors. It will never be known what the letter said: Hosty claimed that it accused him of harrassing Marina; a secretary said 'Oswald' threatened violence. The significance of its destruction is that it establishes how willing the authorities were to destroy documentary evidence. In testimony to the Commission, Hosty did not mention the letter or its destruction.)

On Tuesday, 5 November, Hosty again called to see Ruth to ask if she had obtained 'Oswald's' address in Dallas, but although 'Oswald' had been at her house the previous weekend, she again told Hosty that she did not know the address of the rooming house. She again failed to tell Hosty the telephone number of the rooming house; Hosty remained only for a moment and only to ask where 'Oswald' was living, an address which he was never to ascertain, nor was he to speak to 'Oswald' prior to the assassination.

Hosty informed the FBI in New Orleans that he had traced Marina and partially traced 'Oswald,' and that 'Oswald' was employed in a nonsensitive industry. He was to testify that having checked with the Depository that 'Oswald' was so employed, and 'Oswald' having ceased his FPCC activities, he had decided that he would see him only after he received the complete file with up-to-date information from the FBI in New Orleans; this file was to be received by the FBI in Dallas on 21 November but was not to be studied by Hosty until after the assassination.

'Oswald' had been in no position to report to his contact the extent of FBI interest in him until he knew what it was, and he was not to know this until after Hosty's brief second visit to Ruth's house on 5 November. Although the date for the assassination was approaching, apparently it had been advisable for 'Oswald,' who had visited Ruth's house at weekends, to wait for another weekend to pass to see if Hosty would again visit the house; if Hosty did not do so he could tell his contact that the FBI was no longer interested in his activities.

He was, therefore, in no position to communicate this information until after the weekend of 9-10 November.

On Saturday 9 November, 'Oswald' was spending the weekend in Ruth's house; Hosty had not called there since 5 November. Ruth was to testify that during the morning, having advised 'Oswald' that he should learn to drive, having given him some lessons and told him to obtain a driver's license, she drove him to a Texas drivers' license examining station. But because it was an election day, the station was closed.

Albert Bogard, a car salesman in a large firm sited near the Depository, was to testify that in the early afternoon that day, a man calling himself Lee Oswald asked if he could try out a car with the purpose of buying it. 'Oswald' then drove Bogard along Stemmons Freeway (the last part of the motorcade route) at 60-70 miles per hour, alarming Bogard with his speed and swift cornering; 'Oswald' appeared, however, to be an efficient driver. (After the assassination, the car carrying the dying President was to travel at maximum speed along Stemmons Freeway to Parkland Hospital.) 'Oswald' told Bogard that in several weeks' time he would have money to buy the car. When possible but unacceptable credit terms were discussed with another salesman, Eugene Wilson, 'Oswald' said sarcastically, "Maybe I'm going to have to go back to Russia to buy a car." The salesmen were not to see or hear from him again. (WR.320-321.) (The Warren Report discounts the statements of the salesmen.)

'OSWALD' REPORTS IN

During the afternoon of that day, using one of Ruth's typewriters, 'Oswald' typed a letter from himself and Marina to the Soviet Consulate in Washington, and addressed the envelope to "Reznichenko" but spelled it "Rezneechyenko." (XVIII.539.)

The long Veterans Day holiday weekend having passed without a further visit from Hosty, the letter was posted in Irving on Tuesday, 12 November.

The letter is set out below; for convenience of reference the paragraphs are numbered:

FROM LEE H. OSWALD, P.O. BOX 6225, DALLAS,
TEXAS
   MARINA NICHILAYEVA OSWALD, SOVIET
CITIZEN

                TO: CONSULAR DIVISION
                     EMBASSY U.S.S.R.
                     WASHINGTON D.C.
                     NOV. 9, 1963

Dear Sirs:

1. This is to inform you of recent events since my meetings with comrade Kostin in the Embassy of the Soviet Union, Mexico City, Mexico.

2. I was unable to remain in Mexico indefinily because of my mexican visa restrictions which was for 15 days only. I could not take a chance on requesting a new visa unless I used my real name, so I retured to the United States.

3. I had not planned to contact the Soviet embassy in Mexico so they were unprepared, had I been able to reach the Soviet Embassy in Havana as planned, the embassy there would have had time to complete our business.

4. Of corse the Soviet embassy was not at fault, they were, as I say unprepared, the Cuban consulate was guilty of a gross breach of regulations, I am glad he has since been replced.

5. The Federal Bureau of Investigation is not now interested in my activities in the progressive organization "Fair Play For Cuba Committee", of which I was secretary in New Orleans (state Louisiana) since I no longer reside in that state. However, the F.B.I. has visited us here in Dallas, Texas, on November 1st. Agent James P. Hosty warned me that if I engaged in F.P.C.C. activities in Texas the F.B.I. will again take an "interrest" in me.

6. This agent also "suggested" to Marina Nichilayeva that she could remain in the United States under F.B.I. "protection", that is, she could defect from the Soviet Uion, of course, I and my wife strongly protested these tactics by the notorious F.B.I.

7. Please inform us of the arrival of our Soviet entrance visa's as soon as they come.

8. Also, this is to inform you of the birth on October 20, 1963 of a DAUGHTER, AUDREY MARINA OSWALD in DALLAS, TEXAS, to my wife.

Respecfully,

Lee H. Oswald (Signed)

On 18 November, a confidential informant of the FBI stationed at the Soviet Consulate in Washington obtained a copy of the letter and sent it to the field office of the FBI in Washington, which sent it to the Bureau of the FBI on 19 November. The field office or the Bureau then communicated the contents of the letter to the field office in Dallas, where it was to be received on the morning of 22 November, but was not to be seen by Hosty until shortly after the assassination.

On 26 March 1964, the Commission was to submit a questionnaire to the FBI that asked, among other things, "What was the FBI evaluation of confidential information received on November 18, 1963, regarding Oswald's letter to the Soviet Embassy in Washington?" The answer, contained in a letter dated 6 April 1964 and signed by J. Edgar Hoover reads in part ". . . the information received on November 18, 1963, concerning Oswald's contact with the Soviet Embassy in Mexico City as reported by the CIA, and indicates the reasons for such contact, namely to secure visas to the Soviet Union."

The Warren Commission rejected the FBI evaluation and evaluated it itself; "In the opinion of the Commission, based upon its knowledge of Oswald, the letter constitutes no more than a clumsy effort to ingratiate himself with the Soviet Embassy." (WR. 310.)

My view of the letter, paragraph by paragraph, follows:

1. 'Oswald' was reporting in on "recent events" after the conspiracy at the Soviet Embassy and Consulate in Mexico City, the postal system being a commonly used method of communication in subversive matters.

2. 'Oswald's' admission to the use of a false name shows that the KGB knew that he was using an alias in Mexico City.

3. The KGB had "planned" with 'Oswald' that he go to the Soviet Embassy in Havana, and that "our business" was the transmission to him of most secret instructions for the assassination and escape; the secrecy of the plot dictated that in its entirety it could not be given to 'Oswald,' even by Kostin. There had been no point in 'Oswald' remaining "indefinily" in Mexico; he would have to return to Dallas to await his final instructions direct from Moscow, Washington, or Havana.

4. 'Oswald' intended to enter Cuba but in some way had learned that the Cuban with whom he had spoken at the Cuban Consulate "has since been replced."

5. 'Oswald' was telling the KGB that the assassination could proceed without interruption by the FBI. Hosty, like FBI Agent Quigley in New Orleans, had been tricked by 'Oswald' into considering him only as a nonviolent and halfhearted supporter of the FPCC, and now of little interest to the FBI unless he recommenced his FPCC activities in Dallas.

Further, the need to parenthetically spell out in what state New Orleans is located suggests that the letter was for consumption in Moscow rather than in Washington. Some five months earlier, 'Oswald' had written "New Orleans, La" on his counterfeit vaccination certificate. When filling out forms for the Soviet authorities in Minsk two years before, he had written his place of birth as "New Orleans, *Texas.*" Marina also filled in forms for the Soviets and she, too, wrote her husband's place of birth as "New Orleans, *Texas.*"

6. 'Oswald's' words are intended to confirm Marina's continued loyalty to the Soviet Union (unlike his words about her to the stenographer, Miss Bates, on 18 June 1962).

7. On 1 July, Marina and 'Oswald' had written to Reznichenko

asking for visas to reenter the Soviet Union as soon as possible, but
'Oswald' had put a note in the envelope asking that his visa be considered separately; this paragraph is a reminder to Reznichenko to make
available visas for Marina and her daughters to return to the Soviet
Union immediately following the escape of her husband after the assassination.

8. The omission of the child's call-name Rachel was a signal to the
KGB. Omissions or additions, seemingly insignificant, are often used in
espionage to convey a message.

Several abridged drafts of the letter unaddressed and with omissions
were found; one immediately by Ruth Paine on her desk. Inexplicably
she copied it and kept both original and copy, offering them to Hosty
after the assassination. The paragraph relating to Russian visas was
omitted as this would have alarmed Ruth since she had no knowledge
of Marina's correspondence with the Soviet Embassy in Washington.
Paragraph 8 was also omitted. The drafts deliberately left behind compromised Ruth as they implied that 'Oswald' was a Soviet or Cuban
agent.

The letter is reproduced in the Warren Report in a size 3.1" x 2.2"
that makes it tedious for people with perfect eyesight to read and partly
illegible for those with normal vision. (WR.311.)

The Commission does not discuss the letter as a whole, but prints
and discusses it part by part in different sections of the Warren Report,
thus precluding an understanding of the letter. On page 309 of the
Report, paragraph 1 of the letter is printed and discussed; on page 310
paragraph 2 is printed and discussed; *paragraph 3 is neither printed
nor discussed, thus omitting Oswald's attempt to reach the Soviet Embassy in Havana "as planned"*; on page 735 only the first part of
paragraph 4 is printed, thus omitting the 'replacement' of the Cuban
Consul; on page 739 paragraphs 5, 6 and 7 are printed, 5 and 6 are
discussed, *but there is no discussion of the request for information
about visas in paragraph 7. Paragraph 8, which omitted the name
"Rachel," is neither printed nor discussed.*

When Counsel questioned Marina, he omitted the words "as
planned" and changed "to complete our business," to "complete his
business." (1.47.)

According to the foreword written by "The Editors," just 80 hours
after President Johnson released the Warren Report, the publishers of
Bantam Books published a "completely authoritative edition" of the
Report including "all the text and every single one of the vitally impor-

tant Commission Exhibits necessary to an understanding of the Report." The first printing by W. F. Hall Printing Company in Chicago of 700,000 copies of the Bantam edition of the Report established "a new milestone in book publishing . . . over 150 skilled men and women . . . accomplished this gigantic task by working in eight-hour shifts around the clock. Since President Johnson felt it was of vital importance that the whole truth about President Kennedy's death be given to the world as quickly as possible, special arrangements were made to airlift the books all over the world. Thus, the Warren Commission Report in this edition will be read in London, Paris, Tokyo, Melbourne and other cities throughout the world almost as soon as it appeared in Los Angeles."

Through no fault of the publisher, the vital letter of 9 November "necessary to an understanding of the Report" was reduced even further in size. Only a few thousand copies of the more expensive Report were sold, so that the vast majority of people and politicians throughout the world were never able to read the letter.

THE DAYS BEFORE THE ASSASSINATION

On 14 November 1963, the *Knoxville Journal*, Tennessee, carried a news article reporting that John Howard Bowen had gone on holiday to Europe. (In the long FBI report on Albert Osborne contained in the Exhibits, pages seven and eight are missing. The extraction of these pages was effected after the FBI report was prepared, since the pages are identified in the index as "Knoxville Journal." It would seem that for many years the newspaper had been used by Albert Osborne and John Howard Bowen for the transmission of information to other espionage agents, and that whoever extracted the pages suspected that this had been the case.)

On about 14 November, Albert Osborne, in the name of John Howard Bowen, was to leave New York for Scotland by plane and, on arrival, was to entrain some 300 miles to Grimsby to stay in his real name with his sister, Emily Featherstone, and her daughter, and to visit his brother in "The Old Folks Home." This was the second of two short visits to Grimsby in 44 years, the first having been made in 1953. Having talked incessantly about religion, after three days he was to leave, saying that he was going to London.

The departure of Albert Osborne for Grimsby about a week before the assassination, and his return to the United States about two weeks after the assassination is inexplicable. There must have been a reason for the visit of the man allegedly impoverished and so closely associated with the assassin; his role in the assassination will perhaps never be known. It is possible, however, that as Cambridge is only 75 miles from Grimsby, Albert Osborne was responsible for a brief and dramatic call 25 minutes before the assassination to a senior newspaper reporter in Cambridge telling him to ring the American Embassy in London for "some big news" (a recent CIA release), establishing preknowledge of the assassination.

In interviews with the FBI, John Howard Bowen said he was born in Chester, Pennsylvania, and denied ever having been in England. Later, when forced to admit having been to England, and, indeed, even having been born there, he made a point of omitting his trip to Scotland and Grimsby.

'Oswald' stayed in Dallas and did not visit his family in Irving on the weekend of 16-17 November because, according to Marina's testimony, he had been there for four days during the previous weekend (Friday through Monday), and Marina was worried that he might have outstayed his welcome on that occasion. It is not known what 'Oswald' did on these two days in Dallas, but it was on 16-17 November that the route of the downtown motorcade was finally decided.

On Sunday 17 November, Marina asked Ruth to telephone 'Oswald' at the number that he had given them, but when Ruth rang, she was told by the person who answered the telephone that nobody with the name of Oswald lived there. Neither Ruth nor Marina had ever used the number before; it had not been necessary because 'Oswald' had telephoned Marina twice a day—in the middle of the day and in the evening—always speaking in Russian. From the time 'Oswald' arrived in Dallas from Mexico City, neither Ruth nor Marina had visited him at either of his rooming houses in Dallas, and only on 17 November—five days before the assassination—did they attempt to telephone him.

On the *morning* of Monday 18 November, the motorcade was rehearsed through downtown Dallas and past the Depository. Jack Ruby could have checked the timed rehearsal downtown and its approach to the Depository. 'Oswald' could have watched it pass the Depository.

On the *afternoon* of 18 November, Ruby met at the Carousel with Mrs. Bertha Cheek to discuss opening a new club. Her sister, Mrs.

Earlene Roberts, was 'Oswald's' resident housekeeper at 1026 North Beckley and occupied the bedroom adjoining 'Oswald's'.

When 'Oswald' telephoned Marina that evening, she told him she was upset that he was unknown at the number. 'Oswald' became angry, telling her that he was living under a fictitious name and that she was not to call again. (It is difficult to accept that Marina was upset as she knew he had used a false name in New Orleans. She herself had signed "A. J. Hidell" as the fictitious president of 'Oswald's' New Orleans chapter of the FPCC.) According to Marina, he ordered her to erase the number from Ruth's private book of telephone numbers and, when Marina refused to do so, a quarrel developed. Marina's refusal to erase the number was to place Ruth in a difficult position, for her notebook would be seen by the authorities after the assassination and it would show that she had known but twice failed to give Hosty the telephone number of 'Oswald's' rooming house.

Nothing of importance is recorded for 19-20 November, but on Thursday 21 November, 'Oswald' asked Frazier to drive him to Irving after work that evening and to take him back to the Depository the following morning. Frazier understood 'Oswald' to be going to Irving on Thursday instead of the usual Friday because he wished to pick up a set of curtain rods from Ruth's garage to use in his own room in Dallas. The owners of 1026 North Beckley were to testify that no curtain rods were necessary, the windows in "O. H. Lee's" room being adequately covered with material that did not require rods.

Both Ruth and Marina testified that they were surprised to see 'Oswald' when he arrived on Thursday because he had always asked Ruth's permission to visit, and apart from his visit to Ruth's house on 4 October after he returned from Mexico, he had never come to Irving other than at weekends. Clearly, on this day, he had not wished to risk being refused.

Ruth testified that both she and Marina thought that 'Oswald' had come to Irving to be reconciled with Marina after the quarrel on the telephone; she said that 'Oswald' had talked to Marina and played with his daughter June on the lawn before dinner. Marina testified that she would not talk to him because she was too angry about his use of a false name, but that they all had evening dinner in the house, and after the meal she and Ruth were busy with their children. At some point 'Oswald' must have gone into the garage, where, according to Marina, he kept his rifle wrapped in a blanket. He then packed it in a long paper bag which he had constructed from materials at the Depository.

Marina testified that he went to bed at about 9:00 P.M. but that she did not follow him until about 11:00 P.M. In the morning, he rose early and dressed while talking to Marina, who was feeding the new baby. He left his wedding ring in a cup on Marina's dressing table and $170 in a wallet in the bedroom, retaining less than $14 for himself. He did not leave a note with instructions for Marina as he had done before he shot at Walker. He planned to be out of reach of the United States authorities, probably in Mexico. It is not known what plans he had for Marina, though her own plan was to return to Russia.

After drinking some coffee in the kitchen, 'Oswald' walked about 40 yards to Frazier's house carrying the paper bag. Frazier then drove him to the Depository, where he saw 'Oswald' enter the building carrying the package which Frazier thought contained curtain rods. 'Oswald' must then have taken his rifle to the sixth floor, secreted it among the hundreds of cartons of books on that floor and, so far as is known, proceeded to carry out his normal duties in the building. At some prior time to 12:00 P.M. he made his preparations and lay in wait for the President to pass.

8

The Assassination

"If anybody really wanted to shoot the President of the United States it is not a very difficult job—all one has to do is to get on a high building some day with a telescopic rifle, and there is nothing anyone can do to defend against such an attempt."

—PRESIDENT JOHN KENNEDY, in Fort Worth,
two and a half hours before his premonition
was to be fulfilled

DALLAS, TEXAS, 22 NOVEMBER 1963, 12:30 P.M.

At 11:40 A.M. on Friday 22 November 1963, the President and his wife together with their party had arrived in the Presidential plane at Love Field, Dallas. A motorcade was formed and in the Presidential limousine the President sat in the rear seat with his wife on his left. In the jump seats in front of them sat Governor Connally of Texas and his wife, the governor being immediately in front of the President. A Secret Service agent was driving the limousine and on his right sat another Secret Service agent.

Although there had been some threat of rain, the skies had cleared; it was decided that there was no need for the "bubbletop"—a thin plastic shield to protect passengers against inclement weather.

After a few minutes, the motorcade left Love Field and proceeded toward downtown Dallas, stopping on occasion at the President's request to greet well-wishers among the unexpectedly friendly crowds.

At 12:05 P.M. and just as Kennedy's motorcade was approaching downtown Dallas, according to recently released CIA documents, the senior reporter of the *Cambridge News* (England) received the anonymous call at the newspaper office in Cambridge. The voice said, "Call the American Embassy in London for some big news," and rang off.

At 12:30 P.M., the motorcade made a sharp turn under the windows of the red brick Texas School Book Depository onto Elm Street and proceeded at about 11 mph toward Stemmons Freeway and a luncheon at the Trade Mart.

Suddenly three shots in rapid succession rang out from behind the Presidential car. The first bullet struck Kennedy in the back and exited through his throat. The second hit Connally in the back and wrist before becoming embedded in his thigh. The third struck Kennedy in the back of the head, causing parts of his skull and brain to disintegrate; an immense neuromuscular spasm forced his body to jackknife backwards and upwards, and finally to collapse on the lap of his wife.

In about seven seconds 'Oswald' had fired three bullets from the end window on the sixth floor overlooking the motorcade. The bottom half of the dirty window had been lifted about 16 inches, and it was through this gap that he fired. Just inside the window, stacks of cardboard cartons of books created a "sniper's nest," hiding him from the sight of anyone who might pass through that floor. Inside the "nest" he had placed a carton on the floor on which he could sit and scarcely be visible from inside or outside the building. He had placed three cartons by the window so that his rifle, resting on the top carton, would be aimed directly at the motorcade. Attached to the rifle was a homemade sling which would be used to wrap around the left arm to ensure rigidity in the assassin's grip on the forepart of the rifle. Using the sling and resting the rifle on the carton ensured the assassin of a stable position for accurate fire.

The weapon was the Italian military rifle fitted with a telescopic sight that he had purchased from the mail-order house earlier that year. It had "an inherent capability of great accuracy under rapid fire conditions" and, having less recoil than the average military rifle, was the perfect weapon for the task (FBI report). The first cartridge was already in the chamber and ready to fire, so that 'Oswald' had to work the bolt on the rifle only twice; it was not difficult for him to fire three times in under seven seconds. The telescopic sight was 4-power and, as such, was ideal for the distance at which the assassin would have to fire at his slowly moving target, a range of 55 to 88 yards; by enlarging the target, the scope "reduced" the first shot to a distance of about 22 yards. When the rifle was discovered in the Depository and received by the FBI from the Dallas police and tested by them, it was found that three shots could be fired in seven seconds. The rifle was also found to fire slightly high and slightly to the right of a bull's-eye. This "defect" was one which would have assisted 'Oswald' when he was aiming at a target moving away and slightly to his right; he would not have to make allowances for the apparent upward movement of the car due to the high elevation of the "sniper's nest" and for the movement of the car slightly to the right of his line of vision. He could aim directly at his target and be more certain of hitting it. (WR.194.)

FIFTEEN SECONDS TO FIRE THREE SHOTS

If the motorcade had proceeded along Main Street instead of turning on to Elm Street, the defect in the sight would have assisted 'Oswald' even more; the Presidential limousine would have been moving a fraction more to the right of the assassin's line of fire.

The choice of the Depository as an assassin's base was an excellent and finely calculated not only because the victims appeared "almost stationary" (FBI report) and minimal movement had been all but corrected by the telescopic sight, but because the Presidential car had passed and was going *away* from the Depository; almost all eyes were on the President and his wife, and therefore away from the elevated rifleman. So as not to attract attention before firing, the assassin in the window must have remained out of sight by hiding in the brick corner of his "sniper's nest," only moving into his firing position when the motorcade was below him. He would have about five seconds to align the rifle, seven seconds to fire, and three seconds to withdraw from the window; the barrel of the rifle and his face in the background were visible only for a total of some 15 seconds. As his face was inside the window, it was visible only to a handful of people in front of and immediately in line with him. The window was not overlooked by any high building, and the excellence of the chosen firing point is shown by the fact that only a few people realized that the shots came from the Depository.

One man, Howard Brennan, who was sitting on a nearby wall

below the Depository, heard two explosions like the sound of fire-crackers above him apparently coming from the Depository. He looked up after hearing the second report, and actually saw the third and last shot being fired. (WR.63-71.) But none of the Secret Service agents accompanying the cars of the President and the Vice President for the purpose of observing the crowds and scanning the buildings saw the assassin. Before firing he was hidden, and when he was firing the agents all had their backs to him.

At the sound of gunfire, some of the police escorting the motorcade had rushed to the right and to the front of the Presidential car, the direction from which the shots appeared to have come—an instant reaction to the general commotion and panic in the immediate vicinity of the car, possibly aided by the misleading effect of echoes.

After firing, the assassin hid the rifle among some cartons of books and went downstairs to a luncheon room on the second floor.

The attention of one police officer, Patrolman Marrion Baker, had been drawn to the building because he had seen pigeons fly from the roof at the sound of the shots. He ran to the main entrance, where he was joined by a Depository official, and they ran upstairs to search the roof. On reaching the second floor, the officer noticed 'Oswald' through a glass panel in the door of the lunchroom, and, with drawn revolver, he accosted the youthful-looking man who was attired in torn and shabby working clothes. The officer asked the official who the man was, and the official vouched for him as an employee; both to the officer and to the official the man appeared calm and undisturbed. The officer and the official then continued upstairs to search the roof while 'Oswald,' holding a bottle of Coca-Cola, walked down the last flight of stairs and out the main entrance of the building at approximately 12:33 P.M. It was several minutes before it was realized that the shots had been fired from behind, and the Depository was then sealed off at 12:37 P.M.

THE ESCAPE ROUTE

After leaving the building, 'Oswald' proceeded with his escape by walking northeast for seven blocks, where, at 12:40 P.M., he boarded a Marsalis bus, one of a regular local service that ran from the northeast of Dallas to the south through the center of the city. When he boarded the bus, it was headed in the direction of the Depository, and toward

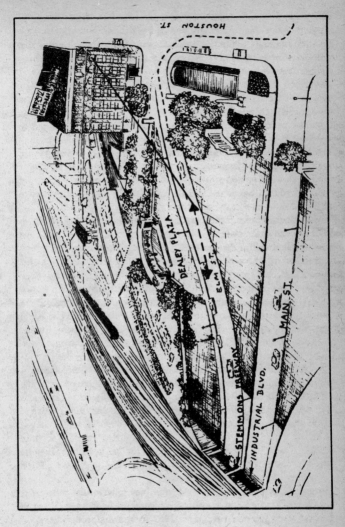

South Dallas. 'Oswald' had in his wallet a counterfeit identity card. He purchased a 23-cent ticket which would take him to a stop at 11th Street and Marsalis, about two city blocks west of Ruby's apartment at 223 South Ewing, some 2¼ miles from the Depository, and one mile from his rooming house.

Seated on the bus was 'Oswald's' former landlady, Mrs. Bledsoe, who was an elderly woman and one of the few people in Dallas who knew him by sight *and* by the name of L. H. Oswald. After watching the motorcade, Mrs. Bledsoe was returning from downtown Dallas to her house at 621 Marsalis, which was situated on the southbound Marsalis bus route and about one and a half miles short of his intended stop. She recognized 'Oswald,' and, since there were only a few people on the bus and he passed in front of her to sit down, it would seem that he recognized her. She noted his attire and later was able accurately to describe it.

The bus was now moving very slowly and reached the 11th Street stop about half an hour late. If by chance one of the employees at the Depository had seen and recognized him at the window and had immediately informed the police, who would speedily broadcast his name, 'Oswald' could have been "trapped" on the bus by Mrs. Bledsoe. Even if Mrs. Bledsoe was to leave the bus before the name of the wanted man was broadcast she would have been able to telephone the police to tell them that he had continued on the Marsalis bus past her house and to describe his attire, perhaps enabling the police to arrest him while he was still on the bus or, at the least, indicating the direction of the escape, thereby limiting the area to be searched.

Apparently dismayed by Mrs. Bledsoe's presence, 'Oswald' took a transfer ticket and left the bus only four minutes after boarding it; the time was now 12:44 P.M. He then took a taxi southwest to his rooming house, 1026 North Beckley, where he had registered in the name of O. H. Lee some five weeks previously. The rooming house was served by a different bus route, Beckley, which had a stop outside 1026. Since a Beckley bus had been immediately behind the Marsalis bus when he had boarded the latter, had he originally intended to go to 1026 he surely would have taken the Beckley bus.

He arrived at 1026 at 1:00 P.M. and, hurrying inside, collected a .38 snub-nosed Smith and Wesson revolver which he had purchased in the name of A. J. Hidell in March 1962 from a mail-order dealer in Los Angeles; also sent to his post office box in Dallas. He altered his appearance by changing his trousers and putting on a zip-up jacket.

After about two minutes, he rushed out of the house and walked rapidly southeast in the direction of the bus stop and Ruby's apartment. The change of clothing had been necessary because he feared that either Mrs. Bledsoe or Patrolman Baker might have noticed his attire during their brief encounters and would describe it were his name to be quickly broadcast.

THE SECOND KILLING

At 1:16 P.M., when most of the 1,200 Dallas police were still surrounding the Depository or searching downtown for the assassin, 'Oswald' was walking rapidly in the direction of the 23-cent bus stop and Ruby's apartment. He was stopped and casually questioned by Dallas patrolman J. D. Tippit—the only police officer patrolling the large Oak Cliff suburb. The officer must have heard on his police radio a rough description of the wanted man but was apparently unaware that he was speaking to the assassin. A short conversation ensued between the seated officer and 'Oswald,' who was resting his arm on the door of the car. Something appears to have aroused the suspicion of the officer, for he got out of his car and was drawing his revolver when he was shot dead by 'Oswald,' who fired four rapid and professional shots to the body and head. The shooting was less than half a mile from Ruby's apartment.

After killing the officer, 'Oswald' ran away in the opposite direction from which he had been walking and, as his clothing might have been noticed by some people who had observed this killing, he again altered his appearance so far as possible by taking off his zip-up jacket, which he hid in a used car lot. He was last observed by two men at about 1:20 P.M., four minutes after killing Tippit.

THE ARREST OF THE ASSASSIN

At about 1:42 P.M. the manager of a shoe shop in Oak Cliff, the shop being about three-quarters of a mile west of Ruby's apartment, noticed 'Oswald' with his back to the street, standing near the shop door and apparently attempting to hide his face from a passing police car searching for the killer of the patrolman. 'Oswald' moved off after the car had gone, but the manager, who had heard a report of the killing on the radio and happened to glance toward the door, followed and saw him enter the nearby Texas (movie) Theater. The manager spoke to the cashier, who had been attracted to the sidewalk by the siren of the approaching police car; she had noticed a man enter the foyer of the theater but had not realized he had gone into the theater without paying. While the shoe shop manager tried to find 'Oswald' in the theater, the cashier telephoned the police. Swiftly, 15 policemen arrived, and, after a violent struggle in which 'Oswald' sustained some head injuries, he was arrested at about 1:50 P.M.

The area around the site of Tippit's murder had been rapidly flooded with police cars drawn from downtown Dallas and outer areas to search for the killer. It would have been dangerous for 'Oswald' to then have run toward the apartment of the man upon whom he probably relied for escape. So although armed and capable of hijacking a car to take him away from Dallas, he had chosen not to flee the city but to hide in the only available place in the area—a theater—perhaps to make a third attempt, possibly after dark, to approach Ruby's apartment or its vicinity.

Although several people had seen 'Oswald' running away after shooting Tippit, his whereabouts from about 1:20 P.M. until just before he entered the theater at approximately 1:42 P.M. are unknown. Similarly, Ruby's whereabouts after about 1:00 P.M. were never satisfactorily determined. (At approximately 1:45 P.M., however, Ruby entered his downtown nightclub. When he was to testify before the Warren Commission on 7 June and 18 July 1964, he was not asked to account for his movements after 1:00 P.M.)

The odds against Mrs. Bledsoe choosing to go downtown to view the motorcade and then return on the bus that was later to be boarded by 'Oswald' must have been very considerable. The odds against the only officer patrolling a large suburb being on the same street at the same time as 'Oswald' and deciding to speak to him must have been equally considerable. The odds against a police car with sirens blaring passing 'Oswald' less than half a minute before he could reach the safety of the theater and forcing him to step into a shop doorway must also have been considerable. The odds against anyone noticing him in the doorway, then being sufficiently alert to follow him, and thereafter for the cashier to decide to call the police must have been fairly considerable. It would seem that but for a series of misadventures—the odds against which must have been substantial—'Oswald' would have been able to escape from Dallas and ultimately from the United States.

On arrival at Dallas police headquarters at 2:00 P.M., and after having loudly protested to onlookers about "police brutality" while giving a clenched-fist sign, the first of a series of interrogations of 'Oswald' commenced. He consistently and vehemently denied the killing of either the officer or the President. He admitted owning the revolver that had been found in his possession on arrest but denied that he possessed a rifle.

THE IMMEDIATE AFTERMATH OF THE ASSASSINATION

Following the assassination, the car carrying the dying President and the wounded governor had rushed to Parkland Hospital, arriving at about 12:35 P.M. Vice President Johnson had been traveling in the motorcade and arrived at the hospital almost simultaneously. Secret Service agents who had accompanied the motorcade and other agents already stationed in Dallas immediately formed a protective circle around Johnson and his wife while taking further emergency security measures to protect them. They took similar security measures to protect the families and relatives of both Johnson and Kennedy. At 1:20 P.M., Johnson was told that the President was dead; agents advised him to leave the hospital for Love Field Airport at once, using an unmarked police car, and instructed him to keep below window level. Security measures had been taken for the Presidential plane, the airport terminal, and the surrounding area, and agents had worked with police clearing all the people from the areas adjacent to the aircraft, including warehouses, other terminal buildings, and neighboring parking lots.

For military reasons, a federal judge was rushed to the airfield to administer the Presidential oath of office, thereby filling the vacuum in the Presidency, and at 2:28 P.M. Johnson became the thirty-sixth President of the United States. Nine minutes later the plane departed for Washington from where, on arrival at 5:58 P.M., the new President went to the White House. Within a few minutes, he was conferring with heads of departments, and that evening he officially appointed the FBI to investigate and report upon the assassination. After learning that a Soviet conspiracy was considered among the possibilities, and having ordered that the facts should be at once suppressed, Johnson left the White House for his own home at 9:00 P.M.

After President Kennedy had been pronounced dead, by state law the body should not have been removed from the city of Dallas until an autopsy had been performed. But, despite the loud protests of Dallas officials and the senior medical staff at Parkland Hospital, Kennedy's body was almost forcibly removed from the hospital by the federal agencies and taken to Love Field, whence it was flown to the National Naval Medical Center at Bethesda, Maryland, where the autopsy would be performed.

PART 2:

THE AFTERMATH

9

Dallas Police Headquarters

The cover-up of the Kennedy assassination began immediately after the assassination.

The first step was to ensure that no notes should be taken of what the arrested man might say; his words might point to a conspiracy. The Dallas police must have been instructed not to take records *before* the first interrogation at 2:30 P.M. on 22 November because during the 12 hours of intermittent interrogation of the assassin on three days—22-23-24 November—by Captain Fritz, Chief of Homicide in the Dallas police, according to the Warren Report no notes, stenographic, or tape recordings were made (WR.180.) The representatives of four and sometimes five investigative agencies were frequently present, the FBI, the Secret Service, the office of the District Attorney, the office of the Sheriff, and the Texas Rangers, and they, too, took no notes. From whom these instructions came is not known.

Finally, the FBI withheld from the Dallas police the contents of their file on "Lee Harvey Oswald." The police had the assassin in their hands, evidence of imposture, and possible Soviet and/or Cuban conspiracy. The FBI file would have supplied enough evidence to have enabled the police to expose imposture and conspiracy and to act accordingly. Though no federal agency had any authority in the matter, not only did the FBI deny the police access to their file in a case of double-murder (the President and Patrolman Tippit), but it removed from police possession all the physical evidence relating to the murders.

Before Kennedy's visit to Dallas, the FBI had failed to supply the Secret Service, entrusted with the protection of the President and Vice President, with the information about 'Oswald' contained in their files.

Chief of Police Curry was later to say that shortly after 2:00 P.M. on 22 November, after he had mentioned to the press that the Dallas office of the FBI had a file on Oswald—which he had just heard from an FBI agent who had rushed to the police station—the head of the Dallas office of the FBI had telephoned him and given him 30 minutes to retract his statement to the effect that the FBI knew Lee Harvey Oswald was in Dallas; Curry did not retract.

At about 2:00 P.M., 10 minutes after his arrest at the theater, 'Oswald' was brought into Dallas police headquarters, having remained silent when asked to give his name. He was wearing a shirt, undershirt, trousers, belt, underpants, socks, shoes, and an inexpensive silver bracelet inscribed with the name "Lee." In his pockets were five revolver cartridges, a Marsalis route bus transfer ticket, a wallet, and the top of a small box, with the words "Cox's. Ft. Worth." (XXIV.345.) (Cox's is a store where Oswald's mother briefly worked in 1959. Espionage agents have been known to use similar box tops for the purposes of identification with other agents. The 3" x 2" box top is conspicuous by its absence from the Exhibits, which contain thousands of less relevant items and documents.)

A senior FBI agent, Manning Clements, appeared at the Dallas police headquarters to obtain "descriptive and biographical data." 'Oswald' told him that his height was 5'9" and that he had *no permanent scars*, which the agent duly recorded. In addition, the agent listed the contents of 'Oswald's' wallet as follows:

1. A Selective Service System notice of classification in the name of Lee Harvey Oswald.

2. A counterfeit Selective Service System notice of classification in the name of Alek James Hidell, recording the height of Hidell as 5'9", with a photograph added. (The name Alek James Hidell was later found to be fictitious.)

3. A certificate of service in the United States Marine Corps in the name of Lee Harvey Oswald.

4. A counterfeit certificate of service in the United States Marine Corps in the name of Alek James Hidell.

5. A Selective Service System registration certificate in the name of Lee Harvey Oswald, recording his height as 5'11".

6. A Department of Defense identification card in the name of Lee

Harvey Oswald, recording his height as 5'11". (The photograph of Oswald had been removed and replaced by another photograph stamped 1963.)

7. A United States Forces Japan identification card issued to Lee H. Oswald on 8 May 1958. (Marine Oswald was on active duty in Japan at that time.)

8. A Social Security card in the name of Lee Harvey Oswald.

9. A card, "Compliments GA—JO Enkanko Hotel," with the telephone number ED-5-0755 (the pay phone in the hall of the apartment block where Marguerite Oswald lived in the summer of 1962) handwritten on the reverse side together with another partially legible handwritten number, apparently 92463 (possibly shorthand for 24 September 1963, a day on which no one knew where he was).

10. A white card with the longhand writing "Embassy USSR, 1609 Decatur NW, Washington, D.C., Consular Reznichenko."

11. A slip of paper with longhand writing, "The Worker, 23 W. 26th St., New York 10, N.Y. The Worker, Box 28 Madison Sq. Station, New York 10, NY."

12. A card for the Fair Play for Cuba Committee with a New York address, issued to Lee H. Oswald and filed by V. T. Lee as executive secretary. (This was the true address, name, and signature of the then secretary of the FPCC.)

13. A card for the Fair Play for Cuba Committee, New Orleans Chapter, issued to L. H. Oswald and signed by the chapter president, A. J. Hidell. (This card was later found to have been printed for 'Oswald' in New Orleans in June 1963, and the name A. J. Hidell written in by Marina.)

14. An undated Dallas Public Library card, with an expiration date of 7 December 1965, issued to Lee Harvey Oswald of 602 Elsbeth, Dallas, correctly stating his business address as Jaggars-Chiles-Stovall, followed by the name Jack L. Bowen of 1916 Stevens Forest Drive, as 'Oswald's' reference. (Jack L. Bowen was the alias of John Caesar Grossi, 'Oswald's' co-worker at Jaggars-Chiles-Stovall.)

15. A check stub from American Bakeries, Dallas, dated 1960, a year when 'Oswald' was in the Soviet Union. (The previous tenant of an apartment on Neely Street, Dallas, occupied by 'Oswald' and Marina in the spring of 1963, had been employed by American Bakeries in 1960. Why it was included in 'Oswald's' wallet has not been resolved.)

16. A snapshot of Lee Harvey Oswald in Marine uniform.

17. A snapshot of a woman (presumably Marina) and a snapshot of an infant.

18. A Marine marksman's medal.

19. $13 in currency, consisting of one $5 bill and eight $1 bills.

(Numbers 6 and 14 do not appear in the Warren Exhibits.)

The contents of the wallet formed a self-identifying "history" of the assassin's operations, and an identification of his wife and (presumably) his first child, born in the Soviet Union, together with the names of his contacts while he was in the United States; it was an all-purpose "passport."

The proposed use of the counterfeits and false photographs remains, of course, obscure, but the methods employed to counterfeit were arduous and required photographic skill, the use of different typewriters, and considerable time.

At 7:10 P.M., after considerable interrogation (and presumably after many telephone calls among the various authorities) a justice of the peace arraigned 'Oswald' for murder with malice of Patrolman Tippit.

THE WHITE HOUSE

President Johnson had arrived at the White House at about 6:00 P.M., and had met with advisers, including FBI director, J. Edgar Hoover. Taking into account the contents of the FBI files at the Bureau in Washington in addition to the discrepancies the Dallas police immediately discovered, Hoover must have realized that the assassin did not act alone and that his identity was in question.

If *The Investigation of the Assassination of President John F. Kennedy: Performance of the Intelligence Agencies. Book V. Final Report of the Select Committee to Study Governmental Operations with Respect to Intelligence Activities. United States Senate.* 23 April 1976, hereafter referred to as Book V, is correct, Hoover did not tell Johnson any of the above or that the FBI had an open security file on 'Oswald.' He gave him only details on 'Oswald's' background and the fact that he had been in Russia. Nonetheless, conspiracy seems to have been considered by Johnson, since shortly before 9:00 P.M. that night, the White House exerted pressure upon Dallas officials and police not to disclose a suspected Russian conspiracy.

Apparently recoiling from the horrendous consequences were he to disclose to the stunned American public that their young President might have been assassinated by the Soviets—particularly so soon after the terror of the Cuban Missile Crisis—Johnson and his advisers had decided that immediate restraint was necessary. Hoover then departed, neither he nor the President issuing any public statement.

Shortly before 9:00 P.M., the White House telephoned Waggoner Carr, the Attorney General of Texas, and asked him to contact Henry Wade, the District Attorney of Dallas, to ensure his cooperation in seeing that no charge suggesting Soviet conspiracy be preferred against the arrested man. Henry Wade testified that, in a telephone conversation with Waggoner Carr, the latter had referred to the undesirability of such an allegation for fear of international complications.

Six months later, Waggoner Carr was to testify in Washington:

As I recall it was around *8 or 9 o'clock at night* on November 22, 1963 when I received a long-distance telephone call from Washington from someone in the White House. I can't for the life of me remember who it was. A rumor had been heard here (Washington) that there was going to be an allegation in the indictment against Oswald connecting the assassination with an international conspiracy, and the enquiry was made whether I had any knowledge of it, and I told him I had no knowledge of it . . . I received the definite impression that the concern of the caller was that because of the emotion or the high tension that existed at the time that someone might thoughtlessly place in the indictment such an allegation without having proof of such a conspiracy . . . There was no direct talk or indirect talk or insinuation that the facts, whatever they might be, should be suppressed.

Carr went on to testify that he was asked to contact District Attorney Wade to find out if such an allegation was in the indictment, and that he telephoned Wade, who told him ". . . that he had no knowledge of anyone desiring to have that or planning to have that in the indictment; that it would be surplusage (*sic*), it was not necessary to allege it, and that it would not be in there, but he would double-check to be sure." Carr then telephoned the White House with the information he had received from Wade, presumably to speak to the man whose name he was unable to recall. (V.258-260.)

FINGERPRINTING THE ASSASSIN

Between 8:40 P.M. and 8:55 P.M. on 22 November, the arrested man's fingerprints were twice taken in Fritz's office. J. B. Hicks testified that he took fingerprints "on an inkless pad. That's the pad we use for fingerprinting people without the black ink that they make for the records." (VII.288.) W. E. Barnes testified that he also fingerprinted the man, using the usual inking and rolling process. He said that the man "would not sign the fingerprint card when I asked him. We have a place on this card for the prisoner's signature, and I asked him would he please sign that, and he said he wouldn't sign anything until he talked to an attorney." Barnes said that when the man said he would not sign the fingerprint card, Barnes had told him that was "all right with me." (VII.285.) The prints taken by Barnes appear in the Exhibits as CE.627, and in the space for the signature of the printed man is handwritten Lee Harvey Oswald.

After the two sets of fingerprints had been taken, the arrested man continued to be questioned in Fritz's office.

THE MIDNIGHT SHOW-UP

Late on the night of 22 November it had been decided to hold a midnight "show-up" of the assassin to the press in the detail room of the police station. At one end stood a platform, in front of which was a "one-way" screen; the police used the platform and the screen for identity parades so that witnesses could identify suspects without themselves being seen. When the assassin was brought in by some 12 policemen and led onto the platform behind the screen, the crowd of newsmen shouted that they could not photograph properly through the screen, and the assassin was brought off the platform onto the floor—where the newsmen literally could touch the prisoner. They continued to shout questions at him. Calmly, 'Oswald' made noncommittal replies, and, after a minute or two, he was taken upstairs to the jail. Ruby, who must have somehow identified himself as a newsman, was one of those present in the room.

After the "show-up," at 12:33 A.M. (23 November), 'Oswald' was delivered to the jailer, who placed him in a maximum security cell on the fifth floor.

SATURDAY 23 NOVEMBER 1963

Films that had been taken on the third floor on the evening of 22 November show that Ruby was near the homicide office just before midnight when it was announced that the assassin would be shown to the press in the detail room. When the assassin was brought down to the room for the midnight "show-up," another film shows Ruby, pencil and notepad in hand, standing on a table at the back of the room with other reporters. After a brief appearance, the assassin was taken away, but Ruby remained in the room to hear Wade answer questions from the press.

Wade said that the assassin would probably be moved to the county jail at the beginning of the following week. When the questioning was over, Ruby followed Wade out of the room and said to him, "Hi! Henry, don't you know me, I am Jack Ruby. I run the Vegas Club (another of Ruby's clubs)." Wade had never heard of Ruby. Ruby then obtained the night telephone number of radio station KLIF, telephoned KLIF, and told them that he would like to bring them some sandwiches and cold drinks; he was invited to their premises. He then observed a reporter holding open a telephone line and trying to attract Wade's attention. Ruby directed Wade to the reporter, who proceeded to interview him. Ruby again telephoned KLIF and offered to secure them an interview with Wade by calling the latter to the telephone, which he did.

Ruby then left the police station and drove to KLIF, arriving at about 1:45 A.M., where he distributed some of his refreshments and remained in the studio for about 45 minutes making friends with some of the staff. On leaving KLIF, at about 2:30 A.M., Ruby went to a point near his club where he met a police officer who was sitting in a parked car with an entertainer from the Carousel Club. All three were to testify that they talked for about an hour in the car and that they were all crying because of the assassination. Ruby then left them and drove to a newspaper office where he told some of the employees about his visit to the police station the previous evening and that he had set up a telephone interview of Wade by KLIF.

In retrospect, it would seem that Ruby had been ingratiating himself with Wade and members of the news media who might later be able to tell him exactly when the assassin would be moved from the police jail to the county jail. Wade was to testify that, when he heard on his car radio on 24 November that the assassin had been murdered by a "businessman," before Ruby's name was announced he had said to himself, "That must be Jack Ruby, the way he looked (after the show-up). He looked kind of wild to me down there Friday night, the way he was running everywhere, you know, and I said to myself that must be him."

Sometime after Hoover left the White House on the night of the assassination, the classification and formula of the first and second sets of prints taken by the Dallas police must have been flashed to him in Washington. These prints would then be found to be the same as the prints of Lee Harvey Oswald on joining the Marines in 1956. Hoover must have been surprised to find that the prints of the arrested man matched those of the Marine, because of the conflicting information revealed in the FBI file. It would seem that in order to be certain that no mistakes could have been made when the first and second sets of prints were taken in Fritz's office, Hoover had asked the Dallas police to *again* print the arrested man in the ID Bureau.

Twelve minutes after the "show-up" (12:35 A.M., 23 November), 'Oswald' was checked out of his cell by Lieutenant Knight and Sergeant Warren of the ID Bureau on the fourth floor. He was fingerprinted for the *third* time and pictures were taken; the police mug shot of the man shows the date on the card around his neck as 11.23.1963. It is not known who took this third set of prints or if the arrested man again refused to sign the card. Neither Knight nor Warren testified, but both Lieutenant Baker and Fritz testified that prints were taken, and that the assassin was returned to his cell at 1:10 A.M. (IV.247-248.) The third set of prints does not appear in the Exhibits.

Some six and a half hours after his first arraignment, and during the second hour of the morning, 'Oswald' was again arraigned, this time for murder with malice of Kennedy. The news went out on the State Department radio, "The Voice of America," that the death of the President was the result of a rightwing conspiracy. The news carried over American radio and television made no mention of any possible conspiracy.

Sometime that morning a director of Jaggars-Chiles-Stovall telephoned the Secret Service to inform it that his firm had employed Lee Harvey Oswald a few months previously. The Service went at once to the firm's premises and, presumably, discovered that the firm had a "secrets" department, that the assassin had obtained employment there by lying, that he had joined the firm on 12 October 1962, and that on the morning of his first working day, 16 October, he had photographed material for the Army Map Service. Following the Secret Service, the FBI also visited the firm's premises, but there is no record in the Exhibits of what, if anything, either agency discovered.

In the early afternoon, 'Oswald's' mother, brother, and wife were allowed to visit the arrested man. The mother and the brother confirmed that the arrested man was the man who had arrived in Fort Worth from Russia in 1962. The wife did not dispute the fact that the man she was visiting was the man she married in Minsk in April 1961.

Late that Saturday night, Chief Curry set 10:00 A.M. Sunday morning as the time when the assassin would be transferred from the police jail to the county jail; he told the exhausted newsmen that if they were back by that time the next morning they would not miss anything.

SUNDAY 24 NOVEMBER 1963

The last interrogation of the assassin commenced at 9:25 A.M. in the homicide office on the third floor of Dallas police headquarters. Present were Captain Fritz, two senior Secret Service agents, three Dallas police detectives, and a senior postal inspector. The inspector was present because the assassin had rented three post office boxes during the past 13 months. In due course, the inspector was to furnish the Commission with a memorandum reflecting his recollections of that last interrogation.

The memorandum stated that 'Oswald' still denied owning a rifle and killing Tippit or the President, and continued:

> Oswald at no time appeared confused or in doubts as to whether or not he should answer a question. On the contrary, he was quite alert and showed no hesitancy in answering those questions which he wanted to answer, and was quite skillful in parrying those questions which he did not wish to answer. I got the impression that he had disciplined his mind and reflexes to a state where I personally doubted if he would ever have confessed.

The interrogation of the assassin ended at 11:15 A.M., after which arrangements were made to transfer him from the city jail at the police station to the county jail. He was taken from the third floor down to the basement of the building and escorted toward a waiting car. For security purposes there were more than 70 police officers in the basement. The assassin was handcuffed to a detective and escorted by other officials during his walk of some 12 yards to the waiting car, with Captain Fritz preceding the group by some five yards. There were numerous newsmen and television camera crews present who were, or were supposed to have been, screened before being allowed into the basement. Somehow Jack Ruby managed to bypass the screen and appear in the basement at 11:19 A.M., having walked from a nearby Western Union office where, at 11:17 A.M., he had dispatched a $25 money order to one of the strippers who worked in his Carousel Club.

At about 11:20 A.M. the assassin arrived from the third floor by elevator in an area separated from the basement by swing doors. The escorting police waited for a minute to see that all was clear ahead of them and then passed into the basement to approach the transit car. When the assassin had taken only a few steps, in full view of television cameras, at 11:21 A.M., Ruby—who had been frequenting the passages of police headquarters from the time of the assassin's arrest, mingling with the local, national, and foreign reporters, photographers, and television crews, pretending to be a reporter himself—lunged through the line of policemen and, thrusting a .38 snub-nosed Cobra revolver close to the assassin's abdomen, murdered him with one professional shot. The assassin collapsed and died shortly afterward without recovering consciousness. Ruby was thrown to the ground and overpowered by the police, to whom he shouted, "I'm Jack Ruby, you all know me."

To kill the assassin, Ruby had taken into the basement the .38 Cobra revolver which he usually kept either in the glove compartment or in the trunk of his car. After the murder he was taken to the jail, where his clothes and possessions were removed; he had more than $2,000 in a pocket and was wearing an expensive suit, shirt, hat, and other clothes including a 100% silk tie, a diamond Le Coultre wristwatch, a gold ring with three diamonds, a gold-plated tie clasp, and a French Melville belt; a further $1,500 was later found in the trunk of his car.

Ruby had been in the basement for not more than two minutes, but how he had known the exact time that 'Oswald' would appear was never established. In the words of the defending attorney at Ruby's trial, "It was the greatest coincidence in history." Had Ruby entered the basement earlier, he would have risked detection and removal. But, as it was, the imminent appearance of the assassin had created activity and excitement, and during the time that Ruby was there, all present were concentrating their eyes and their cameras upon the swinging doors through which the assassin would shortly emerge; such was the timing of Ruby's entry that it passed unnoticed.

Ruby was questioned by the police as to how he had penetrated the security screen in the basement. He at first declined to discuss the matter, and it was only later that he said he had entered the basement by walking down a police-guarded ramp; thereafter he maintained that this had been his means of entry.

He had preferred to attend to his business affairs rather than watch the motorcade which had passed within 100 yards of the club; yet he told the police that he had shot the assassin because he had been grieving over the murder for two days; he wished to save Jacqueline Kennedy the distress of being a witness at the trial of the assassin. Although Ruby maintained that the killing had been emotionally motivated, he was convicted of the premeditated murder of "Lee Harvey Oswald," and died in prison in 1967.

Immediately after 'Oswald's' murder, the FBI in Dallas, Chicago, New York, and elsewhere began wideranging interviews of members or suspected members of organized crime. By the next day, 25 November, they were interviewing the remnants of the Al Capone gang, for whom Ruby is believed to have worked in Chicago when he was a boy.

The initial demand for a public inquiry into the assassination was intensified by the murder of the assassin. Attorney General Waggoner Carr immediately announced that a court of inquiry would be held in Texas "to develop fully and disclose openly the facts of the assassination." But this inquiry was postponed at Chief Justice Warren's request until after the Commission had published its report; Carr accepted the offer of the Commission to work with it. Thus, an independent inquiry was never held in Texas or elsewhere. At the end of his testimony before the Commission, Carr was complimented by Warren and another Commissioner on the fact that "from the very beginning of the Commission's investigation his co-operation had been complete, enthusiastic and most helpful to the Commission"; the Commission had appreciated it very much indeed. Carr replied, "Well, thank you, sir, I will say this, that it has been a very pleasant experience for us, and I think set a good example of how a state government and a federal government can co-operate together where we have common objectives such as this, where we are trying to determine the facts and nothing else."

During 22-23-24 November, Chief of Homicide Fritz, Chief of Police Curry, and District Attorney Wade had severally or jointly given interviews to the news media; these are recorded on television studios' tapes. (XXIV.748-847.) If any statements were to be made to the news media, it would seem that they should have reflected the information already in the hands of the Dallas police. But this was not the case, and it is important for an appreciation of the events of the three days to quote from the tapes and testimony of the three men. The tapes show that Fritz, Curry, and Wade made no comment to the news people about the contents of the wallet or the recorded discrepancies in height. They said twice that the assassin was on his way to the movie theater when he slew Tippit, although reference to a map of Dallas in the police station would have shown that the assassin was walking away from the site of the theater when he encountered Tippit. They were not sure if the arrested man had been a Marine.

Chief Curry was to testify:

. . . we felt that this was a murder that had been committed in the City and County of Dallas and that we had prior, I mean we had jurisdiction over this. The FBI actually had no jurisdiction over it, the Secret Service actually had no jurisdiction over it. But in an effort to co-operate with these agencies we went all out to do whatever they wanted us to do that we could do to let them observe what was taking place, but actually we knew that this was a case that happened in Dallas, Tex., and would have to be tried in Dallas, Tex., and it was our responsibility to gather the evidence and present the evidence. We kept getting calls from the FBI. They wanted this evidence up in Washington, in the laboratory, and there was some discussion. Fritz told me, he says, "Well, I need the evidence here. I need to get some people to try to identify the gun, to try to identify this pistol and these things, and if it is in Washington how can I do it?" But we finally, the night, about midnight of Friday night (22 November), we agreed to let the FBI have all the evidence and they said they would bring it to their laboratory and they would have an agent stand by and when they were finished with it to return it to us.

Curry said that, to his knowledge, no agent of the Dallas police was sent to Washington with the evidence (thereby destroying the chain of evidence). When asked whether that arrangement worked out alright, Curry replied:

Well, not exactly, because they were to give us pictures of everything that was brought to Washington, and Fritz tells me that some of these little items that it was very poor reproduction of some of the items on microfilm. Subsequently they photographed these things in Washington and sent us copies, some 400 I think, 400 copies of different items. So far as I know, we have never received any of that evidence back. It is still in Washington, I guess. Perhaps the Commission has it.

Counsel then informed Curry that the Commission was still working with it, and Curry continued:

. . . they were in a tremendous hurry to get all of these items to the laboratory here in Washington, and our only concern was this, that if this case is tried in Dallas, we need the evidence to be presented here in court in Dallas and we were a little bit apprehensive about it if it gets to Washington will it be available to us when we need it. If we need somebody to identify, attempt to identify the gun or other items would it be here for them to see? And that was our only concern. We got several calls insisting we send this, and nobody would tell me exactly who it was that was insisting, "just say I got a call from Washington and they wanted this evidence up there," insinuating it was someone in high authority that was requesting this, and we have finally agreed as a matter of trying to co-operate with them, actually . . . I had a lot of communications from the local FBI who inferred that those orders were coming out of Washington, or the questions were coming out of Washington, about various things, insisting that the evidence be shipped up there immediately, and the fact that we shouldn't show anything on television. (IV.150-152.)

Had the contents of the wallet been shown on television, disclosing counterfeiting, forgery, differing heights, a substituted photograph with the date 1963 impressed, a reference to Reznichenko on a piece of paper, and the Communist newspaper, *The Worker*, evidence of conspiracy would have been apparent and immediately publicized.

Chief Fritz was to testify that, although he was the only police officer who interrogated 'Oswald,' officers from the FBI and the Secret Service had also done so. He did not say whether he had been under any pressure. He said that there had been fairly continuous questioning by him, although interrupted by identity parades and other matters. The interrogation had started shortly after 2:30 P.M., on Friday 22 November, and covered a period of some 12 hours between that time and 11:15 A.M. on Sunday 24 November. (Allowing for interruptions, this period could perhaps be reduced to six to eight hours, but it is impossible to identify more than a few questions asked of the arrested man at any time. Many more questions must have been asked, and it is not the replies of the assassin that would be interesting—for he could be silent, evasive, truthful, or untruthful at will—but the nature of the questions that were asked, for there must have been many that inquired in depth into the making and purpose of counterfeit cards (2 and 4), why Oswald's photograph had been removed from card (6) and 1963 stamped on the substituted photograph, how the Marines twice had come to measure him at 2" above his height of 5'9", as to his name, as to his and the "American male's" visits to the Soviet Embassy in Mexico City, as to the identity of Jack L. Bowen on the library card (14), and where he was going when he shot Tippit. Since nobody took notes, the extent and essence of the questioning cannot now be discovered.)

The arrested man had denied killing Tippit or the President, or wounding the governor, and when Fritz asked if he thought the country would be better off with the President killed, he had replied, "Well, I think that the Vice President has about the same views as the President has," adding that Johnson "would probably do about the same thing" that President Kennedy would have done. When Fritz was asked by Counsel whether he had asked 'Oswald' about "this card he had in his pocket with the name Alek Hidell?" Fritz replied that he believed that the man had three of those cards, if he remembered correctly, and that "one of the cards looked like it might have been altered a little bit . . ." On being shown the bus transfer ticket on 23 November, 'Oswald' had revised the story that he had told on 22 November in which he had said that he had taken a bus to his rooming house, now admitting that he left the bus "because the traffic was heavy" and that he then took a taxi to his rooming house.

He said that he was a Marxist but that he was not a Marxist-Leninist and repeated—what he had several times told Fritz—that he believed in the Castro revolution. Fritz said that the arrested man had acted like a person who was prepared for what he was doing and that he suspected that he had been "trained in sabotage from the way that he talked and acted." But when 'Oswald' was asked about this, he replied that, while in the Soviet Union, he had worked only in a radio factory. Fritz said that if he asked him a question that "meant something," 'Oswald' immediately replied that he would say nothing about it and he seemed to anticipate what Fritz was going to say. "In fact, he got so good at it, one time I asked him if he had had any training, if he hadn't been questioned before." Fritz thought that the arrested man had shot the President "because of his feeling about the Castro revolution," and that he did not think that he was "afraid at all" and "was a person who had his mind made up what to do . . . like a person dedicated to a cause." Fritz also thought that he was of above-average intelligence and "was not a 'nut,' which people had been saying."

With regard to Ruby, Fritz said that the nightclub owner had told him he had been "all torn up about the Presidential killing, that he felt terribly sorry for Mrs. Kennedy. He didn't want to see her to have to come back to Dallas for a trial, and a lot of things like that." When Fritz had asked him how he had entered the basement, Ruby said that he had walked down a ramp. When Fritz pointed out that since there had been "an officer at the top and an officer at the bottom" Ruby could not have entered that way, Ruby replied, "I am not going to talk to you any more, I am not going to get into trouble." And Ruby "never talked any more about it." When Fritz asked Ruby when he had first decided to kill the assassin, Ruby avoided the question and talked about something else. (IV.202-249.XV.145-153.)

As with Curry and Fritz, District Attorney Wade was to testify at length and said that Fritz "ran a kind of one-man operation where nobody else knew what he was doing," but that "Fritz was about as good a man at solving a crime as he had ever known." He said that on the evening of 22 November he had heard on the radio or on television that the police were going to charge Lee Harvey Oswald with being part of an international conspiracy to murder the President. He then talked to United States Attorney Barefoot Sanders and discussed these media statements with him. Since there was no such crime in Texas as being part of an international conspiracy, the only charge could be "murder with malice." Anything else alleged had to be proved. He said he thought that if somebody was going to charge the arrested man with being part of an international conspiracy "it had to be a publicity deal, somebody being interested in something other than the law because there was no such charge in Texas." He said that he also talked to Waggoner Carr on the evening of Friday 22 November, and that Carr had mentioned there was a rumor circulating that the police were getting ready to file a charge on Lee Harvey Oswald as being part of an international conspiracy, but that he had told Carr that this was not going to be done. Both Sanders and Carr had told him that they were concerned about having received calls "from Washington and somewhere else," and they had said that if it was not absolutely necessary they thought that it should not be done.

When Wade was asked by Counsel whether in his conversations with Carr he could remember anything else that Carr had said to him, Wade replied:

> I don't actually even remember, you know. He said that he had had a call from Washington; I don't actually remember anything about that. I remember he said that about this charge that this is going (*sic*), "This would be a bad situation, if you allege it as part of *a Russian, the Russian conspiracy*, and it may affect your international relations, a lot of things, of the country," and I said it was silly because I don't know where the rumor started, but I will see even if it was so we could prove it, I wouldn't allege it. Isn't that about it, the way you recall it, Mr. Carr?" (Carr apparently was sitting near Wade during the latter's testimony and, according to the transcript, did not reply.)

(The *Dallas Morning News* of 6 December 1975 reported that Assistant District Attorney Alexander told them that Wade, acting on a call from President Johnson's aide, Cliff Carter, told him on 22 November 1963 to stop talking about a "Communist conspiracy"; "Knock that off," Alexander quoted Wade. "What are you trying to do, start a war with Russia?")

After agreeing with a Commissioner that the law in Texas permitted a charge of conspiracy to commit murder, Wade said that no evidence had been brought to him upon which he could have based an indictment or warrant for conspiracy to commit murder, and he had never seen any of the physical evidence in the 'Oswald' case other than one or two statements and the assassination rifle. But he added that he thought that 'Oswald' had planned the assassination, had practiced shooting, and had his inspiration from someone else.

Wade said that before he had called a press conference at about 8:00 P.M. on the night of Sunday 24 November, he and Fritz had listed about seven pieces of evidence that he was going to give to the news media, but Curry had told them that they should not do this because he had told the FBI that there would be nothing said about the assassination of the President and the murder of the assassin. Wade, however, had considered it to be in the interests of the police that he should dispel rumors that the police had arrested the wrong man and had arranged to have him killed, and he thought that somebody ought to go on television and state the evidence against 'Oswald', telling the public everything. He said that immediately after he held the televised press conference, an FBI inspector called him and asked him not to say anything further about the case. (V.213-254.)

10

The Elusive 'Oswald'

HIDELL AND 'OSWALD'

It would seem that 'Oswald' never committed himself to any name while in police custody. Immediately upon arrival at the police station when he was briefly interrogated by Detective Guy Rose, the assassin said that his name was Hidell. Rose testified, ". . . In a minute—I found two cards—I found a card that said 'A. Hidell.' And I found another card that said 'Lee Oswald' on it, and I asked him which of the two was his correct name. He wouldn't tell me . . . he just said, "You find out." (VII.288.)

Apart from the contents of the FBI file which appeared to show two different Lee Harvey Oswalds, the authorities discovered at least two additional pieces of evidence which showed some systematic effort on 'Oswald's' part to establish two separate identities.

A. Two "photographs," alleged to be montages, were found and, because they were left lying around, were presumably intended to be found by the police among 'Oswald's' possessions in Ruth Paine's house after the assassination. In the "photographs," 'Oswald' was dressed in black and stood holding a rifle, with a revolver strapped around his waist; he resembled the popular idea of a guerrilla (associated at that time with Castro). The "photographs" were taken in the backyard at 214 Neely Street, where the 'Oswalds' were living at the time of the attempted murder of General Walker in April 1963.

In one "photograph," 'Oswald' is holding the rifle in his left hand

Marine Oswald, about September 1959.

The impostor 'Oswald,' about August 1963.

'Oswald' and Marina on their wedding day, April 1961.

George and Jeanne De Mohrenschildt, 1974.

Left-handed 'Oswald' with Trotskyite newspaper *The Militant*.

Right-handed 'Oswald' with American Communist Party
newspaper *The Worker*.

Blowup of head belonging to the left-handed 'Oswald.' The horizontal shadow below the mouth suggests that the upper part of the face was super-imposed upon a figure whose face had a broad chin.

Photo taken in Dallas Police Headquarters, 22 or 23 November 1963, shows the assassin with a vertical cleft in an angular chin.

Above: Ruth Paine's house in Irving. Rifle was stored in the garage.

Assassination rifle fitted with sight and sling.

Shield of cartons surrounding the sniper's nest.

Right:
FBI photo reproducing the assassin's view of Elm Street as seen through the telescopic sight.

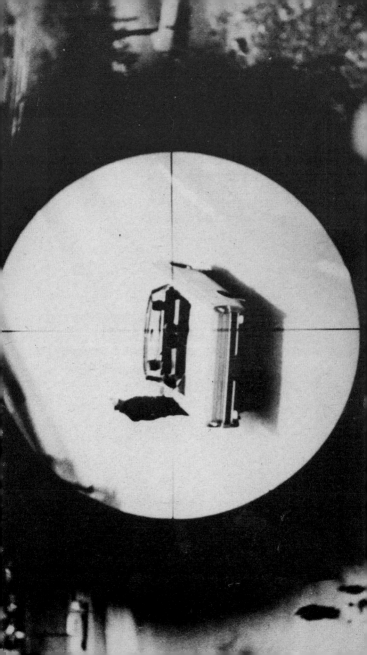

Name Oswald, Mr. Lee Harvey
M. Address 602 Elsbeth
City Dallas   Zone   Phone

Signature
Address Same
City   Zone   Phone
School or Business Jaggers-Chiles-Stoval
Name Jack L. Bowen ←
Home Address 1916 Stevens Forest Dr.
Phone WH8-8997   Expires 12-7-65
DALLAS PUBLIC LIBRARY   cr
(See Reverse Side)

Genuine library card proving 'Oswald's' acquaintanceship with Jack L. Bowen. Not shown in Warren Report or Exhibits.

Department of Defense Identification Card prepared by Marine
Lt. Ayers on 11 September 1959 but exhibiting a picture (stamped 1963)
the Warren Report claims was taken of Oswald in Minsk.
Not shown in Warren Report or Exhibits.

EXAMPLES OF 'OSWALD'S' ALL-PURPOSE IDENTIFICATION

SELECTIVE SERVICE SYSTEM
NOTICE OF CLASSIFICATION   Approval not required

Lee   Harvey   OSWALD
(First name)   (Middle name)   (Last name)

Selective Service No.   ☐ 41 114 39 532 ☐   has

been classified in Class ....IV-A.... (Until ....

19........) by   ☒ Local Board   ☐ Appeal Board,

by vote of .... to .... ☐ President
(Show vote on appeal board stamp only)

FEB 2 1960 ...., 19 ....
(Date of mailing)   (Member or clerk of local board)

The law requires you, subject to heavy penalty for violation, to carry this notice, in addition to your Registration Certificate, on your person at all times—to exhibit it upon request to authorized officials—to surrender it to your commanding officer upon entering the armed forces,

The law requires you to notify your local board in writing (1) of every change in your address, physical condition, and occupational, marital, family, dependency, and military status, and (2) of any other fact which might change your classification.

FOR ADVICE, SEE YOUR GOVERNMENT APPEAL AGENT

Marine Oswald's Notice of Classification without Oswald's signature.

SELECTIVE SERVICE SYSTEM
NOTICE OF CLASSIFICATION
Approval not required

ALEK   JAMES   HIDELL
(First name)   (Middle name)   (Last name)

Selective Service No. 42 224 39 532 has

been classified in Class _____ (Until _____

19_____) by   ☐ Local Board   ☐ Appeal Board,

by vote of _____ to _____   ☐ President
(Show vote on appeal board cases only)

_____, 19____   _____
(Date of mailing)   (Member or clerk of local board)

(Registrant must sign here)

The law requires you, subject to heavy penalty for violation, to carry this notice, in addition to your Registration Certificate on your person at all times—to exhibit it upon request to authorized officials—to surrender it to your commanding officer upon entering the armed forces.

The law requires you to notify your local board in writing (1) of every change in your address, physical condition, and occupational, marital, family, dependency, and military status, and (2) of any other fact which might change your classification.

FOR ADVICE, SEE YOUR GOVERNMENT APPEAL AGENT

Counterfeit Notice of Classification for Alek James Hidell. Legend at bottom reduced to create space for photograph matching that on Identification Card.

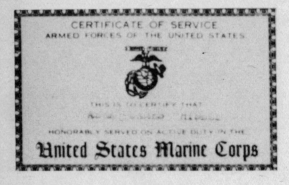

Counterfeit Certificate of Service showing the name Alek James Hidell.

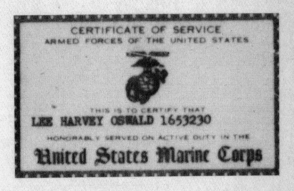

Marine Oswald's genuine Certificate of Service.

REL 11 Sept; 1959

REPORT OF MEDICAL EXAMINATION

1. LAST NAME—FIRST NAME—MIDDLE NAME	2. GRADE AND COMPONENT OR POSITION	3. IDENTIFICATION NO.
OSWALD, Lee Harvey	Pfc	1653230

4. HOME ADDRESS (Number, street or RFD, city or town, zone and State)	5. PURPOSE OF EXAMINATION	6. DATE OF EXAMINATION
3124 West 5th St. Fort Worth, Texas	Seperation	3 Sept 1959

7. SEX	8. RACE	9. TOTAL YRS. GOVT. SERVICE	10. DEPARTMENT, AGENCY, OR SERVICE	11. ORGANIZATION UNIT
M	C	MILITARY 03 / CIVILIAN	USMC	H&HS SEP SEC

12. DATE OF BIRTH	13. PLACE OF BIRTH	14. NAME, RELATIONSHIP, AND ADDRESS OF NEXT OF KIN
18 Oct 39	Louisiana	Mrs. M. OSWALD, Same as line #4 (M)

15. EXAMINING FACILITY OR EXAMINER, AND ADDRESS

U. S MARINE CORPS AIR STATION
EL TORO (SANTA ANA), CALIF.

16. OTHER INFORMATION

Rel: Luthern

17. RATING OR SPECIALTY

TIME IN THIS CAPACITY: TOTAL   LAST SIX MONTHS

NOTES—Describe every abnormality in detail. (Enter pertinent item number before each
comment; continue in item 73 and use additional sheets if necessary.)

NORMAL	ABNOR-MAL	CLINICAL EVALUATION (Check each item in appropriate column; enter "N E." if not evaluated)
X		18. HEAD, FACE, NECK, AND SCALP
		19. NOSE
		20. SINUSES
		21. MOUTH AND THROAT
		22. EARS—GENERAL (Int. & ext. canals) (of auditory acuity under items 70 and 71)
		23. DRUMS (Perforation)
		24. EYES—GENERAL (Visual acuity and refraction under items 55, 56, and 57)
		25. OPHTHALMOSCOPIC
		26. PUPILS (Equality and reaction)
		27. OCULAR MOTILITY (Associated parallel movements, nystagmus)
		28. LUNG AND CHEST (Include breasts)
		29. HEART (Thrust, size, rhythm, sounds)
		30. VASCULAR SYSTEM (Varicosities, etc.)
		31. ABDOMEN AND VISCERA (Include hernia)

(39) S operation, 1" left mastoid
S operation, 1" ULA
S gunshot, left elbow
S 2" left hand
VSULA

(18) Mastoid operation 1945 NCD

Marine medical report, 3 September 1959, noting the mastoidectomy.

'Oswald' after arrest in November 1963, his short haircut exposing open area behind ear. Photograph shows no trace of mastoidectomy scar or depression.

CIA SURVEILLANCE PHOTOGRAPHS
"American male" in dark jacket, Mexico City, 4 October 1963.

"American male" opening or closing pouch. Date not disclosed

"American male" examining contents of pouch. Date not disclosed.

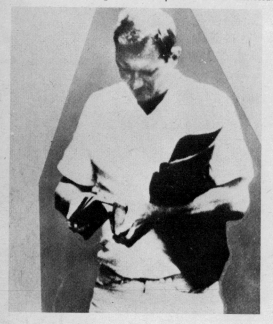

Card A, dated 15 October 1956, apparently forged by the KGB and inserted into the FBI files before Marine Oswald left for the Soviet Union.

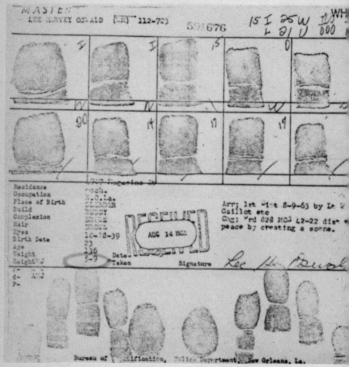

Card B, taken 9 August 1963 by the New Orleans Police stating that Oswald has brown eyes. Signature does not match signatures on Cards A and D.

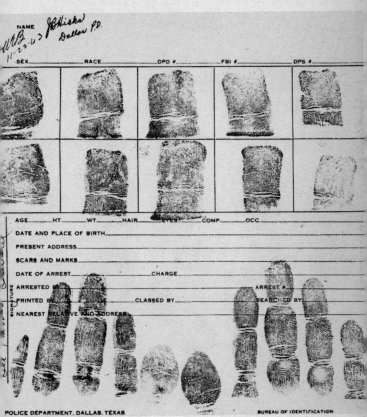

Card D, dated November 1963, taken by the Dallas Police. Signature apparently not that of the assassin as Barnes claimed he would not sign.

Mystery Card E, dated 25 November 1963, taken by the Dallas Police on FBI print card indicating that the assassin, already dead, "Refused to sign."

Ruby posing as a journalist at midnight press "show-up."

Waiting for 'Oswald' in the basement on Sunday morning.

The murder.

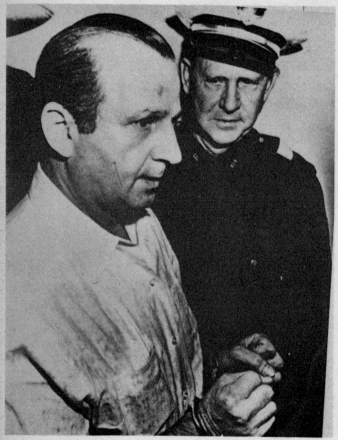

Handcuffed Ruby.

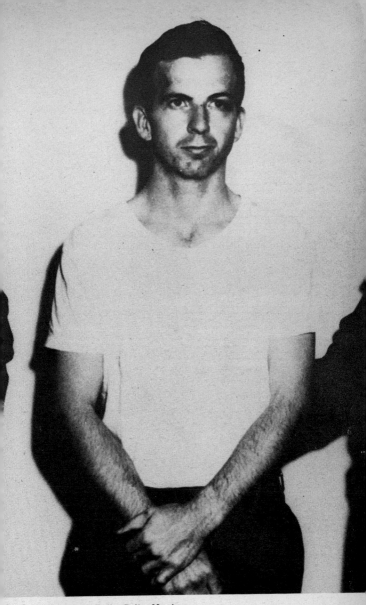
The assassin, Dallas Police Headquarters.

and a copy of the *Militant*, a Trotskyite paper, in his right hand; in the other "photograph," he is holding the rifle in his right hand and a copy of the *Worker*, the organ of the Communist Party of the United States, in his left hand. Marguerite Oswald was to testify that 'Oswald' was left-handed, but Robert Oswald was to testify that 'Oswald' was right-handed.

The upper part of the face on the "photographs" is that of 'Oswald' except for the chin, which is rounded like Oswald's, whereas the chin of 'Oswald' was narrower and with a perpendicular cleft. From the size of the head, the man in one of the "photographs" appears to be taller than the man in the other "photograph."

A commercial photographer and lecturer on photography, Jack White of Fort Worth, concluded that the "photographs" are montages, a photographed figure of a man having been placed upon a photograph of the yard at Neely Street. The upper part of 'Oswald's' face was then superimposed upon another face, the join in the face being made along the horizontal cleft between lower lip and chin. From the evidence supplied by the shadows, a stationary camera perhaps on a tripod had been used to photograph the background.

In summation, the discovered "photographs" show two faces, two heights, one man left-handed and the other right-handed—two men apparently representing two differing political views.

When 'Oswald' was shown the "photographs" by the police, he claimed that the police had had several opportunities to photograph him, and that they had superimposed his face upon that of another man. He told Captain Fritz that he knew all about photography and that in due course he would be able to establish the truth of his allegation.

More interesting, perhaps, than the "photographs" is the fact that Marina's memory should have failed her in testimony, for she said that she had taken one photograph, but, when shown a second photograph, she recollected that she had taken two. Two similar and almost identical "photographs" have recently surfaced in the National Archives, both apparently having been taken at the same time and with the same camera.

The Warren Report states that Marina took two photographs and that she had been asked to do so by 'Oswald' while she "was hanging diapers" in the backyard. (WR.125.) The two surfacing "photographs" are not mentioned. An FBI expert was to testify that in his opinion the photographs were not composites of two different photographs, and that Oswald's face had not been superimposed upon another body. (WR.127.)

B. During his stay in the United States, 'Oswald' had used the name Hidell to suggest that there had been a second Oswald whose real name was Hidell. Among 'Oswald's' possessions were found and, presumably, intended to be found by the police, four 3" by 5" index cards bearing the names G. Hall, A. J. Hidell, B. Davis, and V. T. Lee. (CE.2003, p. 269.) Gus Hall is Secretary General of the United States Communist Party and the late Benjamin J. Davis was a member of the National Administration Committee of the Communist Party. Vincent T. Lee was the executive secretary at the headquarters of the FPCC in New York. To include with these cards one with the name A. J. Hidell would suggest that a pro-Castro Hidell really existed and that A. J. Hidell was the real name of the second 5'9" "Lee Harvey Oswald" who first appeared on the scene when he took a job at Leslie Welding Co. in Fort Worth in July 1962.

MARINA'S 'OSWALD' AND MARGUERITE'S OSWALD

The Secret Service had been in constant contact with the assassin from the time of his arrival at Dallas police headquarters. On 23 November they took charge of Marguerite, Marina, and Robert Oswald.

When on the morning of 24 November Jack Ruby killed the assassin, the Service must have suspected conspiracy and that the killing had been engineered to avoid the trial of the assassin, and they must have realized that Marguerite, Marina, or Robert might also be killed. The Secret Service agents attempted to persuade them to move at once from the hotel where they had been secreted to the home of Robert's father and mother-in-law some 45 miles from Dallas. The agents did not immediately tell Marguerite that 'Oswald' had been shot, and she refused to move so far away, saying that she wanted to be near her imprisoned son. The agents then moved all three to a safer hotel outside of Dallas where they could be better guarded.

After the assassination, according to Marguerite's testimony, she and Marina had an amiable relationship, and the two women had discussed setting up a joint household with Marina's two daughters. This rapport disintegrated under the promptings of the Secret Service, who, by this time, probably understood that 'Oswald' was an impostor. Had the two women been permitted to live together on intimate terms, Marguerite might have brought up details of Oswald's background or physical data that would not jibe with what the impostor 'Oswald' had told Marina, or vice versa. They would have realized they were talking about two different people.

Marguerite stated that from the evening of 27 November 1963, the Secret Service agents had treated her with disdain. The agents had been respectful to Marina although, two days before, Secret Service agent Patterson had interviewed her and reported in writing: ". . . She advised that she was a Castro supporter and from the interview it was felt that she is still a hard-core Communist . . . She stated that she did not know the man who killed her husband. It was felt by the interviewer that she was not telling the truth and still believes in Communism." (XXIII.390.)

What transpired between the various Secret Service agents and Marina is not known, but on the evening of 27 November the agents, according to Marguerite's testimony, separated Marina and Marguerite in their two-room suite and arranged for Marina to sleep on the couch in the sitting-room. When Marguerite attempted to speak to Marina, the latter "shrugged her off" and walked away. (I.164-186.)

On the morning of 28 November 1963, Marina was moved to another part of the hotel entirely. Marguerite was not allowed to see or speak to her and, according to Marguerite and Marina, has never seen her since.

Immediately after the Warren Report and its 26 Volumes of Testimony and Exhibits were published, Marguerite Oswald acquired the entire set and has subsequently made them her life study. When I interviewed Mrs. Oswald, first in 1973 and again in 1975, we discussed the assassination in general terms and I deliberately avoided the subject of imposture. During the course of our conversation, however, Mrs. Oswald, herself, produced a list she had made of discrepancies in Oswald's height, asking what they could mean. Two years later, in the *Dallas Morning News*, she publicly expressed her doubts about the identity of the man known as her son.

11

Jack Ruby

Jacob Rubenstein, a United States citizen whose father was born in Poland, arrived in Dallas early in 1947 contemporaneously with the arrival there of some 25 underworld figures sent by Chicago mobsters to "organize" existing crime and to convert Dallas and the adjacent city of Fort Worth into what came to be known in the underworld as Little Chicago. In December 1947, Rubenstein legally changed his name to Jack Leon Ruby. While in Dallas, he cultivated the friendship of police and other officials, but, although arrested on several occasions for a variety of offenses, he never spent a day in prison. As a young man in Chicago, Ruby had a reputation as a street fighter and he is known to have assaulted many people. Although only 5'9" tall, Ruby was immensely strong: he used to boast that he could hit harder than Joe Louis. In Dallas, there were many records of his violence: he attacked women as well as men, usually without warning, using fists, knees, blackjack, revolver, and knuckle dusters. After he murdered 'Oswald' the police found "new" and "used" knuckle dusters in the trunk of his car.

The Warren Report tends to minimize Ruby's significance in the Dallas underworld. In the popular coverage of the assassination, he comes across as an eccentric if somewhat tawdry figure. It is closer to the truth to see him as a figure of some calculation. Ruby knew of or was known to most of the underworld figures in Chicago and probably throughout the United States, his known contacts ranging down both the East and West coasts, all of Texas, New Orleans, Mexico, and Cuba. The list of his contacts interviewed by the FBI and the other persons referred to reads like a *Who's Who* of the Chicago underworld, past and present.

His association with convicted drug smugglers is well established. In 1956, a woman reported to the FBI that her husband had disappeared on a long trip to Mexico while dealing in drugs on behalf of Jack Ruby whom, she alleged, controlled vice in Dallas: "Nothing could be started without Ruby's consent."

Nevertheless, he abandoned his full and apparently enjoyable life when he killed the man who throughout had protested his innocence. Although Ruby claimed his act was emotionally motivated, the evidence indicates that it was a calculated act. It is a fair presumption that Ruby must have been a conspirator, for otherwise, so far as he knew, he might have been killing an innocent man. The motive for the murder must always remain mysterious but would seem to be to silence a man he knew was guilty and had been unable to escape.

There is an early chronological parallel in Ruby's and Oswald's activities. On 11 March 1959, according to a recently released Commission document, Ruby was made an informant for the Dallas FBI, having been recruited to supply information about the underworld in Little Chicago. But although Ruby had eight meetings with the FBI, he did not provide any information and ended his "federal service" some six months later on 2 October 1959. (CD.1052.)

(It is interesting to note that Oswald took the first step in his plan to go abroad on 4 March when he applied to the college, the same week that Ruby became an FBI informant.)

This experience of Ruby's was divulged in a letter on 27 February 1964 from Hoover to Rankin, and only after Ruby had been convicted of the murder of the assassin. Ruby, on the other hand, did not mention his informant role in testimony to the Warren Commission in June 1964; the Commissioners present did not ask him about it, and it is not mentioned in the Warren Report.

While Ruby was still an FBI informant, Oswald separated from the Marines in Santa Ana, California, on 11 September 1959. On 12 September, Ruby, who lived and worked in Dallas, flew from Miami to Havana (CE.1442.), spent the night in Havana, and returned on 13 September to New Orleans. (CE.1443.) In the meantime, Oswald on leaving the Marines had traveled by bus from California to his mother's apartment in Fort Worth,.arriving there on 14 September.

He left Fort Worth on the evening of 16 September and arrived at the Liberty Hotel in New Orleans on 17 September.

How long Ruby remained in New Orleans is not known, but it *is* known that Oswald arrived there during the same week. It is conceivable that Oswald through the Cuban Consulate in Los Angeles expected to meet someone in New Orleans, and that Ruby was in New Orleans for the purpose of giving Oswald the money to finance a trip to Russia. If this were the case, his FBI informant role could be useful as a cover.

It has never been ascertained where Oswald received the money to finance his expensive trip abroad. The Warren Report states that he saved it, but no record of substantial savings has been recorded. Since Ruby was on record as an FBI informant, anything that happened in New Orleans between 17 September and 20 September (the day Oswald left for the Soviet Union) could have embarrassed the FBI should anything later go wrong—as it did. Ruby's informant role ended on 2 October when Oswald was safely in mid-Atlantic on his way to Russia.

Ruby's testimony in June 1964 and the reaction of the Commission thereto make clear that there was more significance to Ruby's role and to the coincidence of the presence of the two men in New Orleans within four days of each other than would otherwise be suspected.

Ruby had paid an eight-day visit to a prominent underworld figure in Havana in August 1959, about which he willingly testified to the Commission. But Ruby on four occasions *denied* his one-day September trip. In reply to a question about whether he had made a trip to Cuba other than the one in August, he said: "Never; that is the only one that I made." (V.205.) When asked about the step-by-step process by which he had arrived in Havana in August, he replied, ". . . I only went to Cuba once, so naturally . . . I only made one trip to Havana." (V.207.) In reply to the question, "This (August) trip to Cuba was the only time you left the country other than military service?" Ruby replied, "Actually I didn't leave in the military . . . Let's see, never out of the United States except at one time to Havana, Cuba." (V.208.)

During the first week of December 1963, the FBI had obtained the details of Ruby's one-day trip to Havana as set out in CE.1442/3. So it should have been clear to the Commissioners that he was lying in testimony, but they neither confronted him with this evidence nor asked him to explain his failure of memory and the purpose of his trip. Although Oswald's two passports appear in the Exhibits, Ruby's passport is not shown, and the Warren Report does not mention the one-day trip.

OTHER ITEMS OF CIRCUMSTANTIAL EVIDENCE

There are several more items of circumstantial evidence that appear to link Ruby to the assassination from the time that 'Oswald' entered the United States in June 1962 until 22 November 1963. Although none of it can prove that Ruby was a conspirator—for, like 'Oswald', he never confessed to conspiracy—the following matters appear to be significant.

In the first week of June 1963 while 'Oswald' was organizing his FPCC campaign in New Orleans, Ruby visited the city ostensibly to pick up a stripper for his club, again placing the two in proximity.

On 1 November 1963, the same day that 'Oswald' rented a post office box in Dallas, Ruby ordered handbills for a new business which purported to manufacture special boards, an aide in mastering a dance called the Twist.

Six days later, on 7 November, Ruby was to rent a post office box for his business, the box being eight feet from the box rented by 'Oswald' on 1 November, and the first he had rented during his 16 years in Dallas. The handbills had established the existence of the business, and the business provided him with a legitimate reason to rent a box; whatever use Ruby anticipated for his rented box apparently never materialized. According to the Commission Exhibits, when it was opened after Ruby shot 'Oswald,' a thin layer of dust was found on its floor.

On 1 November, Ruby also advertised in a newspaper for a partner with capital in connection with an expensive club-restaurant that he said he was proposing to open in Dallas. Further, he took an impoverished middle-aged man, George Senator, to live with him in his apartment at 223 South Ewing, and hired an itinerant laborer, Larry Crafard, to sleep in his nightclub and act as an extra but unpaid handyman. Senator had been close to Ruby for many years, but Crafard had known Ruby for not more than two months; neither had a criminal record, but both were penniless and had been dependent upon Ruby.

Crafard must have suspected or known that Ruby was expecting soon to receive a large amount of money, but not why or from whom.

Senator had the loan of a Volkswagen microbus in connection with his somewhat unremunerative work filling up card racks and selling novelties. The microbus belonged to a friend of Ruby's and would have been an ideal vehicle to "putter" its way to the large private Dallas Airport, Red Bird, with the assassin hidden in the back. In testimony, Senator was not asked and did not explain the whereabouts of his microbus on 22 November, nor was he able fully to account for his own movements on that day.

It would seem that Ruby's activities on 1 November were connected with the escape of the assassin from Dallas and the reward that Ruby expected to receive.

Similarly, on 8 November, Ruby and Crafard purchased a safe for Ruby's office in the Carousel Club; the safe was capable of accommodating a large sum of money. During his years in Dallas, there is no evidence that Ruby had ever before required a safe; he had always worked "out of his pocket," the trunk of his car accommodating the takings from his clubs. When the safe was opened by the police after Ruby shot 'Oswald,' it was found to be empty.

On the morning of 18 November, the Presidential motorcade was rehearsed through Dallas by the Secret Service and the police, passing close to the Carousel Club and proceeding past the Depository during 'Oswald's' lunch break. Mrs. Bertha Cheek testified that on that afternoon she had a long conversation with Ruby at the Carousel Club about Ruby's proposed new club-restaurant. Ruby told her that he had found a good site and wished her to invest in it. Although she had some capital and previous club-restaurant experience, as well as rooming-house ownership, she was not enthusiastic.

About half an hour after Mrs. Cheek said good-bye to Ruby at the Carousel Club, 'Oswald' was greeting Mrs. Earlene Roberts, the housekeeper of his rooming house at 1026 North Beckley, Mrs. Cheek's sister, who occupied a room next to 'Oswald's'.

At the time that Ruby was advertising for a club-restaurant partner, he owed more than $44,000 in excise and income taxes, and the authorities were about to impose liens on his two clubs. Unless he was expecting to receive a substantial sum of money sufficient to settle his tax indebtedness, the tax authorities would have looked askance at a third club-restaurant, and no doubt would have demanded settlement of the outstanding debts.

Ruby, in fact, had no money other than what he had in his possession when he shot the assassin, about $3,500, plus a few hundred dollars in his apartment, all this money apparently being the takings of his two clubs for, perhaps, the previous week; accounts for goods still to be settled.

On 20 November, Ruby had discussed his new club-restaurant venture with an old Dallas friend named Rossi. Rossi had grown up with Ruby in the area of Chicago known as the "bloody 24th ward." In a newspaper report shortly after Ruby shot 'Oswald,' Rossi said that he was aware of Ruby's tax problems and had suggested to Ruby that these problems would interfere with his new venture. According to Rossi, Ruby said that ". . . he had accumulated or gotten some money or was in the process of getting this all taken care of." Ruby suggested, according to Rossi, that he had the tax problem "settled or finalized," and that he could come to some agreement as to how much the authorities would settle for. "He was going to get that all squared off, and I believe he made mention of the fact that he had some money set aside for that required settlement." Rossi said he did not know the exact amount of money, but he thought "it ran up a fair size sum."

On the morning of 22 November, the *Dallas Morning News* ran an ominous full-page advertisement headed "Welcome to Dallas, Mr. Kennedy," and under which was asked a series of political questions derogatory of the President. At the bottom of the advertisement appear a name, Bernard Weissman, and an address, P.O. Box 1792, Dallas 21, Tex., the whole advertisement being surrounded by a thick black border as in an obituary notice. On seeing this advertisement, Ruby became greatly agitated. He telephoned his lawyer and questioned newsmen in an endeavor to find out if they had heard of Weissman. When nobody could help him, he checked the telephone directories, but to no avail.

The advertisement had been drawn up by Weissman in league with a self-styled "conservative" group of young men who had come to Dallas to start a political movement. The advertisement had been approved and paid for by a few Dallas residents who were opposed to the policies of Kennedy.

That day or earlier, Ruby had noticed a billboard poster in a street headed "Impeach Earl Warren." Ruby had never heard of Warren, but the similarity of the box number, 1757 (with a Massachusetts address) at the bottom of the poster to the box number used in the newspaper advertisement, 1792, interested him greatly.

At the time of the assassination Ruby was in the *Dallas Morning*

News office as he always was on Fridays, checking his weekend advertisements. He complained of their bad taste in accepting the Weissman advertisement, asking "Are you that money greedy?" From the window of the room he could see the Presidential motorcade pass the Depository a quarter of a mile away.

About the time of 'Oswald's' arrest at 1:50 P.M., Ruby arrived at the Carousel Club "incoherent" and "mumbling," and immediately embarked on a series of long-distance telephone calls. He then left for his sister's apartment at 3929 Rawlins in North Dallas, which was about four miles from where he then lived in South Dallas. According to his sister, he took with him enough food for "12 to 20 people," apparently intending to remain there for some days. He had three times asked Crafard to leave the Carousel Club and to accompany him; Crafard had been surprised by the invitation and refused, preferring to remain in the club. After arriving at his sister's apartment, Ruby embarked upon another round of long-distance calls. He was able to eat very little, became ill, and vomited. He remained there until about 7:30 P.M., when he left to go to a synagogue, arriving after the Friday night service but joining in the refreshments. According to the rabbi who talked to Ruby, the latter did not mention the assassination.

From then on Ruby "haunted" the police station, talked with District Attorney Wade and members of the news media after the midnight show-up, and visited a policeman and one of his strippers in a car near the Carousel Club.

Ruby returned to his apartment from downtown Dallas at about 3:00 A.M. on Saturday 23 November, and awakened Senator, whom he told to dress and to accompany him downtown. He telephoned Crafard at the Carousel Club telling him to bring the Polaroid camera and to meet him and Senator outside the club. After picking up Crafard, they went in Ruby's car to the Warren impeachment poster, where Ruby instructed Crafard to take three flashbulb photographs. The three men then drove to a coffee shop, where for the next half hour Ruby continued to discuss the advertisement and the poster. On leaving the coffee shop, they all drove to the Dallas Post Office, where Ruby tried to find out if the box number in the advertisement existed. He discovered that there was a box of that number and found it to be full of mail. He rang the night bell and spoke to a postal employee, asking for the name of the man who had rented the box; he was advised to seek information next day from the man in charge. Ruby then dropped off Crafard at the Carousel Club at about 6:00 A.M. and returned with

Senator to their apartment. Crafard was to testify that at some point during this episode, Ruby, referring to the box numbers in the advertisement and the poster, "said something about the numbers were the same if turned around a little bit."

During the Polaroid episode, Ruby wrote the box number of the poster in one corner of an old envelope and the box number of the advertisement in the other corner, and underneath the box number of the advertisement, 1792, he added 1192; he could not have been in doubt because he had the advertisement in his pocket. He then wrote sideways on the envelope the word "MON," and above it a telephone number, EM-1-1197. The envelope was found among Ruby's possessions after he had murdered the assassin. The address on the envelope and phone number belonged to two members of an extreme rightist group and were apparently deliberately left to throw suspicion on them.

RUBY'S COMPANIONS RECOUNT TWO STORIES

Crafard had been known in the Carousel Club only as Larry, his last name having been unknown to anyone except Ruby. During Crafard's 22 days in the club, Ruby had made him his "close confidant" (the Commission's own words in an interrogatory to the CIA), taking him around with him so that he became known as Little Ruby or Jack Ruby Junior.

About five hours after Crafard had been driven back to the club, at about 11:00 A.M., he packed his clothes and "fled" (the Commission's own word), hitchhiking to his sister's cabin in a remote part of faraway Michigan. He left no message for Ruby.

The next day Ruby shot the assassin. When he was interviewed by the FBI shortly thereafter, he omitted Crafard's name from the list of his few employees at the Carousel Club.

A few hours after the murder of 'Oswald,' Senator went to Dallas police station and, identifying himself as Ruby's friend, was briefly interrogated by the police before being handed over to the FBI for extensive questioning. He volunteered to swear an affidavit for the police, and in the affidavit said that he had been awakened by Ruby at about 3:00 A.M. on Saturday and that Ruby was crying—something Senator had never before seen—and "too sad" about the assassination of the President to go to bed. Senator got up, dressed, and drove to downtown Dallas with Ruby to the Southland Hotel Coffee Shop before returning to their apartment. (XXI.427-432.) Senator had omitted from the affidavit the Polaroid episode, as he did when interrogated by the FBI later that day.

Crafard's name and whereabouts were found through the address of a relative on a piece of paper that he had left in a wastepaper basket at the Carousel Club. When he was discovered and questioned four days later by the Michigan FBI, Crafard described the whole "Polaroid episode," which established that Senator's volunteered affidavit to the police and his signed statement to the FBI had been contrived. (XIX.353-359.)

After Crafard's information had been relayed to Dallas, the Secret Service interviewed Senator on 3 December 1963, and the FBI reinterviewed him on 20 December 1963. Senator then admitted he had been untruthful. (XXI.433-440.)

After the Polaroid episode, Ruby had telephoned a friend at KLIF radio station *only* to ask, "Who is Earl Warren?" (XV.262.) Nevertheless, when Ruby was to testify to the Commission seven months later, his Counsel said to the Commissioners: "I think if you asked him why he went out about 4 o'clock in the morning with George Senator and Larry and took that picture of the sign of Chief Justice Earl Warren, he would tell you that he did it because he was going to turn it over to the FBI and some attorneys, because he thought it was un-American and he did it because he's a 100 percent patriotic American citizen, and he's telling the truth."

During his Counsel's statement, Ruby had tried to prevent him from mentioning the Polaroid episode at all by interrupting and saying enigmatically, "Don't mention anything about that—we're in a bad spot down here because of that." (XIV.567.)

During the rest of that Saturday Ruby was intensively active: police headquarters, court building, taverns, and telephone calls. The next time for which Ruby's movements can be confirmed is his appearance at the Western Union office four minutes before his murder of the assassin at 11:21 A.M. on Sunday.

THE ASSASSIN'S ESCAPE PLAN

Accepting for the moment that Ruby was the conspirator who would have arranged the escape of the assassin from Dallas, how could the escape from the vicinity of Ruby's apartment at 223 South Ewing have been effected?

Red Bird airfield is about four and a half miles and an almost direct drive from the apartment, this airfield being as large as the public airfield at Love Field, and surrounded by hangars for private planes. If it was intended that the assassin should escape from Dallas by plane, a simple method would have been for him to enter an unobtrusive car near the bus stop and Ruby's apartment, and, hiding in the back, be driven for 10 minutes to Red Bird and deposited near a plane. After a nonstop flight to Mexico, the plane could have landed on a secret landing strip; further arrangements could have been made to remove the assassin from Mexico.

Immediately after the assassination, the 1,200 Dallas policemen could not, in one hour, have searched the tens of thousands of houses and automobiles in Dallas. They could have grounded every public and private plane at the several airfields in and around Dallas but did not. As it was to happen, from the time of the assassination at 12:30 P.M. until 2:00 P.M., most of the police and other security forces were searching the Depository and downtown areas; at no time was Red Bird airfield—about seven miles from the Depository—either watched or closed.

Given this reconstruction of events, the assassin would have arrived in the vicinity of Ruby's apartment before 1:30 P.M.; by 1:40 P.M. he could have been at Red Bird, and by 1:45 P.M. on his way to Mexico.

(Testing this theory, at a similar time of day and month in 1973, I traveled by car down the Marsalis bus route to the bus stop near Ruby's apartment, walked west to the site of the Tippit killing, and then east past the bus stop to 223 South Ewing. Although I walked around Ruby's block of apartments and looked in many windows, I saw nobody and apparently was not observed. Between 1:20 P.M. and 1:30 P.M. on the day of the assassination even less interest in a stranger would have been evinced, for the occupants of the apartments would have been listening to their radios or watching television; it seemed to me unlikely that the unremarkable 'Oswald' would have had any difficulty in entering unobserved a strategically parked car near the block. I was then driven for about 10 minutes on an almost direct and somewhat deserted road to Red Bird; once there it would have been a simple matter to board a plane unobserved.)

In testimony, as a convicted murderer about to appeal or ask for a new trial, Ruby was allowed to tell his own story and did not have to account for his movements between 1:00 P.M. and 1:45 P.M. on the day of the assassination. Very much in control of the situation, he told the Commissioners that if he was not allowed to take a polygraph test, to prove that he had absolutely no connections with Oswald, he and all his relatives would be killed, adding that even his own Counsel and Warren were in danger. When asked who would be responsible, he said it was the John Birch Society. (Ruby was familiar with polygraphs; he had the address of a private polygraph firm in his notebook and a sign behind the bar at the Carousel Club threatened employees with a polygraph test if they were suspected of stealing. As a lifelong liar, he had little to fear, since the test depends for its readings upon the subject's "stress" when untruthfully answering questions.)

Although not present when other witnesses testified, the Secret Service were present when Ruby testified.

On the day that Ruby shot 'Oswald,' two journalists accompanied Senator and one of Ruby's lawyers to 223 South Ewing to pick up Senator's clothes. Soon after, one of the journalists was accidentally shot to death in a California police station by a policeman, and the other died of a karate chop in his Dallas apartment; the lawyer died of a heart attack. During this time, Senator would not sleep at 223 South Ewing, would not spend two nights in the same place, would not be out after dark, and would not be in an isolated area. Five weeks after the assassination and still fearing for his life, Senator left Dallas and was never again to live there.

The young stripper to whom at 11:17 A.M. on Sunday morning Ruby had dispatched a $25 money order, when seen by the Secret Service within an hour of the murder of 'Oswald' was incoherent and on the point of collapse. At first, she refused to talk saying that if she said what she suspected—that Ruby and 'Oswald' were conspirators with others—she would be killed. Her few words were then recorded by the Secret Service and appear in the Exhibits. Although changing her name and moving to another part of the United States, she was shot dead in the street. It appeared that several other people who had knowledge of or demonstrated an interest in Ruby's actions were also silenced.

Despite Ruby's connection with the underworld, it is difficult to believe that the underworld, as such, was involved either in the conspiracy to assassinate the President or in the escape of the assassin. It is possible that Ruby was a low-level KGB agent, and George Fehrenbach, who testified, appears to support this view. In the early 1940s Fehrenbach had met Jack Rubenstein in Muncie, Indiana, while the former was working as an apprentice to a jeweler, Sam Jaffe. There was a meeting hall above Jaffe's shop, and it was there that Communist meetings were held with several of Jaffe's relations coming from Chicago, including their friend, Jack Rubenstein. (XV.289-321.)

It may be that—just as it seems to have been in the case of the 16-year-old Oswald, whose name was probably noted in the KGB "apparatus" in Moscow for future use following his application to the Socialist Party of America for information—Jacob (Jack) Rubenstein's name was recorded at the "apparatus" for future use.

12

The Autopsy

On the afternoon of 24 November 1963, Dr. Earl Forrest Rose, Dallas County Medical Examiner, together with Dr. Sidney Stewart, in the presence of Dr. Karl Dockery, performed an autopsy on the body of the assassin in Parkland Hospital. They recorded the length of the corpse as 5'9". The doctors examined the body externally from the crown of the head to the soles of the feet, recording some slight wounds, scratches, and bruises on the head that the assassin had sustained in his struggle with the police on arrest, and other wounds, marks, and scars on his body. Incisions were made behind both ears over the mastoid area preparatory to cutting round the back of the head and peeling the scalp to expose the skull so that the upper part of the skull could be removed for the purpose of extracting the brain and examining the interior of the head. The upper neck was also examined, and this took the doctors up to the mastoid areas. The postmortem report on the autopsy (XXIV.7-11.) states, under the heading "Scalp, Skull, Cranial Cavity and Dura," "Not remarkable. No evidence of injury is noted." Under the heading "Neck Organs," the report says, "They are not remarkable. The hyoid is intact. No evidence of injury is noted. The thyroid is not remarkable grossly."

A MASTOIDECTOMY

When the real Oswald was six years old, he had been admitted to a hospital with acute mastoiditis and a mastoidectomy was performed behind his left ear. The operation leaves a lifelong scar of about one to one and a half inches and a depression where bone has been removed, the depression sometimes filling up but not until middle age. The part of the bone cut away would not have filled up in someone of 'Oswald's' age. The mastoidectomy and the scar were noted on Oswald's Marine health records in 1956 and 1959. (XIX.582-590.)

Neither the mastoidectomy scar nor bone removal was recorded in the postmortem report of 24 November, and it is difficult to accept that the two doctors who carried out the autopsy could have missed the external and internal evidence of mastoidectomy had such an operation been performed. That the autopsy was carried out with special interest is established by the fact that Dr. Rose took 27 Kodachrome slides during the autopsy, retaining them in his possession until he later exhibited them to the FBI. Dr. Karl Dockery took nine rolls of 35-mm film of the body. His films should be in the National Archives, because a recently released Commission Document refers to them.

THE SCARS ON THE LEFT ARM

In addition to this apparent absence of mastoidectomy, there were discrepancies between certain scars on the left upper arm of the assassin and the scars on the left upper arm of Marine Oswald. After considering all the medical records, a British surgeon, Mr. Whittam, prepared for this author an analysis of the scars, accompanied by a drawing showing the left arm of the Marine and the left arm of the assassin with the positions and discrepancies in these scars marked on the drawing. The postmortem report had disclosed only two scars on the left upper arm of the assassin, whereas there had been three scars on the left upper arm of Marine Oswald. Both the position and description of the two scars recorded in the postmortem report differ from two of the three scars recorded in the Marine medical reports.

THE SCAR ON THE LEFT WRIST

The postmortem report discloses that there was a one-and-three-quarter-inch transverse scar on the inner aspect of the left wrist. No such scar was recorded in the Marine records.

The importance of the apparently absent mastoidectomy, the number, position, and description of the scars on the left upper arm, and the scar on the left wrist does not lie in the unlikely possibility that either the Marine Corps or autopsy doctors might have been in error, but in the reaction of the FBI to these physical discrepancies.

Late on 24 November, 'Oswald's' body had been released by the Dallas police and taken by the Secret Service to the morgue of Miller's Funeral Home in Fort Worth, some 35 miles from Dallas, to await burial at about 4:00 P.M. on 25 November. On the morning of 25 November, according to the *Fort Worth Press*, while the assassin's body lay unattended in the morgue "an FBI team with a camera and crime lab kit" spent a long time checking over the body and, according to yet another local source, taking an additional set of fingerprints.

Apparently puzzled by the contradiction presented by the Marine Corps medical record, the postmortem report, and the body of the assassin, the FBI decided to find out whether the Marine records could possibly have been erroneous.

On 3 December, an FBI agent went to Harris Hospital in Fort Worth, where he discovered from the Medical Records Libraries that, in February 1946 and at the age of six, Lee Harvey Oswald had been admitted to the hospital with acute mastoiditis of the left ear. The Operative Record bore the notation: "A simple mastoidectomy was done. The wound was closed with dermal. A rubber dam drain was used." (XXV.118.)

On 25 February 1964, some three months after the postmortem report and the visit to Harris Hospital, agents of the field office of the FBI in Dallas, Tom Carter and Manning Clements, interviewed Dr. Rose regarding the scars mentioned in the postmortem report. Carter had been the senior of the two agents who had interrogated "Lee Harvey Oswald" in Fort Worth on 26 June 1962, and had been told by 'Oswald' that his height was 5'11". On 22 November 1963 in Dallas police headquarters, Clements had been told by 'Oswald' that his height was 5'9", and that he had "no permanent scars."

The report that the two agents wrote of their February 1964 interview with Dr. Rose appears in the Exhibits. (XXVI.161-162.) Among the color slides made by Dr. Rose were some showing the left upper arm, but the slides were so overexposed that the light portions of the slides obscured them entirely. The scars could not be seen, much less identified from the slides.

As the Dallas field office of the FBI had been designated by Hoover to conduct the postassassination investigation, the FBI agents must have read the Historic Diary allegedly kept by the real Oswald in the

Soviet Union and found among the assassin's possessions after the assassination. It recorded a slashed left wrist, the alleged attempted suicide having occurred, according to the diary, at about 8:00 P.M. on 21 October 1959 in Oswald's room at the Hotel Berlin (Moscow), which was four hours after the Botkin Hospital records said that he had been admitted to the hospital; the FBI agents must have noticed and been puzzled by the discrepancy.

Clearly, given the evidence it had collected about the mastoidectomy and the scars on the upper left arm, the Dallas FBI had been unable to reconcile the corpse of the assassin with the body of the real Oswald. They therefore asked Dr. Rose if the scar on the wrist could, in fact, have been the result of a genuine attempt at suicide. He replied that the scar "might possibly be associated with a suicide attempt."

According to the published Exhibit, Dr. Rose was not asked to confirm that there was no evidence of a mastoidectomy on the corpse of the assassin.

In an article in the *Dallas Morning News* of 24 November 1975 discussing the autopsy, both Dr. Rose and Dr. Stewart said they were not looking for a mastoidectomy because the FBI had not told them of any possible discrepancies when the autopsy was performed at Parkland Memorial Hospital.

"I won't say that we couldn't have overlooked a mastoidectomy," Rose said. "That is a possibility and I certainly won't deny it. You know it could have been in the hair." Stewart, however, recalled that "We went into very careful details to note as many of the abrasions or scars or any type of skin blemish to help in identification in case this question arose."

In 1975, Dr. Rose and Dr. Stewart could not, of course, recollect the hairline of the assassin which, as an illustration in this book shows, was considerably above the area where any mastoid scar or depression could have been located.

The question must be asked why, in so important an autopsy, the FBI did not supply the doctors with a copy of the Marine medical reports to assist them in their autopsy, a part of which is concerned with the identification of the subject. It must also be asked whether an examination of the subject's teeth was performed, and, if so, whether there are dental charts which could and still can be compared with the detailed charts prepared by the Marine medical officers.

On the morning of 25 November, the FBI had been in no position to pursue their investigation into the identity of the assassin because at about 4:00 P.M. that afternoon the body was buried. They had had no opportunity, nor perhaps the desire, to ask Dr. Rose or Dr. Stewart to come to Fort Worth from Dallas in order to confer with them over the postmortem report and the corpse of the assassin.

The body was buried in a sealed concrete vault and covered with earth, and Robert Oswald records on pages 168-9 of his book *Lee. A Portrait of Lee Harvey Oswald* (1967):

> That Wednesday evening (27 November, the day that the Secret Service separated Marina and Marguerite), the fire marshal of Tarrant County came out to see me . . . He told me as quietly and gently as he could that some people in Fort Worth had object- ed to Lee's burial at Rose Hill Cemetery. They were bringing some pressure to have the body moved from the Fort Worth area . . . Briefly that evening I considered the possibility of having Lee's body cremated to protect it from the ghouls who might try to break into his grave. The fire marshal had anticipated this possi- bility, and he left three forms with me. If I did decide on crema- tion, he said, I should sign those three forms and he would help me make the arrangements. I said nothing at all about this to Marina, and I still have the blank forms . . .

Insofar as the FBI was concerned, it would have been preferable for the body to have been cremated rather than buried, thus destroying the incontrovertible evidence of imposture.

The Warren Report does not discuss the postmortem report, and mentions only the recorded approximate weight of the corpse. As a result, the contradictions presented by the Marine medical records and the postmortem report are not discussed in the Warren Report, and neither Marina nor any of the witnesses who knew the assassin socially or at work were asked if he had a scar or any depression behind the left ear.

Since the Marine and the autopsy medical staff were not asked to testify, the apparent physical discrepancies remain unresolved.

13

Fingerprints

The fact that the fingerprints in the Texas School Book Depository and those of the assassin matched, satisfied the authorities that the arrested man had fired the rifle killing the President. Nor can it be disputed for a moment that those prints matched the prints taken when Oswald was in the Marine Corps. (As part of my research, I had the 1956 prints of Marine Oswald compared with those of the impostor by the retired head of the Scotland Yard Fingerprint Department. The prints were indeed the same.)

There is no easy way to traverse the fingerprint evidence. If the facts that speak for an imposture were not so compelling, it would be logical to accept the evidence of the fingerprints at face value and to accept the Commission's findings—that the assassin was the former Marine, Lee Harvey Oswald. Because the evidence leads to conspiracy and imposture, the validity of the fingerprints needs to be tested.

In 'Oswald's' notebook appear the words "FINGER PRINTS." (XVI.67.) 'Oswald's' purpose in writing these words, as with the word "microdots" discussed earlier, indicated espionage and were calculated to embarrass the FBI when found in the notebook after the assassination. (The Warren Report makes no mention of either the words "FINGER PRINTS" or the word "microdots.")

It must be considered whether at some early date the Soviets managed to infiltrate the fingerprint filing system of the FBI in order to substitute the impostor's prints for those of the real Oswald. It has to be determined whether the FBI itself in the interests of national security made the switch. Until these questions are asked and resolved no official body can accept the fingerprints that have been introduced into the Warren Commission Exhibits as a last word.

Before the assassin was buried on 25 November 1963, there were six extant fingerprint cards in the name of Lee Harvey Oswald, as follows (the names of the persons who took the prints are included when available):

A. Marine Corps card
    Taken in Fort Worth by Melam.   15 October 1956
B. New Orleans police card
    Taken in New Orleans police
    station.   9 August 1963
C. Dallas police card
    Inkless prints taken in Dallas
    police station by Hicks.   22 November 1963
D. Dallas police card
    Taken in Dallas police
    station by Barnes.   22 November 1963
E. Dallas police card
    Taken in Dallas police station.   23 November 1963
F. FBI card
    Taken by the Dallas police,
    time and place contradictory.   25 November 1963

The original Marine Corps prints (Card A) were extracted from the FBI file eight times to check and to compare with other prints. Following are the dates appearing on the back of the Marine Corps card together with some surrounding circumstances which may or may not throw light on the purpose of the extractions.

1. *29 October 1956* (stamped on card is "RECORDED, IDENT DIV. 32."). This was the day on which Oswald's prints were filed in the fingerprint department of FBI headquarters, having been sent there by the Marines for checking against a possible prior criminal record.

2. *26 February 1957* (stamped on card). This was the day before Oswald was granted his first two weeks' leave.

3. *31 October 1959* (handwritten, with the words "Quoted Info to Reddy, Div. S."). This was the day on which a man calling himself Lee Harvey Oswald appeared for the first time at the United States

Embassy in Moscow and attempted to renounce his American citizenship by handing over ex-Marine's Oswald's passport to Embassy officials. ("Div. S." signifies "Division. Sov." at the Department of State.)

4. *5 November 1959* (handwritten, with "CL. CH." stamped against the date). On or about this date, the Embassy received a letter from 'Oswald' dated 3 November, which again requested that his citizenship be revoked. ("CL. CH." possibly signifies Classification Checked.)

5. *16 November 1959* (stamped on card). On 13 November, the American journalist Aline Mosby interviewed 'Oswald' at the Hotel Metropole in Moscow and three days later the second American journalist, Priscilla Johnson, interviewed him at the same hotel. If, as is likely, the Embassy had encouraged both Mosby and Johnson to interview 'Oswald' in an attempt to dissuade him from renouncing his American citizenship and/or to ascertain his motive, Embassy officials, reading the journalists' descriptions conflicting with each other and Miss Mosby's with the passport, possibly reacted by calling immediately for a fingerprint check.

6. *1 March 1960* (stamped on card). I cannot account for the fingerprint check being made at this time; 'Oswald' had been living in Minsk for some six weeks, and was just about to be allotted an apartment.

7. *15 December 1961* (stamped on card). I do not know why the FBI deemed it necessary to extract the card on this date.

8. *15 August 1963* (stamped on card). The card was extracted for comparison with the prints taken by the New Orleans police on 9 August following 'Oswald's' arrest for a minor street disturbance, the police prints having been forwarded to the FBI for recording, and received by the FBI on 14 August.

My theory is that at some time prior to the impostor's first visit to the Embassy in Moscow (31 October 1959) but after Oswald had left the United States, a period of five weeks, the KGB had substituted a forged print card in the FBI fingerprint files, the forgery substituting the impostor's prints in place of the ex-Marine's prints. Such a substitution would explain why the Embassy could so summarily dismiss the discrepancies in the journalists' descriptions, as well as put aside the warnings against imposture later to be given by Hoover, Hickey, and Rusk.

Sebastian Latona, supervisor of the Latent Fingerprint Department of the Identification Division of the FBI, testified that the FBI fingerprint files contained 77½ million civil and 15 million criminal prints, and that the FBI received between 23,000 and 25,000 prints every day, all these being processed within 30 days. When asked by a Commissioner, "What is your card system like? If this is too confidential I don't want to get anything in the record that is too secret. We can take it off the record," Latona replied, "Nothing is secret about our files."

(In order to better follow this discussion, the reader should turn to the illustrations of fingerprints; they are copies of Cards A, B, D, and F, the *only* prints appearing in the Exhibits.)

Latona was called by the Commission on 2 April 1964, principally to testify about finger and palm prints found on cardboard boxes and paper in the "sniper's nest" at the Depository, and to compare them for the Commission with the fingerprints taken from the assassin on 22 November by the Dallas police. (IV.1-48.)

Extracts from his testimony relating to a comparison of fingerprint cards are as follows:

Counsel: Mr. Latona, you have handed me three cards, one of which appears to be a standard fingerprint card (Card D) and the other two of which appear to be prints of the palms of an individual. All these cards are marked "Lee Harvey Oswald." Are these the cards which you received from your Dallas office which you just described as being the prints of Lee Harvey Oswald?

Latona: They are.

Counsel: Mr. Chairman, I would like these admitted into evidence as 627 (Card D), 628 and 629 . . . Did you receive a second submission of known prints? (Card F)

Latona: Yes; we did . . .

Counsel: Do you know why the second submission (Card F) was made?

Latona: The second submission was made, I believe, in order to advise us formally that the subject, Lee Harvey Oswald, had been killed, and it has the notation on the back that he was shot and killed 11-24-63 while being transferred in custody.

Counsel: And did you examine that second submission? (Card F)

Latona: Yes, I did.

Counsel: And is it in all respects identical to the first? (Card D)

Latona: The fingerprints appearing on this card (Card F) are exactly the same as those that appear on the card which you have previously referred to as Commission Exhibit 627 (Card D) . . .

Counsel: May I mark that (Card F) as (Commission Exhibit) 630? . . . Now in addition, did the Federal Bureau of Investigation have in its files prints of Lee Harvey Oswald which it had received at some earlier date, prior to November 22?

Latona: Yes, sir; I believe there is a Marine Corps print (Card A).

Counsel: Did you compare the 10-finger card (Card D) which you received from the Dallas office of the FBI (Cards D and F had been given to the Dallas FBI by the Dallas police) and compare it with the Marine Corps fingerprint (1956) card? (Card A)

Latona: Yes, sir.

Counsel: Were they identical?

Latona: They were the same . . .

Counsel: Could you submit to us a copy of the 10-print card which you received (in 1956) from the Marine Corps? (Card A)

Latona: Yes; I could.

Counsel: With the Chairman's permission, that will be appended as an exhibit to Mr. Latona's testimony.

A Commissioner: Do you wish to identify it by a number at this time?

Counsel: Yes. If we could give it a number in advance of receiving it, I would like to give Commission Exhibit No. 635 (Card A) . . .

A Commissioner: Do you know whether any fingerprints were taken after Lee Harvey Oswald returned from the Soviet Union?

Latona: Those after he was arrested in connection with this particular offense.

A Commissioner: Apart from the fingerprints obtained in connection with the assassination.

Latona: I do not.

Counsel: Mr. Latona, Exhibit 630 (Card F), which is one of the known 10-print cards submitted by the Dallas office, is marked "Refused to sign" in the box with the printed caption "Signature of person fingerprinted." Do you recall whether Lee Harvey Oswald signed the Marine Corps card? (Card A)

Latona: Offhand, I do not.

Counsel: I think it would be interesting, for the record, to see if that (Card A) is signed, and, of course, as we read and get the card, we will be able to note that information . . .

For some reason Counsel did not ask (1) how the date, 25 November, appeared on Card F, since on all of this day the corpse of the assassin was in Fort Worth, some 35 miles from Dallas police headquarters; (2) how the corpse had "Refused to sign"; (3) why the authority taking the prints was said to be the Dallas police, although the last they had seen of the corpse was on the evening of 24 November before it was taken that night to Fort Worth; and (4) who fingerprinted the assassin or his corpse on this occasion and placed an initial which looks like *L* in the appropriate space. Counsel should not have accepted what on its face appears to be a contradictory fingerprint card, but should have identified *L*, calling him to testify and clarify the taking of the prints.

It is surprising that while Latona was unsure whether Marine Corps prints (Card A) existed and, if it did, whether Oswald had signed the card, he still testified in no uncertain terms that he had compared them with the Dallas prints and found them to be "the same." But it is even more surprising that he did not know of the existence of the New Orleans prints (Card B), particularly as his testimony was required in connection with an official investigation into the murder of a President of the United States. The only way to make sense of Latona's remarks, then, is to presume that he was instructed to give testimony only to show that the prints found in the "sniper's nest" and on the rifle matched those of the arrested man. He needed to produce only Cards D and F for that purpose. At the same time, for whoever needed to effect a cover-up, it was necessary that Cards A and B must be concealed from the Commissioners. Furthermore, they could not allow the Commissioners (which means the public) to see a Dallas police print card that did not have the signature, "Lee Harvey Oswald" on its face.

I can think of two reasons why it had been necessary to conceal Card A:

1. If this card had been produced, the Commissioners would have seen that it had been extracted for comparison purposes on five occasions while the subject of the inquiry, whoever he was, was in the Soviet Union.

2. The signature of the young Marine, "Lee Harvey Oswald," appears on the concealed Card A and is unlike the signature, "Lee H. Oswald," on concealed Card B (but not unlike the signature on produced Card D, apparently not written by the assassin.)

I can also think of two reasons, however trivial they may seem, why Card B was concealed:

1. If this card had been produced, the Commissioners could hardly have failed to note that the signature, "Lee H. Oswald," was unlike the signature, "Lee Harvey Oswald," on produced Card D.

2. The police had also recorded on the card that the color of the man's eyes was "brown."

The authorities were forced to produce for the Commissioners prints of the assassin that had been taken in Dallas police station (Card D), and which would show that apparently it had been signed by ex-Marine Lee Harvey Oswald.

But five days *after* Latona's appearance before the Commission, Dallas police officer Barnes testified in Dallas, with no Commissioners present, that the arrested man would not sign anything until he had seen an attorney, which he never did. Had Barnes testified before Latona, it might have occurred to the Commission to ask Latona to explain the presence of the signature, "Lee Harvey Oswald," on the card. It would, in fact, have been preferable and correct practice for Barnes to be examined *before* Latona (with Commissioners present) so that Barnes could produce Card D and identify his initials, W. E. B., on a card which he and not Latona had created. He could then have been asked if he knew who had signed the name "Lee Harvey Oswald" on Card D.

In addition to not insisting on having the Marine Corps prints on Card A compared for them with the Dallas prints on Card D, the Commissioners should have preceded Latona's testimony with a proper chain of evidence by calling the Marine Corps official who took the prints to testify that it was his signature on the Marine Corps print card and to certify that the prints on the card were those taken by him when Lee Harvey Oswald joined the Marines in October 1956. He should have been asked to confirm that these prints had been routinely sent to the FBI at that time for checking against a possible criminal record.

The Commissioners had even been reminded by Latona of the necessity for a proper chain of evidence with respect to fingerprint cards when he testified that he could not certify the prints on Card D as being those of Oswald. Asked to explain what he meant, he said, "As I am not the one who fingerprinted Oswald I cannot tell from my own personal knowledge that those are actually the fingerprints of Lee Harvey Oswald."

(It is unheard of, or should be, for a fingerprint card to be produced as evidence in legal proceedings without the certifying testimony of the official taking the prints.)

As a result of the wrong ordering of witnesses and improper production of Card D, the public had no reason to suspect that the signature on Card D must have been written by someone else. Moreover, the public never realized that the arrested man refused to sign anything nor that—in the opinion of this author—had he ever committed himself to any name while in police custody.

In view of the warnings against imposture and the physical evidence of imposture, it is beyond comprehension 1) that the fingerprints of Oswald, taken when he joined the Marines in 1956, were not compared before the Commission with the prints of the arrested man, 2) that the Marine who took the prints was never called to testify that the prints had been taken by him, and asked to verify his signature, 3) that the prints taken in New Orleans were not shown to the Commission, 4) that, of the two print cards taken after the assassin had been arrested and shown to the Commission, one had the signature of Lee Harvey

Oswald written in by someone other than 'Oswald,' and the other showed the typewritten words "Refused to sign" in the space reserved for the fingerprinted man's signature when, according to the date on the card, he was already dead. A more haphazard presentation of vital evidence to a judicial body can hardly be imagined.

14

The Authorities

The omissions in the testimony of J. Edgar Hoover of the FBI, John A. McCone and Richard M. Helms of the CIA, C. Douglas Dillon of the Secret Service, and The Honorable Dean Rusk of the Department of State, when considered in conjunction with similar omissions in the Warren Report, establish beyond reasonable doubt that there was a cover-up. First, the authorities needed to cover up their own incompetence in preventing an impostor from assuming the identity of an American citizen, entering the country, and proceeding to assassinate the President. Second, the assassination having occurred, in the interest of national security they needed to cover up the identity of the assassin and the facts of espionage and conspiracy.

Far from taking an independent line in the inquiry into the events surrounding the assassination, all of the investigative agencies subordinated their private judgments to the need for hiding their mistakes under the umbrella of national security. Their individual words would appear on the record; their knowledge and opinions would not.

Rusk, in stressing the necessity for learning the truth, nonetheless emphasized that any evidence of conspiracy discovered would raise "the gravest issues of war or peace."

This seemingly coincidental concurrence of testimony by the agencies involved was cast in a new light on 26 April 1976 by the Senate's publication of *Book V of the Senate Select Committee.*

Among other things, this report disclosed that CIA and Secret Service personnel reviewed Hoover's testimony prior to the testimony of their own agents in order to ensure that there were no conflicts in testimony. One can presume that Rusk followed suit, since his testimony in no way contradicted that of Hoover.

Even more telling was Hoover's postassassination assessment (meant to be kept within the confines of the Bureau) of the operations of some of his subordinates before the assassination. Noting on internal FBI memoranda, Hoover observed that they ". . . could not have been more stupid," "asinine," and charged them with ". . . gross incompetence." In a memorandum disseminated to senior Bureau officials on 12 October 1964, Hoover also noted: "There is no question in my mind but that we failed in carrying through some of the most salient aspects of the Oswald (preassassination) investigation. It ought to be a lesson to all, but I doubt if some even realize it now. . . ."

Another of Hoover's notes reads: ". . . I do not intend to palliate actions which have resulted in forever destroying the Bureau as the top level investigative organization."

On 10 December 1963, 17 Bureau employees (five field investigative agents, one field supervisor, three special agents in charge, four headquarters supervisors, two headquarters section chiefs, one inspector, and one assistant director) were censured or placed on probation for "shortcomings in connection with the investigation of Oswald prior to the assassination."

Four days after the Warren Report was published in September 1964, eight of the 17 employees were again censured, put on probation, or transferred. In addition to the above eight, three other employees who had not been disciplined in December 1963 were disciplined as follows:

1. A Special Agent in Dallas was censured and placed on probation for failing to properly handle and supervise this matter;

2. An Inspector at FBI headquarters was censured for not exercising sufficient imagination and foresight to initiate action to have Security Index material disseminated to Secret Service;

3. An Assistant to the Director at FBI headquarters was censured for his overall responsibility in this entire matter.

None of the investigative deficiencies was brought to the notice of the Warren Commission. If the Commissioners had been informed of Hoover's actions, they would surely have asked for explanations, and certainly the conclusions in the Warren Report would have been different. Book V does not disclose the identities of any of the 20 employees.

The reports of the heads of the CIA, the FBI, the Secret Service and the Department of State to the Warren Commission—in particular their testimony given in person—are of vital importance to the story

of the cover up and the Russian conspiracy. These men omitted significant events that had occurred within their separate provinces. Selected
passages appear in the following pages.

FBI LETTERS TO THE COMMISSION

On 6 April 1964, J. Edgar Hoover wrote the following to the Commission's General Counsel:

Dear Mr. Rankin:

Your letter dated March 26, 1964, transmitted specific questions
pertaining to the investigation of Lee Harvey Oswald prior to the
assassination of President Kennedy and requested a reasoned response to each question.

At the outset, I wish to emphasize that the facts available to the
FBI concerning Lee Harvey Oswald prior to the assassination did
not indicate in any way that he was, or would be, a threat to President Kennedy; nor were they such as to suggest that the FBI
should inform the Secret Service of his presence in Dallas or his
employment in the Texas School Book Depository.

The Oswald case was one of many thousand investigative matters
handled by the FBI. During the fiscal year ending June 30, 1963,
the FBI handled 636,371 investigative matters in the criminal,
civil and security fields. The extent, depth and urgency of each investigation necessarily are dependent on the available facts in the
case. A file concerning Oswald was opened at the time newspapers
reported his defection to Russia in 1959, for the purpose of corre-
lating information inasmuch as he was considered a possible security risk in the event he returned to this country. When we learned
in 1960 that his mother was sending him money, we interviewed
her and his brother, Robert Oswald, to determine the reason.
Again in 1960 investigation was conducted to determine if he was
in Switzerland, as we were advised he contemplated enrolling in a
College there. The investigation was re-instituted at the time of
his return to the United States in 1962, and he was interviewed on
two occasions in 1962 in an effort to ascertain if he had been
recruited by the Soviet intelligence services and to evaluate him as
a possible security risk.

The investigation was continued in 1963 when it was reported that Oswald had corresponded with "The Worker," an east coast communist newspaper, and it was also reported he was engaged in activities on behalf of the Fair Play for Cuba Committee. This investigation was in progress when he was reported in October, 1963, to be in contact with the Soviet Embassy in Mexico, and on November 18, 1963, in contact with the Soviet Embassy in Washington, D.C. The purpose of the investigation was to determine the extent of his activities on behalf of the Fair Play for Cuba Committee and the reasons for his contacts with the Soviet Embassy.

In short, Oswald had gone to the Soviet Union at the age of 19 and attempted to renounce his American citizenship. He had recanted; his passport had been returned to him and he had been permitted by the Department of State to return to the United States as an American citizen. After his return, he had subscribed to "The Worker," had distributed pamphlets for the Fair Play for Cuba Committee and had admitted publicly that he was Marxist. He had been in contact with the Soviet Embassy in Washington, D.C.; and it was reported, but not confirmed, that he had been in contact with the Soviet Embassy in Mexico. The reason indicated for his contacts with the Soviet Embassies was to obtain visas to re-enter the Soviet Union. As previously indicated, his activities as known at the time of the assassination did not suggest in any way that he was a dangerous subversive; that he was violating any federal law; or that he represented a threat to the personal safety of the President. There was no basis for the FBI to keep him under observation. In the absence of any information showing Oswald to be a possible threat to the President, there was no basis to inform the Secret Service concerning Oswald's presence or employment in Dallas, Texas.

The answers to your specific questions are set forth in the attached memorandum.

Sincerely yours,

(Signed) J. Edgar Hoover (XVII.787-788.)

When Hoover wrote, of course, he had known from the afternoon of 22 November that it was not the slender assassin who twice visited the

Soviet Embassy in Mexico City, but an approximately 6' tall 35-year-old "American male" of athletic build. He knew that the impostor would hardly have required a stand-in to assist him "to obtain visas to re-enter the Soviet Union." Further, he made no mention of the "American male," Albert Osborne or John Caesar Grossi, both Osborne and Grossi using the alias Bowen; he failed to mention the discrepancy in heights and backgrounds recorded by Carter and Fain in Fort Worth in June 1962, and by Quigley in New Orleans in August 1963, and he omitted any reference to his own warning against imposture.

Attached to Hoover's letter was a list of questions asked by Rankin on behalf of the Commission, and the answers supplied by the FBI. (XVII.789-803.) The list contained 30 questions and the answers thereto; five are pertinent here.

Question 5: What was the FBI evaluation of Oswald as a result of the June, 1962 interview?

The answer dealt with the FBI evaluation of 'Oswald' resulting from the first FBI interview with him on 26 June 1962 by Carter and Fain in Fort Worth, but it did not inform Rankin that the agents had recorded 'Oswald's' height as 5'11'', and Marina's as 5'5''.

Question 6: Why was Oswald interviewed so soon thereafter on August 14, 1962? What was the FBI evaluation of Oswald as a result of this interview? Where was this interview held, how long did it take, and was there anything remarkable about Oswald's demeanor during the course of the interview?

The answer dealt in full with the question, but Hoover did not disclose to the Commission that after this interview the file on Lee Harvey Oswald was given a "closed status." This fact was later to appear during the testimony of FBI agent Fain.

Question 12: Did SA. Quigley, who interviewed Oswald at the New Orleans jail, or SA. Kaack (FBI, New Orleans) who prepared the report on Oswald, review earlier FBI reports on Oswald? Were they aware that, contrary to his statement, Oswald had not lived with his mother following discharge from the Marine Corps, but rather had gone to Russia. Were they aware that, contrary to his statement, his wife's maiden name was not

Prossa and that they had not married in Fort Worth but in Russia.

The answer dealt with Quigley's interview with 'Oswald' on 10 August 1963 and said, ". . . SA. Milton R. Kaack, who prepared a report concerning Oswald dated October 31, 1963, did review the results of prior FBI investigation concerning Oswald and he, of course, was aware of the various contradictions in the information furnished by Oswald. In the event the investigation of Oswald warranted a further interview, these discrepancies would have been discussed with him." Hoover did not inform Rankin that FBI agent Quigley had recorded 'Oswald's' height as 5'9": all of Quigley's report was included in Kaack's report. Rankin must have failed to notice the difference in the FBI recorded heights of 5'11" and 5'9".

Question 23: What was the FBI reaction to the CIA report of October 10, regarding Oswald's visit to the Soviet Embassy in Mexico City? Why did the FBI not request additional information or follow-up information by the CIA? What was the FBI evaluation of Oswald in view of the CIA report?

The question is impossible to understand. If Rankin had been provided with and had read the full CIA report he could not have failed to see that the approximately 35-year-old "American male" of athletic build in no way resembled the younger, slender assassin. It would seem that Rankin could not have appreciated that two men were involved; he would have asked the FBI to identify the "American male" and to evaluate *his* visit to the Soviet Embassy on 1 October 1963 in the name Lee Oswald.

The answer to this question was, *verbatim*:

The investigation of Oswald in 1963, prior to receipt of the Central Intelligence Agency communication dated October 10, was directed toward the primary objective of ascertaining the nature of Oswald's sympathies for, and connection with, the FPCC or other subversive elements. The Central Intelligence Agency communication which reported that a man, tentatively identified as Oswald, had inquired at the Soviet Embassy concerning a telegram which had been sent to Washington did not specify the nature of the telegram. This contact with the Soviet Embassy interjected a new aspect into the investigation and raised the obvious question of why he was in Mexico and exactly what were his relations with the Soviets. However, the information available was not such that any additional conclusions could be drawn as to Oswald's sympathies, intentions or activities at that time. Thus, one of the objectives of the continuing investigation was to ascertain the nature of his relations with the Soviets considering the possibility that he could have been recruited by the Soviet Intelligence services. The Central Intelligence Agency communication dated October 10, 1963, stated that any further information received concerning Oswald would be furnished and that our liaison representatives in Mexico City were being advised. On October 18, 1963, one of our FBI liaison representatives in Mexico City was furnished this information by Central Intelligence Agency and he arranged to follow-up with Central Intelligence Agency in Mexico City for further information and started a check to establish Oswald's entry in Mexico. Subsequent to the assassination, Central Intelligence Agency also advised us of Oswald's contact with the Cuban Embassy in Mexico City at the time of his visit there.

The first part of the answer dealt with the CIA teletype message to the FBI on 10 October and does not mention that after 10 October the FBI do not appear either to have noticed or acted upon the description of the "American male," such description fitting neither Marine Oswald nor the assassin. This answer should have apprised Rankin that the approximately 35-year-old "American male" who visited the Soviet Embassy on 1 October, although using the name Lee Oswald, was not the assassin, which Hoover knew from the CIA photographs of the man, one photograph having been supplied to him on 22 November and (at least) two others on or just after 23 November 1963. Hoover should have mentioned KGB officer Kostikov and that it was not the assassin who spoke with him. The whole answer is misleading because it makes it appear that the assassin and the "American male" were the same person, and that that person was the real Oswald. The question had referred only to the CIA message of 10 October, and it would appear that Rankin was unaware of the message of 18 October 1963 involving Kostikov; none of Rankin's other questions refers to this matter.

Question 28: What was the FBI evaluation of confidential information received on November 18, 1963 regarding Oswald's letter to the Soviet Embassy in Washington?

The answer to this question was, *verbatim*:

The information received on November 18, 1963, concerning Oswald's contact with the Soviet Embassy tended to confirm his contact with the Soviet Embassy in Mexico City as reported by the Central Intelligence Agency and to indicate the reasons for such contact, namely to secure visas to the Soviet Union.

This answer implies that the assassin, "Lee H. Oswald" (who wrote the letter of 9 November to the Soviet Embassy in Washington) was the "American male" who had contacted the Soviet Embassy in Mexico City on 28 September and 1 October 1963; this is misleading because it again makes it appear that the assassin and the "American male" were the same person.

After requests from the Commission for more details from the FBI master file on Oswald, Hoover wrote to Rankin on 4 May 1964 as follows:

Dear Mr. Rankin:

Reference is made to the discussion *between staff members of the Commission* and Mr. A. H. Belmont of this Bureau, May 4, 1964.

In accordance with this discussion, there are listed below the contents of the FBI headquarters file concerning Lee Harvey Oswald up to the time of the assassination of the late President John F. Kennedy on November 22, 1963.

The letter then lists in summary form the 69 items contained in the master file on Lee Harvey Oswald. (XVII.804-813.) Only 13 of these are pertinent to this discussion.

Item 5: A copy of an Office of Naval Intelligence memorandum dated November 2, 1959, containing the results of a check of the U.S. Marine Corps file regarding Oswald.

This memorandum should have contained the physical data of ex Marine Oswald, including his height of 5'11".

Item 14: A letter from this Bureau to the Department of State dated 3 June 1960, furnished the State Department data in the possession of the FBI concerning Lee Harvey Oswald and requesting the State Department to furnish this Bureau any information it may have concerning Oswald.

This summary excludes the fact that the letter of 3 June 1960 included Hoover's now historic warning to the State Department of the possibility of impersonation of the "defecting" Marine. This item is *written* evidence that the warning was withheld from the Commission.

Item 17: A letter to this Bureau from the Legal Attaché in Paris dated October 12 (1960), advising that information from his sources indicated that Oswald was not in attendance at the Albert Schweitzer College in Churwalden, Switzerland.

Item 18: A letter to this Bureau from the Legal Attache in Paris dated November 3, 1960, which set forth additional data developed from officials of the Albert Schweitzer College regarding Lee Harvey Oswald.

This additional data should have disclosed Lee Harvey Oswald's application form for enrollment at the college on which he had written his height as 5'11" and his weight as 160 pounds.

Item 21: A letter from the Washington Field Office to this Bureau dated May 23, 1961, setting forth results of a review of the files in the Passport Office, Department of State, concerning Oswald.

This should have included Lee Harvey Oswald's application for a passport dated 4 September 1959, on which he had stated his height to be 5'11", and the physical data stated on the face of the passport including the 5'11" height.

Item 25: A letter from the Washington Field Office to this Bureau dated September 1, 1961, which set forth results of a review of the records of the Passport Office regarding Oswald.

See comment on Item 21 above.

Item 31: A copy of a communication classified "Confidential" from the Director of Naval Intelligence to the Naval Attaché in Moscow dated March 3, 1962, which set forth information in Office of Naval Intelligence files regarding Oswald.

The information in the Navy files should have contained the Marine's recorded height of 71'' or 5'11''.

Item 41: A report of SA. John W. Fain dated July 10, 1962, at Dallas, which set forth results of investigation regarding Oswald and his wife, Marina. This report also set forth results of the interview of Oswald on June 26, 1962, by SA.s John W. Fain and B. Tom Carter.

The report dated 10 July 1962 contained the height of 5'11'' for Lee Harvey Oswald obtained by Carter and Fain from "observation and interrogation," and 5'5'' for Marina, but Hoover did not advise Rankin of this.

Item 57: An airtel from Dallas to this Bureau, dated October 22, 1963, reporting that INS in Dallas had received a communication classified "Secret" from the Central Intelligence Agency Mexico City, which indicated that an individual, possibly identical with Lee Harvey Oswald, was in contact with the Soviet Embassy in Mexico City.

The contents of this airtel and the CIA communication are probably the same as Item 58 or 61 below.

Item 58: A CIA Release dated October 10, 1963, which was sent to the FBI, Department of State, and Department of the Navy classified "Secret" which reported that an "American male" who identified himself as Lee Oswald had contacted the Soviet Embassy, Mexico City, on October 1, 1963. The CIA release indicated Oswald, born October 18, 1939, in New Orleans, Louisiana.

Item 61: A cablegram to this Bureau from our Legal Attaché in Mexico dated October 18, 1963, which furnished information from CIA classified "Secret"—Not To Be Further Disseminated, reporting that Lee Harvey Oswald had contacted Soviet Vice Consul Valeriy V. Kostikov of the Soviet Embassy, Mexico City, Mexico on September 28, 1963. Our Legal Attaché indicated he was following this matter with CIA and was attempting to establish Oswald's entry into Mexico and his current whereabouts.

At the time Items 58 and 61 were prepared, Hoover was aware that "Lee Oswald" was the "American male," and was neither ex-Marine Lee Harvey Oswald nor the assassin, but he did not advise Rankin of this. Nor did he advise Rankin that Kostikov was suspected by the FBI to be a veteran member of Department 13.

Item 63: The Report of SA Milton R. Kaack dated October 31, 1963, at New Orleans, Louisiana, which set forth results of additional investigation regarding Oswald.

The Report of Kaack included the Report of FBI agent Quigley regarding his interview with a man calling himself Lee Harvey Oswald in New Orleans Police Station on 10 August 1963, when Quigley recorded from "observation and interrogation" that the height of the man was 5'9". When this Item was prepared, Hoover was aware from his own file of the 5'11" height for the assassin recorded by his agents, Carter and Fain, in Fort Worth in June, 1962, and of the height of 5'9" recorded by his agent, Quigley, in New Orleans in August 1963, but he did not advise Rankin of this.

Item 69: An airtel from the Washington Field Office (FBI) to this Bureau dated November 19, 1963, reporting that an informant advised on November 18, 1963 that Lee Harvey Oswald had been in contact with the Soviet Embassy, Mexico City, Mexico.

This airtel was the result of the discovery of the letter of 9 November 1963 written by "Lee H. Oswald" from Irving, Texas, to Consul Reznichenko at the Soviet Embassy in Washington. The letter referred to "Lee H. Oswald's" "meetings" with comrade Kostin at the Soviet Embassy in Mexico City, stated that it was through the "stupidity" of the Cuban Consul in Mexico City that he had been unable to reach the Soviet Embassy in Havana "as planned," stated that he had not used his real name in Mexico, and that the FBI were not "now interested" in his activities. Hoover did not tell Rankin that the FBI informant had obtained the complete letter; he told him only "that Lee Harvey Oswald had been in contact with the Soviet Embassy, Mexico City, Mexico." Although this letter indicated that the assassin had "meetings" with Kostin, Hoover did not tell Rankin that these meetings were in addition to the meeting of the 'American male' with Kostikov and probably Yatskov.

FBI TESTIMONY

On 6 May 1964, Alan H. Belmont was to testify before the Commission. (V.1-32.) He said that he had joined the FBI in 1936 and that about June 1961 he had been made assistant to the Director in charge of all investigating work of the FBI in Washington, and that that was his present position. As the individual in charge of all investigative operations, the Lee Harvey Oswald investigation was his responsibility, but prior to the assassination the Lee Harvey Oswald case was not of such importance or urgency that it was considered necessary to call it to his attention for personal direction. In regard to Lee Harvey Oswald, he said: ". . . we have no reason to believe that he was an agent of any other country . . . and I could support no conclusion that this was other than an act of Oswald." He said that there was no credible evidence which would support a conclusion or an opinion that the death of the President was the result of a conspiracy. In regard to Ruby, he said that the FBI had found no evidence to the effect that Ruby was a Communist. In regard to Lee Harvey Oswald and Ruby, he said, ". . . we did not come up with anything of a solid nature, that is anything that would stand up to indicate that there was any association between Ruby and Oswald. We had numerous allegations which we ran out extensively and carefully, but there is nothing, no information, that would stand up to show there was an association between them."

Belmont said that he had supervised the preparation of the FBI answers to the 30 questions contained in Hoover's letter to Rankin of 6 April 1964 and the summaries of the 69 documents in the FBI file contained in Hoover's letter to Rankin of 4 May 1964. When testifying, he said that he had brought the "actual file" as it was maintained at the Bureau "with all information in it," and offered to leave it for a reasonable time in case any of the Commissioners wanted to examine it personally. Three Commissioners were present, two wished to inspect the file, but Warren discouraged this on the ground that it contained confidential material; the file was never examined by any Commissioner at any time; Belmont mentioned nothing that would incline the Commission toward the idea of conspiracy.

Then, on 14 May 1964, a few days after his deputy, Belmont, had laid out the agency's line of reasoning, Hoover was to testify:

When President Johnson returned to Washington (from Dallas) he communicated with me within the first twenty-four hours, and asked the Bureau to pick up the investigation of the assassination because, as you are aware, there is no Federal jurisdiction for such an investigation. It is not a Federal crime to kill or attack the President or the Vice President or any of the continuity of officers who will succeed to the Presidency. However, the President has a right to request the Bureau to make special investigations, and in this instance he asked that this investigation be made. I immediately assigned a special force headed by the special agent in charge at Dallas, Tex. to initiate the investigation, and to get all the details and facts concerning it, which we obtained, and then prepared a report which we submitted to the Attorney General for transmission to the President . . . I have read all of the requests that have come to the Bureau from this Commission, and I have read and signed all the replies that have come to the Commission. In addition, I have read many of the reports that our agents have made and I have been unable to find any scintilla of evidence showing any foreign conspiracy or any domestic conspiracy that culminated in the assassination of President Kennedy . . . I, personally, feel that any finding of the Commission would not be accepted by everybody, because there are bound to be some extremists who have very pronounced views, without any foundation for them, who would disagree violently with whatever findings the Commission makes. But I think it is essential that the FBI investigate the allegations that are received in the future so it can't be said that we had ignored them or that the case is closed and forgotten. I would estimate . . . that there are at least 50 or 60 men giving their entire time to various aspects of the investigation, because while Dallas is the office of the origin, investigation is required in auxiliary offices such as Los Angeles or San Francisco, and even in some foreign countries like Mexico. We have representatives in Mexico City.

A Commissioner urged Hoover to go further, saying:

. . . the point that I think ought to be made is that despite the magnitude of the effort that has been made by the FBI and by other agencies, and despite the tremendous effort that has been made, I believe, by the Commission, to help and assist and to consolidate all of the evidence that we possibly could, and there is always the possibility at some future date that some evidence might come to the surface . . . I want just to be sure that no leads, no evidence regardless of its credibility will be ignored, that it will be pursued by the Bureau or any other agency to make certain that it is good, bad, or of no value.

Hoover replied:

Well, I can assure you so far as the FBI is concerned, the case will be continued in an open classification for all time . . . I think this will be a matter of controversy for years to come, just like the Lincoln assassination. There will be questions asked by individuals, either for publicity purpose or otherwise, that will raise some new angle or some new aspect of it. I think we must, and certainly intend in the FBI to continue to run down any such allegations or reports of that kind.

A Commissioner then said:

I read the FBI report (on the assassination: a four-volume summary on 9 December 1963 and one supplement on 13 January 1964) very carefully and the whole implication of the report is that No. 1, Oswald shot the President; No. 2, that he was not connected with any conspiracy of any kind, nature or description. Do you still subscribe to that?

Hoover replied:

I subscribe to it even more strongly today than I did at the time the report was written. You see, the original idea was that there would be an investigation by the FBI and a report would be prepared in such form that it would be released to the public (before the assassin was shot) . . . Then a few days later (after the assassin was shot), after further consideration the President decided to form a Commission, which I think was very wise, because I feel the report of any agency of Government investigating what might be some shortcomings on the part of other agencies of Government ought to be reviewed by an impartial group such as this Commission. And the more I have read these reports, the more I am convinced that Oswald was the man who fired the gun; and he fired three times; killed the President and wounded Governor Connally. And I also am further convinced that there is absolutely no association between Oswald and Ruby. There was no such evidence ever established . . . There was suspicion at first this might be a Castro act.

Hoover said that although the FBI knew of 'Oswald's' contact with the Soviet Embassy in Washington by letter of 9 November 1963, this contact gave no "indication of any tendency to commit violence." As in his letter to Rankin, he remained silent about anything that might suggest conspiracy and the agency's failure to discover it. He did not mention that the contents of the letter were not passed on to the Dallas field office until the morning of 22 November 1963 even though the FBI in Washington had the information in hand on 18 November. Nor did he say that the FBI agent in charge of Lee Harvey Oswald's file in Dallas had failed to read this communication until shortly after the assassination. He also said nothing about 'Oswald' and the 75-year-old Albert Osborne, nothing about 'Oswald' and the 38-year-old John Caesar Grossi, nothing about 'Oswald' and the approximately 35-year-old "American male's" two visits to the Soviet Embassy in Mexico City, nothing about 'Oswald's' "meetings" with comrade Kostin, and did not mention any of the Russian intelligence officers or officials named in this book. Neither did he mention Major Yuri Nosenko's alleged defection to the United States some three months prior to his (Hoover's) testimony, which he himself knew about. The FBI had interrogated Nosenko but never revealed its findings, which, at the very least, raised some questions about conspiracy. Neither did Hoover mention his own warning of 3 June 1960 against the possibility of imposture. Instead he testified of Lee Harvey Oswald:

. . . We went back into his Marine Corps record. He was a "loner." He didn't have many friends. He kept to himself, and when he went abroad he defected to Russia . . . and then later, about 22 months later, he returned to the (United States) Embassy there and according to the report at the Embassy we have and which the Commission has furnished, the Embassy gave him a clean bill. He had seen the error of his ways and disliked the Soviet atmosphere, et cetera, and they, therefore, cleared him, paid his way and paid his wife's way to come back to this country . . . He had been over there long enough but they never gave him citizenship in Russia at all. And I think they probably looked upon him more as a kind of queer sort of individual and they didn't trust him too strongly.

Although Hoover mentioned 'Oswald's' alleged training at an espionage school in or near Minsk, when he came to discuss the real Oswald's Marine Corps record, he again failed to inform the Commission that Marine Oswald's height was 5'11", nor did he mention the mastoidectomy and the other scars stated on the Marine records, and that the postmortem report on the body of the assassin indicated discrepancies.

Regarding the assassination, Hoover said:

There was no question but that the gun and the telescopic lens could pinpoint the President perfectly. The car was moving slowly. It wasn't going at a high rate of speed, so that he had a perfect opportunity to do it.

About Ruby, Hoover testified that he came from Chicago:

. . . he was on the fringe of what you might call the elements of the underworld there. He came to Dallas, opened up a nightclub and it was a place where, certainly not the better class of people went, but it wasn't any so-called joint, to use the vernacular. It was just a nightclub.

Hoover apparently was suggesting that Ruby was unimportant and murdered the impostor for the emotional motives that Ruby had proffered at his trial, and not for the apparent purpose of silencing him. Yet Hoover well knew that Ruby had associated with major criminals all his life and was a man of unbridled ferocity. Hoover's studied indifference to anything or anyone suggesting conspiracy extended to the dichotomy in his statements about Marina and Marguerite Oswald:

I think his wife was a far more reliable person in statements that she made so far as we were able to ascertain, than his mother. I think the mother had in mind, naturally, the fact that she wanted to clear her son's name, which was a natural instinct, and more importantly she was going to see how much money she could make, and I believe she had made a substantial sum . . . There is no way of knowing whether she (Marina) belonged to the Russian Communist party in Russia. She is a rather intelligent woman, and notwithstanding that you have to talk with her through an interpreter, we have no indication of her association with communists in this country, nor have any of her close friends or relatives. As to his (Oswald's) mother, we found no indication she is associated or closely associated with the communists. She is the only one of the group that we have come in contact with that I would say is somewhat emotionally unstable. Our agents have interviewed her. She sometimes gets very angry and she won't answer questions.

Hoover did not mention that from 1959 through 1961, Oswald's mother had made substantial efforts in person and by correspondence to persuade the authorities in Washington to recover her son from the Soviet Union, wrongly believing him to have gone there as an agent on behalf of an agency of the United States. Nor did Hoover mention the large amounts of money Marina had received from various sources (perhaps as much as $200,000) allegedly from the media and private well-wishers after the assassination, and that they greatly exceeded the amount that Marguerite may have received (perhaps some $2,000).

Hoover knew, moreover, (a) that Marina had told the United States Embassy in Moscow that she had not been a member of Komsomol—the Communist League of Youth—and that her untruthful denial, if known at the time, would have prevented her admittance to the United States; (b) that the uncle with whom she lived in Minsk was a colonel in the MVD and a member of the Communist Party; (c) that after the assassination she had been interviewed on some 46 occasions by FBI agents and had been consistently untruthful when denying any prior knowledge of her husband's secret trip to Mexico seven weeks previously; and (d) that when testifying to the Commission in February 1964, through an interpreter, she had said obscurely, "I will not be charged with anything," but that under oath, she would tell the truth. (I.14.) (Marina's reference to not being "charged with anything" carries with it the sense of an arrangement of some sort, an exchange, with the authorities that allowed her to stay in the United States after her husband's death, and not be "charged with anything.")

Judging from his testimony, Hoover appears to have wished to discredit the testimony of the mother, who appears to have said and been dangerously near the truth in saying, someone was using her son. In contrast, he emphasized Marina's reliability which was the keystone of the conclusions of the Commission; the Warren Report was to quote extensively from her supporting testimony.

Hoover said at one point:

> In going back over the record, and I have read each of the reports dealing with that and the reports of Mr. Hosty who had dealt with the Oswald situation largely in Dallas, we have the matter that I have previously referred to, the report of the State Department that indicated that this man was a thoroughly safe risk, he had changed his views, he was a loyal man and had seen the light of day, so to speak. How intensive or how extensive that interview in Moscow was, I don't know. But, nevertheless, it was in a State Department document that was furnished to us.

Hoover neglected to tell the Commission that, after Ruby had killed the assassin, Hosty had destroyed a letter from 'Oswald' addressed to Hosty and hand-delivered by 'Oswald' in November. (Testimony of Hoover: V.97-120.)

When Hosty's tampering was discovered some 12 years later by the *Dallas Times Herald*, he claimed he had acted on orders from "above." According to the *New York Times* of 13 December 1975, Hosty, when testifying to a House Judiciary subcommittee that was looking into charges that the FBI withheld information from the Warren Commission, said that he "was instructed both by Commission and FBI personnel only to answer questions put to him and not to volunteer."

CIA TESTIMONY

When Hoover had completed his testimony, the Commission took the testimony of John A. McCone and Richard M. Helms, respectively Director and Deputy Director of the CIA. According to Book V of the

Senate Report, Helms testified that he, too, had been instructed only to answer questions. Neither Hosty of the FBI nor Helms volunteered the name of the person who issued these instructions.

Helms and McCone testified together:

We made an investigation of all developments after the assassination which came to our attention which might possibly have indicated a conspiracy, and we determined after those investigations,
which were made promptly and immediately, that we had no evidence to support such an assumption.

When asked whether their agency had made a particular investigation in connection with any allegations about a conspiracy involving the
Soviet Union or people connected with Cuba, they replied:

Yes, we did. We made a thorough, a very thorough investigation
of information that came to us concerning an alleged trip that Oswald made to Mexico City during which time he made contact
with the *Cuban* Embassy in Mexico City in an attempt to gain
transit privilege from Mexico City to the Soviet Union via
Havana. We investigated that thoroughly.

They said that they had found no evidence of conspiracy in all of
their investigation. When asked specifically whether the CIA investigated any aspects of Lee Harvey Oswald's trip to Mexico, they replied:

We were aware that Oswald did make a trip to Mexico City and
it was our judgment that he was there in the interest of ensuring
transit privileges and that he made contact with the *Cuban* Embassy while he was there. We do not know the precise results of
his efforts, but we assume, because he returned to the United
States, he was unsuccessful. We have examined to every extent we
can, and using all resources available to us, every aspect of his activity, and we could not verify that he was there for any other purpose or that his trip to Mexico was in any way related to his later
action in assassinating President Kennedy.

Although it was their own informant who had twice reported the
presence of the "American male" in the *Soviet* Embassy in Mexico

City and some of his activities while there—in addition to the CIA having photographed him—McCone and Helms made no mention of it. Like Hoover, they made no reference to anything hinting at conspiracy. Helms, in fact, did not even mention his own two affidavits relating to the possibility of conspiracy in Mexico City, the earlier and definitive one of which was to be hidden in the National Archives. (Testimony of McCone and Helms: V.120-129.)

SECRET SERVICE TESTIMONY

In support of the view that the Secret Service had an important role in the postassassination investigations, Lt. Martello of the New Orleans police was to testify that at 3:00 A.M. on 23 November 1963 he was contacted by Secret Service agent Vial, who told him that "the Secret Service was conducting *an official investigation* regarding the assassination of the President of the United States."

On 2 September 1964, Secretary of the Treasury, C. Douglas Dillon, testified before the Commission. He was responsible for Secret Service activities, and it was hoped he would shed some light on the Service's involvement in the postassassination investigation. But his testimony was almost entirely devoted to the past, present, and future protection of the President, Vice President, and others in line for the Presidency; during his lengthy testimony there was only a short reference to the assassin. After denying the rumor that the assassin might have been an agent of the Secret Service, Dillon was asked, "Do you know of any area of the investigation of the Commission that you would like to suggest that we do more than we have insofar as you are familiar with it?" "As far as I know," Dillon replied, "the investigation has been very thorough." When asked, "Do you know of any credible evidence that would lead you or anyone to believe that there was a conspiracy, foreign or domestic, involved in the assassination of the President?" he replied, "From all the evidence that I have seen, this was the work of one deranged individual . . . Lee Harvey Oswald." When asked, "Is there anything that you would like to call to the attention of the Commission at this time that we should know or that we should cover?" he replied, "I think we have covered my area of competence pretty thoroughly this morning. I can't think of anything else."

Dillon neglected to mention that it was Secret Service agents who, on 23 and 24 November, went to the premises of Jaggars-Chiles-Stovall to investigate and presumably to discover "the work of one deranged individual" in that "sensitive" firm. (Testimony of Dillon: V.573.588.)

DEPARTMENT OF STATE TESTIMONY

On 10 June 1964, the Honorable Dean Rusk, Secretary of State, testified: "I would like to be just as helpful as possible to the Commission. I am not quite clear of testimony in terms of future publication. There may be certain points that arise where it might be helpful for the Commission for me to comment on certain points but there—it would be a very grave difficulty about publication, so I wonder what the Commission's view is on that." Chief Justice Warren replied, "Well, Mr. Secretary, our purpose is to have available for the public all the evidence that is given here. If there is any phase of it that you think might jeopardize the security of the nation, have no hesitation in asking us to go off the record for a moment, and you can tell us what you wish." A Commissioner asked, "Would it be feasible to have a discussion here of the points that are vital from the point of view of our record, and so forth, and maybe a little informal conversation afterward to cover the other points?" The Commission then recessed; when back on the record, Rusk was asked, "In your opinion, was there an (sic) substantial interest or interests for the Soviet Union which would have been advanced by the assassination of President Kennedy?" Rusk replied,

I would first have to say on a question of that sort that it is important to follow the evidence. It is very difficult to look into the mind of someone else and to know what is in someone else's mind. I have seen no evidence that would indicate to me that the Soviet Union considered that it had an interest in the removal of President Kennedy or that it was in any way involved in the removal of President Kennedy . . . I was with several colleagues in a plane on the way to Japan at the time the assassination occurred. When we got the news we immediately turned back. After my mind was able to grasp the fact that this event had in fact occurred, which was the first necessity, and not an easy one, I then, on the plane, began to go over the dozens and dozens of implications and ramifications of this event as it affects our foreign relations all over the world . . . But one of the great questions in my mind at that time was just that question could some foreign government somehow be involved in such an episode. I realized that were this so this would raise *the gravest issues of war or peace*, but that nevertheless it was important to try to get at the truth—the answer to that question—wherever that truth might lead; and so, when I got back to Washington I put myself immediately in touch with the processes of inquiry on that point and as Secretary of State had the deepest possible interest in what the truthful answer to those questions would be, because it would be hard to think of anything more pregnant for our foreign relations than the correct answer to that question. I have not seen or heard of any scrap of evidence indicating that the Soviet Union had any desire to eliminate President Kennedy nor in any way participated in any such event.

Rusk proceeded to develop this argument and said,

I think also that it is relevant that people behind the Iron Curtain, including people in the Soviet Union and including officials in the Soviet Union, seemed to be deeply affected by the death of President Kennedy. Their reactions were prompt and, I think genuine, of regret and sorrow. Mr. Khrushchev was the first to come to the Embassy to sign the book of condolences. There were tears in the streets of Moscow. Moscow radio spent a great deal of attention to these matters. Now they did come to premature conclusions, in my judgment, about what this event was and what it meant in terms of who might have been responsible for it and—ideology effect has crept into that. But I have the impression that the regret was genuine and that the ordinary Soviet citizens joined with ordinary people in other parts of the world in feeling the loss of the President in a very genuine sense.

Rusk was then asked if he could give an opinion to the Commission in regard to Cuba in the same general way, and he replied,

Well, I would again repeat that the overriding consideration is to make every possible effort to find evidence and follow the evidence to wherever it leads. I think it is, at least for me, more difficult to try to enter into the minds of the present leadership in Cuba than, perhaps, even of the present leadership of the Soviet Union. We have had very few contacts, as the Commission knows, with the present government of Cuba. But again, I have seen no evidence that seems to point in that direction. There were some exchanges, with which the Commission is familiar, that seemed to be—seemed to come to another conclusion. But I would think that objective considerations would be that it would be even greater madness for Castro or his government to be involved in any such enterprise than almost for anyone else, because literally the issue of war and peace would mean that the issue of the existence of his regime and perhaps of his country might have been involved in that question. We were under the impression that there was very considerable concern in Cuba as to whether they would be held responsible and what the effect of that might be on their own position and their own safety. But I have seen no evidence that points to involvement by them, and I don't see any objective facts which would seem to make it in their interests to remove Mr. Kennedy. You see, this embarks upon, in any event it would embark upon, an unpredictable trail for them to go down this path, but I would think again the Commission would wish to examine the evidence as it had been doing with meticulous care and follow the evidence in these matters.

When asked whether there was any possibility that the Mexican government could have been in any way involved, Rusk replied,

. . . we never had the slightest view that Mexico was involved in this, the problem, the question arose because Mr. Oswald had been in Mexico, and was known to have been in touch with some Cubans at the *Cuban* Embassy in Mexico. But the Mexican authorities gave us complete and most helpful cooperation in full investigation of this matter.

Counsel said to Rusk: "There has been some suggestion that possibly the leadership of the Soviet Union would not have been politically interested in the death of the President but possibly a distant wing of the Party might have been so involved. Can you throw any light on that, Mr. Secretary?" Rusk disposed of this suggestion by saying that the primary problem of dissidents is within the Soviet Union, and that, although it was "a matter of some speculation," he doubted that there would be either motive or opportunity.

Finally, Counsel asked Rusk, "Mr. Secretary, will you tell us whether you know of any credible evidence to show or establish or tending to show any conspiracy either domestic or foreign involved in the assassination of the President?" Rusk replied: "No, I have no evidence that would point in that direction or to lead me to a conclusion that such a conspiracy existed."

Rusk omitted any reference in his testimony to the Soviet Embassies in Havana, Mexico City, and Washington, to any of the Soviet intelligence officers and officials named in this book, to the defector Nosenko, to Hoover's memorandum to the Department of State of 3 June 1960 and several State Department memoranda relative thereto. In particular, he failed to tell the Commission that Edward Hickey of his Department's passport office in March 1961 had warned against handing Oswald's passport to a suspected impostor. Nor did he remind the Commission of his own warning against imposture of July 1961. (Testimony of Rusk: V.363-371.)

THE AUTHORITIES AGREE

The following is taken from Book V of the Senate Investigation. Passages are reproduced as printed. My additions are initialled ME.

Almost immediately after the assassination, Director Hoover, the Justice Department and the White House "exerted pressure" on senior Bureau officials to complete their investigation and issue a factual report supporting the conclusion that Oswald was the lone assassin.

In a telephone conversation with White House Aide Walter Jenkins immediately following Oswald's murder, Director Hoover stated:

> The thing I am most concerned about, and so is Mr. Katzenbach, is having something issued so we can convince the public that Oswald is the real assassin.

The pressure to issue a report that would establish Oswald as the lone assassin is reflected in internal Bureau memoranda. On November 24, 1963, Assistant FBI Director Alan Belmont informed Associate FBI Director Clyde Tolson that he was sending two Headquarters supervisors to Dallas to review

> the written interview and investigative findings of our agents on the Oswald matter, so that we can prepare a memorandum to the Attorney General . . .

(setting) out the evidence showing that Oswald is responsible for the shooting that killed the President.

The performance of these agencies should not be evaluated in isolation. Senior government officials, both within the agencies and outside them, wanted the investigation completed promptly and all conspiracy rumors dispelled. For example, only three days after the assassination (25 November: ME), Deputy Attorney General Nicholas Katzenbach wrote Presidential Assistant Bill Moyers:

> It is important that all of the facts surrounding President Kennedy's assassination be made public in a way which will satisfy people in the United States and abroad that all the facts have been told and that a statement to this effect be made now.
>
> 1. The public must be satisfied that Oswald was the assassin; that he did not have confederates who are still at large; and that the evidence was such that he would have been convicted at trial.
>
> 2. Speculation about Oswald's motivation ought to be cut off, and we should have some basis for rebutting thought that this was a Communist conspiracy or (as the Iron Curtain press is saying) a right-wing conspiracy to blame it on the Communists.

On November 26, 1963, J. Edgar Hoover spoke with Deputy Attorney General Katzenbach. According to Alan Belmont, Hoover relayed:

> Katzenbach's feeling that this (FBI) report should include everything which may raise a question in the mind of the public or press regarding this matter.
>
> In other words, this report is to settle the dust, insofar as *Oswald and his activities* are concerned, both from the standpoint that he is the man who assassinated the President, and relative to Oswald himself and his activities and background. (Emphasis added.)

The next day Belmont responded.

> Relative to the Director's question as to how long we estimate the investigation in this matter will take, we plan to have the report on this matter, and on the Jack Ruby matter, this Friday, 11/29/63.

In a November 29, 1963, memorandum, Hoover recounted a telephone conversation he had that day with President Johnson:

> The President called and asked if I am familiar with the proposed group they are trying to get to study my report—two from the House, two from the Senate, two from the courts, and a couple of outsiders. I replied that I had not heard of that but had seen reports from the Senate Investigation Committee.

The President stated he wanted to get by just with my file and my report. I
told him I thought it would be very bad to have a rash of investigations. He
then indicated the only way to stop it is to appoint a high-level committee
to evaluate my report and tell the House and Senate not to go ahead with the
investigation. I stated that would be a three-ring circus.

On December 9, 1963, Deputy Attorney General Katzenbach
wrote each member of the Warren Commission recommending that
the Commission immediately issue a press release stating that the
FBI report clearly showed there was no international conspiracy,
and that Oswald was a loner.

FBI documents also reveal that James Angleton of the CIA passed
information he received about the Warren Commission investigation to the FBI. On May 13, 1964, he contacted William Sullivan
(FBI Supervisor: ME), stating "that it would be well for both
McCone and Hoover to be aware that the Commission might ask
the same questions, wondering whether they would get different
replies from the heads of the 'two agencies'. Angleton then informed
Sullivan as to the questions he believed McCone would be asked
and the "replies that will be given."

15

George De Mohrenschildt

George De Mohrenschildt has always been a significant figure in the investigation but when on 29 March 1977 he committed suicide, his relationship to the assassin took on a new aspect. What is known of his history is deserving of attention.

'Oswald's' only friend in Fort Worth and Dallas from August 1962 until about 15 April 1963, according to Marina Oswald's testimony to the Warren Commission, was the aristocratic and talented 52-year-old Russian- or Polish-born geologist and petroleum engineer, George De Mohrenschildt, a man of many social graces, fluent in many languages, and more given to associating with professional people than with a person of 'Oswald's' background. Although De Mohrenschildt admitted to this friendship in testimony, it was such an improbable relationship that it always appeared to have deeper implications. His Russian-born wife, Jeanne, equally talented as an architect and a dress designer, in testimony admitted her friendship with Marina.

The testimony of De Mohrenschildt shows that, carrying a Polish passport, he entered the United States in 1938 and within a short time attracted the attention of the FBI. In late December 1941, he was already under surveillance as a suspected spy, and remained in the FBI open "Internal Security" files up to the time of the assassination.

His testimony indicates that he was an agent, having spent considerable time purposefully sketching and photographing coastal and inland areas that would be of interest to a hostile power. It appears that when taking photographs of coastal areas, he would have with him a young woman and, in the process of taking snapshots of each other, a "sensitive" background would be included. It appears that his cover was either genuine employment as a geological explorer or, on occasion, a pleasure trip. He visited Mexico, all of Central America, most of the countries in South America, islands in the Atlantic, Poland, Yugoslavia, Denmark, Sweden, France, and areas of Western Africa.

A reading of De Mohrenschildt's testimony suggests that while living in Dallas he had been instructed (a) to make contact with 'Oswald' and Marina (August 1962) after their arrival in Fort Worth (June 1962), (b) to help to infiltrate the assassin into Jaggars-Chiles-Stoval (October 1962), (c) to help in assisting in the introduction of Marina to Ruth Paine, who made the call to the Depository (February 1963), and finally (d) to arrange the attack on General Walker (April 1963). A few days later he would remove himself from Dallas and the United States by going to Haiti until after the assassination.

GARY TAYLOR

These views are supported by the testimony of Gary Taylor who, when 19 years of age, in November 1959 had married Alexandra, De Mohrenschildt's 16-year-old daughter by a previous marriage. Taylor, a member of a prominent family, was probably closer to the De Mohrenschildts than anyone else during the time they were acquainted with 'Oswald' and Marina.

During the Cuban Missile Crisis of October 1962, at the De Mohrenschildts' request, the Taylors had allowed Marina to stay with them. During this time, 'Oswald' and both the De Mohrenschildts occasionally visited Marina at the Taylors' apartment.

Gary Taylor testified to the Warren Commission in March 1964, his testimony indicating the control that his father-in-law had exercised over 'Oswald,' and disclosing Taylor's opinion that if there had been a conspiracy to assassinate the President, then the De Mohrenschildts were probably involved.

An extract from Taylor's testimony (IX.72-102) (one Counsel but no Commissioner being present, and the testimony not being mentioned in the Warren Report) is as follows:

(Describing De Mohrenschildt): He is a rather overbearing personality; somewhat boisterous in nature and easily changeable

moods—anywhere from extreme friendliness to downright dislike—just like turning on and off a light . . . he is athletic . . . I
would say that he has an inflammable personality. And he's very
likable, when he wants to be, and he oftentimes uses this to get
something he wants, puts a person in a good mood and then, by
doing this, he tries to drag whatever it is that he wants out of
them. I would say that they (the De Mohrenschildts) lead a somewhat Bohemian life . . . (He) oftentimes wearing merely bathing
trunks, and things like this, that—for a man of his age, which is
about 50 to 52—is a little unusual on the street as a constant ap-
parel. He does not often work. In fact, during the time that I was
married to his daughter (4 years), I have not known of him to
hold any kind of a position for which he received monetary re-
muneration . . . They are very active, outdoor sort of people.

When asked to give his judgment as to the relationship between 'Oswald' and George De Mohrenschildt, Taylor replied:

It's difficult to assess their relationship because there probably was
more to it than I ever saw. But what little of it I saw, they were
quite in opposition to each other—such as the lessons in English
for Marina. But I certainly think that they must have been closer
than they appeared or the De Mohrenschildts wouldn't have been
so active in seeing that they got along well.

When asked if he had any opinion about whether De Mohrenschildt
exercised any influence over 'Oswald,' he said:

Yes, there seemed to be a great deal of influence there. It would be
my guess that De Mohrenschildt encouraged him to move to
Dallas (from Fort Worth), and he suggested a number of things to
Lee—such as where to look for jobs. And it seems like whatever
his suggestions were, Lee grabbed them and took them—whether
it was what time to go to bed or where to stay or to let Marina
stay with us while he stayed at the YMCA.

When asked about De Mohrenschildt's political philosophy, Taylor
testified:

I have heard them (the De Mohrenschildts) say everything—from
saying that he was a Republican and she expressed democratic

ideals, and they expressed desires to return to Russia and live—so,
it's all colors of the spectrum. Anything that—again, so much of
what they do is what fits the moment. Whatever fits their designs
or desires at the moment they do it.

When asked by Counsel if he had anything to add that would be
helpful, his testimony was as follows:

Well, the only thing that occurred to me as to that—and I guess it
was from the beginning—that if there was any assistance or plot-
ters in the assassination that it was, in my opinion, most probably
the De Mohrenschildts.

Counsel: On what do you base that?

Taylor: I base that on—their desire, first of all, to return to Russia at one time and live there; they have traveled together behind
the Iron Curtain; they took a trip to Mexico, through Mexico, on
the avowed purpose of walking from Laredo, Tex., to the tip of
South America—

Counsel: Panama?

Taylor: And—

Counsel: On beyond that?

Taylor: Beyond—to the tip of South America—the southern tip
of South America.

Counsel: All right.

Taylor: And this they claim to have done, yet further information
(correctly) indicated to me that their trip extended only to the por-
tion of South America where the Cuban refugees were being
trained to invade Cuba and that this trip coincided and that they
were in the area while all this training was going on. And, so,
from that—from these observations—

Counsel: Do you conclude that they were attempting to spy on
that invasion preparation?

Taylor: Yes; because where—they went to Guatemala where the
invasion troops were being trained, or they were in Guatemala
when they were supposed to be on a walking trip, and had taken

up residence in the unoccupied home of some acquaintances there
. . . the De Mohrenschildts were evicted when the people who
owned it returned . . .

Counsel: This was the trip during the time you were married to
their daughter?

Taylor: Yes.

Counsel: You are basing this information on communications
from them, conversations with your wife; conversations that occurred after they returned?

Taylor: Yes . . . there was an indication here that they had been
in the area (Guatemala) where some spying or information-
gathering might be valuable to Communist interests. They had
expressed a desire to live in a Communist country; and that they
had traveled extensively through Communist countries.

One month after Gary Taylor had testified, the De Mohrenschildts
voluntarily came from Haiti to Washington to testify at length to the
Warren Commission, the testimony covering 166 pages, with one
Counsel but no Commissioner present. After testifying, they returned
to Haiti.

The FBI had supplied the Commission with its suspicions of De
Mohrenschildt's espionage, and had chronicled his activities while in
the United States from 1938, including such details as his mode of travel and the hotels he visited. During testimony Counsel referred to the
"mountains of reports" that had been supplied to him; the details
brought out so astounded De Mohrenschildt that he frequently ex-
claimed, "How did you know that?"

It is, of course, impossible in this book to do more than select or
paraphrase parts of De Mohrenschildt's testimony; the parts chosen
relate to De Mohrenschildt's own admission to espionage, other apparent espionage, his derision of the FBI, his denigration of both 'Oswald'
and Marina, and his insistence that, after leaving Dallas for Haiti in
April 1963, he and his wife had "put the Oswalds out of our minds."

THE TESTIMONY OF GEORGE AND JEANNE DE MOHRENSCHILDT

Attempting to be disarming, at the commencement of his testimony, De Mohrenschildt minimized the value of the "file," and said that his appearance before the Warren Commission was "hurting" him in his present work in Haiti; he said that President Duvalier had received a letter from the FBI saying that De Mohrenschildt was a "very close friend of 'Oswald's', a Polish Communist, and a member of an international band of assassins," and he said that his job in Haiti, which was the result of many years of preparation, was very important to him; "it would be very unpleasant, just to be kicked out of that country because of the rumors . . . all sorts of speculation have arisen from time to time . . . I don't mind, frankly . . . when you don't have anything to hide, you see, you are not afraid of anything . . ." He hoped that the Commission's inquiry could be conducted "somewhat delicately."

De Mohrenschildt admitted spying in the United States after World War II broke out, understanding the operations to be on behalf of the French. In December 1941 he was accused of making sketches and taking photographs of military installations near the Bay of Corpus Christi at Aransas Pass while on a trip to Mexico with a girl friend, Lilia Pardo. He testified, "Around Corpus Christi—really, . . . you would laugh about some of the activity of the FBI, and the money they spend following false trails . . . I don't know whose advice they followed . . ."

De Mohrenschildt had at first avoided mentioning Aransas Pass, but when asked by Counsel if he had taken photographs there, he said, "Possibly, of each other." He admitted making sketches because "I like to sketch, I sketched the dunes, the coastline, but not the Coast Guard Station. Who gives a damn about the Coast Guard station in Aransas Pass?"

Counsel: You apparently were not aware of the fact that this country was then at war (8 December 1941).

De Mohrenschildt: But nobody told me there was any military installations around Aransas Pass.

Counsel: Well, you were seen sketching the countryside . . . and that aroused suspicion.

De Mohrenschildt: (On the way back from Aransas Pass) Some characters stopped the car and came out of the bushes, "You are a German spy." . . . It was very strange. Here is my Polish passport . . . I think they said they were from the FBI . . . and they (five men) followed me all the way from New York . . . searched the car, found absolutely nothing.

De Mohrenschildt was reportedly arrested by the United States Coast Guard, but the outcome of the incident is not known. It appears that his camera was confiscated, because when he and Lilia entered Mexico, it was not among the items they had with them.

He said that he had done a lot of painting while in Mexico, although not of military installations. "Girls, tropical jungle, Mexican types—I am very fond of Mexico." He said that he was thrown out of Mexico as "persona non grata" by General Maximo Comacho because the general wanted to take Lilia away from him; eventually he returned to New York by train.

The CIA must have kept him under close surveillance while in Mexico for several months because they knew the date of his reentry into the United States and his actual method of travel.

Counsel: When you got back to the United States . . . the records indicate that you made some effort here in Washington to obtain reentry into Mexico and you were unable to do so . . . and that Lilia attempted to assist you.

De Mohrenschildt agreed with this and also admitted that Lilia had attempted to return to the United States but was refused entry as "persona non grata."

On a business trip to Yugoslavia in 1957, Jeanne LeGon (later Jeanne De Mohrenschildt) joined him for several weeks and De Mohrenschildt testified about his altercation there:

De Mohrenschildt: . . . The same thing happened to me in Yugoslavia except that this time they were the (anti-Soviet) Communists who thought I was making sketches of their fortifications.

Actually, I was also making drawings of the seashore. And this time they shot at us.

In testimony, Jeanne De Mohrenschildt referred to the incident, ". . . and all of a sudden we hear shots. We thought it was old fortifications . . . but they were actually their fortifications and they thought we were interested in it. They were pointing a rifle at us and shooting."

On another occasion offshore in a boat they were again shot at, this time by cannon, the first shell hitting the water about one yard from the boat. They had been taking photographs of each other in front of some caves on an island; "The little island we thought was completely empty, not a soul on it, they had fortification on that island."

Jeanne De Mohrenschildt testified that during the several weeks in 1957 that she had been with De Mohrenschildt in Yugoslavia, her husband, Robert LeGon, accused her of being a Communist and a spy, writing letters to her employers and creditors, expressing in a "horrible way" that she was "a spy or something." He had signed some of the letters with his own name and others as "some kind of FBI" agent. She said that the letters had quite an effect because she had lost the work she had, was unable to find work, and it took almost a year to "get everything straightened out." A short time later, LeGon was committed to a mental institution, by whom is not known, and was to remain there up to and including the time the De Mohrenschildts testified to the Commission, Jeanne saying that he was "incurable."

De Mohrenschildt testified further about a walking trip of almost a year (1960-1) from the United States-Mexican border down to Panama, during which he and his wife covered about 5,000 miles.

Counsel: Now, this trip of yours down through Mexico, and the Central American countries—wasn't that about the time of the Bay of Pigs invasion (17 April 1961)?

De Mohrenschildt: It was indeed; yes. And we didn't know anything about it.

Counsel: You didn't?

De Mohrenschildt: We didn't know anything about it.

Counsel: Your trip had nothing whatsoever to do with that?

De Mohrenschildt: Nothing to do with it—except I remembered we arrived in Guatemala City, and by God you know we walked on the street, we were trying to get some visas to get to the next country—you have to get visas and permits to carry guns. We had to carry a revolver with us to protect us, because we were going constantly through a jungle . . . We were walking around the town trying to get a permit to Nicaragua, and to San Salvador, and to Honduras. And as we were walking on the street we saw a lot of white boys, dressed in civilian, but they looked like military men to me. And I said to Jeanne, "By God, they look like American boys." . . . and then we left Guatemala City—two days later—we read the paper on the road about the Bay of Pigs invasion. That is all we knew about it.

Speaking of Guatemala City, Mrs. De Mohrenschildt testified:

Mrs. De Mohrenschildt: . . . it was very funny. There was such a commotion, such confusion in the American Embassy, we just remarked about it. They were running around, busy, busy . . . (The American Consul) was on the phone all the time, such a confusion was going on. So we noticed that. And we noticed those funny looking boys running around. I thought they were Canadian boys. And later on we learned that there was an invasion. So maybe that was the people that were involved in it.

Counsel: That is all you know about the Bay of Pigs invasion?

Mrs. De Mohrenschildt: That is all we know about it.

The De Mohrenschildts made an 8-mm movie of 1,200 feet giving a complete sequence of the journey because "they went to places where no white man had ever been before." They lived exactly like the natives, poorly dressed, and with all their cameras, equipment, and money covered by a piece of old rag on a mule. The trip ended at the Panama Canal, where they visited the United States Ambassador.

Counsel: It has no political implications whatsoever?

De Mohrenschildt: No political implications. I am not interested at all in politics. Naturally, when I was going there I could not help seeing what was going on. The dictatorship in Honduras, the civil war in Panama, the guerrilla fights. It is all recorded in my book . . . But I had nothing to do with it . . . When we completed the trip we were very tired and we decided to go and take a rest in Haiti . . . I had a very close friend of my father's who lived in Haiti. I speak French and I like the country . . . and I started preparing my contract with the Haitian Government at the same time . . . until finally there was the contract in March 1963 two years later.

Counsel: Here again this is all business?

De Mohrenschildt: Purely business.

Counsel: No political or like consideration?

De Mohrenschildt: No.

Counsel: You have never been a member of any subversive group?

De Mohrenschildt: Never have.

When asked by Counsel about his work in Haiti after 1963, De Mohrenschildt identified his marks on a map of Haiti of coastal areas, beaches, and small islands, and explained that they were sites for "new resorts" and "oil possibilities." (XIX.554.)

Counsel inquired, "And this is in no way linked, directly, indirectly, or in any remote possibility, with any mapping of this country with great care for the possibility of its being employed by any other nation or group?" De Mohrenschildt replied, "No, no other nation could use my maps, and no other project, except our own commercial and geological project—nothing else."

In 1965, a revolution erupted in the Dominican Republic. Though the revolution taken over by the Cubans ultimately did not succeed, there is no doubt that plans had been made to absorb an almost defenseless Haiti. In 1967, peace was restored and the De Mohrenschildts returned to Dallas.

In testimony, Jeanne De Mohrenschildt told of sketching while walking in the mountains of Haiti, "In fact, I try to help him whenever I can. I draw maps. Just now I made for him some maps in the Dominican Republic about this nickel mine and everything. He couldn't have it photostated. They were too old. So I sit down and draw it any time I can, because I really love that."

In testimony, the De Mohrenschildts admitted their friendship with the 'Oswalds' from August 1962 until about the middle of April 1963. It was easy for De Mohrenschildt to make it appear that their "involved" relationship with the newly arrived 'Oswalds' was a natural occurrence as the De Mohrenschildts were well-established members of the Dallas Russian émigré community, many of whom were trying to help the impoverished young couple with their various problems. At the same time the De Mohrenschildts denigrated both 'Oswald' and Marina, De Mohrenschildt making it appear that neither of the 'Oswalds' could be considered as suitable persons for employment by a hostile power.

De Mohrenschildt testified that at first he was doubtful about 'Oswald' because he had been in Russia. He did not want to get involved and distinctly remembered that a friend of his had "checked" on 'Oswald' at the FBI, which had alleviated his fears. He said that one of the reasons he was interested in 'Oswald' was that 'Oswald' had been in Minsk, where De Mohrenschildt said he had lived as a child.

Counsel: I think I will ask you at this point, Mr. De Mohrenschildt, you are a man of very superior education and extremely wide experience and acquaintance here and in Europe, South America, West Indies—you have lived an extremely colorful life. You are acquainted to a greater or lesser degree with a great variety of people.

De Mohrenschildt: Yes.

Counsel: Did there go through your mind speculations as to whether Oswald was an agent of anybody?

De Mohrenschildt: No.

De Mohrenschildt said that "I certainly can evaluate people just by looking at them—because I have met so many people in my profession—you have to evaluate them by just looking at them and saying a few words."

De Mohrenschildt said that he had not even thought about 'Oswald' being an agent, because he was too "outspoken about his ideas and attitudes," and if he really were an agent, De Mohrenschildt thought he would have kept quiet. De Mohrenschildt did not take 'Oswald' "seriously" because he was not "sophisticated . . . a semi-educated hillbilly." 'Oswald's' opinions were "crude," but at the time De

Mohrenschildt thought he was "rather sincere." He said that 'Oswald'
read books but did not understand them, and "loved to use difficult
words to impress" De Mohrenschildt, so, although he could "not take
Oswald seriously and just laughed at him," nevertheless he and Jeanne
always had an "element of pity" for "a forlorn individual groping for
something." He would never believe that any government would be so
stupid as to trust 'Oswald' with anything important because he was
"unstable, mixed-up, uneducated and without background"; no government would have given him any type of confidential work. "Oswald
hated his jobs, and switched all the time."

(De Mohrenschildt's testimony does not jibe with that of William
Stuckey, the radio panel moderator, whose testimony portrays an intelligent and articulate 'Oswald' during radio debates in New Orleans
in August 1963, nor does it jibe with the opinion of the Jesuits who met
with him in Alabama.)

De Mohrenschildt maintained that 'Oswald' continually told him
that he was not a Communist, and when asked point-blank, "Are you
a member of the Communist Party?" 'Oswald' replied that he was a
Marxist, and kept on repeating it. De Mohrenschildt did not explore
the matter further with 'Oswald' because the "sound of the word
Marxism is very boring to me."

When asked by Counsel whether 'Oswald' ever discussed with him an
attempted defection to Russia, De Mohrenschildt said that he could
"remember a few words now." 'Oswald' had said that while he was in
Japan he saw tremendous injustice, meaning, De Mohrenschildt
thought, the material disparity between the proletariat and the rich in
Japan. He had also told De Mohrenschildt that he had some contact
with Japanese Communists in Japan and they had "got him interested
to go and see what goes on in the Soviet Union . . . and that was one
of his inducements in going to Soviet Russia."

Counsel: He always knew what the answer was (to political questions).

De Mohrenschildt: He always knew what the answer was. And
possibly that is why he was clinging to us, to my wife and me,
because we did not discuss it with them, because we did not give a
damn. After we found out what was going on in that town of
Minsk, what was the situation, what were the food prices, how
they dressed, how they spent their evenings, which are things interesting to us, our interest waned. The rest of the time, the few

times we saw Lee Oswald and Marina afterwards, was purely to give a gift, to take them to a party, because we thought they were dying of boredom.

In testimony, De Mohrenschildt had said that after he and his wife had left Dallas for Haiti in April 1963, the only communication he received from 'Oswald' was a card saying that he and Marina were now in New Orleans. Yet while in Haiti De Mohrenschildt had received a photograph of 'Oswald' which was inscribed in Russian with the words "Fascist hunter. Ha Ha Ha. To my friend George. Lee Oswald. 5.IV.1963." Only after De Mohrenschildt's death was the photograph discovered.

Four years after the assassination, in 1967 the De Mohrenschildts returned to Dallas where in 1969 De Mohrenschildt took a post at Bishop College as a teacher of Russian and French. If De Mohrenschildt was under any pressure from his immediate environment, he managed to keep it hidden. But in August 1976, he began to exhibit anxiety amounting to what is known as "psychotic depression," according to his doctor. In October 1976, he asked a psychiatrist to commit him as a patient to Terrell State Hospital; four days later he changed his mind. In vain, his wife sought to commit him to Parkland Hospital, saying that he had tried to commit suicide four times, that he thought he was under surveillance—either by the CIA, the FBI, the KGB, or a "Jewish Mafia,"—and that his telephone and house were being bugged. On 9 November, he finally agreed to commit himself to Parkland Hospital and, after undergoing shock therapy, was released on 30 December 1976.

In mid-February Jeanne De Mohrenschildt left George and went to California, probably never seeing him again. On or about 17 February 1977, De Mohrenschildt was visited by a Dutch journalist, Willem Oltmans, who lived in Brussels and who has stated that he was an old friend of De Mohrenschildt's.

On 1 March, De Mohrenschildt took a three-day leave of absence from the college, ostensibly to see his daughter in New Orleans, but, instead of going to New Orleans, he flew to Holland with Oltmans. According to Oltmans, they drove to Brussels, where De Mohrenschildt disappeared, leaving behind his suitcases and clothes; what De Mohrenschildt did or what happened to him over a period of some ten days is unknown.

On 14 March he arrived in New York, and on 15 March Oltmans told the present House Select Committee on Assassinations in Washington that De Mohrenschildt had told him on or about 17 February, that 'Oswald' had acted with his knowledge when he killed President Kennedy; he said De Mohrenschildt had also asked him, "How do you think the media would react if I came out and said I feel responsible for 'Oswald's' behavior?"

Oltmans' information interested the House Committee, although they were apparently highly skeptical of De Mohrenschildt's statements. A Committee investigator was quoted in the press as saying that although the Committee did want to see De Mohrenschildt, "It doesn't sound like fertile ground to me. It sounds like a man who has cracked." Whatever the case, the Committee were never to reach De Mohrenschildt.

According to what has been reported in the press, he arrived in Florida on 17 March to stay at the home of a relative in Palm Beach where his daughter, Alexandra, was then living. On the morning of 29 March, an investigator for the Committee, Gaeton Fonzi, called at the house and asked Alexandra if he could interview her father. On being told that he was out, Fonzi said he would return at 8:30 P.M. that evening. After Fonzi's departure, Alexandra went out. When she returned home at 3:32 P.M., she found her father dead, a 20-gauge shotgun by his body. De Mohrenschildt had apparently placed the gun in his mouth and killed himself. Alexandra was later to say that her father had been "terrified" of Oltmans.

Although all suicides challenge one's sense of the credulous, this one had an added dimension of the bizarre because someone had left a tape recorder working to record a television soap opera. Against the background of the program were recorded someone's footsteps crossing a room, the opening of a drawer (where there was a 20-gauge shotgun), and someone walking away. The machine then recorded a single shot, the continuing television program, Alexandra's calls to her father, and her scream on finding her father's body.

On 1 April, in statements made to the Associated Press and the National Broadcasting Company, but without any substantiating documents, Oltmans said that De Mohrenschildt had told him that he and 'Oswald' had been hired by anti-Cubans and Dallas oilmen to assassinate Kennedy, and that 'Oswald' was to be paid a large sum of money. He said that De Mohrenschildt had told him that he was "very, very much involved," and asserted that De Mohrenschildt had committed suicide rather than face being exposed as responsible for the assassination. Oltmans also said that De Mohrenschildt had told him that "Kennedy had actually been shot by anti-Cubans and not by 'Oswald'." These statements once again play into the hands of those who maintain that the Soviets were not the source of the conspiracy.

When Oltmans made these statements, an unaddressed letter written by De Mohrenschildt and dated 17 March had been found in the room in which he killed himself. According to television reporters who claim to have read the letter, it said that De Mohrenschildt had traveled from Houston to Amsterdam with Oltmans and Carl Angelier of the Dutch TV Network. When they reached Holland, Oltmans tried to bully him into admitting things he didn't do, gave him drugs, and then interviewed him. Oltmans then drove him to Brussels, where Oltmans met with a friend, Denisov, from the Soviet Embassy, a meeting that De Mohrenschildt did not attend. De Mohrenschildt ended the letter, "As I see it, the main reason Oltmans took me to Amsterdam was to ruin me financially and completely."

It is possible that De Mohrenschildt went to Europe with Oltmans in the expectation that the KGB would help him to disappear; but his hope was dashed in Brussels, since neither the Russians nor the Poles would accept him into their country. If the KGB's past performance is any indication, De Mohrenschildt was possibly threatened with death or exposure as a longtime Soviet agent. Whatever the case, De Mohrenschildt's final flight and suicide indicated a man in a state of extreme terror.

THE DALLAS TRIANGLE

It is a remarkable coincidence that in a city of 300 square miles and thousands of blocks, during 1956-7-8 and perhaps thereafter, De Mohrenschildt and Ruby had access to apartments in the same block, less than 100 yards apart. None of this was mentioned in testimony or in the Warren Report and Exhibits.

The above suggests that there was an early connection between De Mohrenschildt and Ruby, and that after the assassination the authorities suspected this to be so.

It is my belief that these three men—George De Mohrenschildt, Jack Ruby and the impostor 'Oswald'—were the three primary operatives at work in Dallas for the purpose of killing President Kennedy.

Epilogue

I believe there is overwhelming evidence of conspiracy in the assassination of President John F. Kennedy and that this evidence was suppressed in the interest of national security. I also believe there is powerful evidence that the assassin was a Soviet agent. Furthermore, I believe there is persuasive evidence that the Soviet agent was an impostor.

The difficulty in condensing the great volume of material gathered over the years has been enormous. Equally formidable has been the task of fitting together the pieces of the puzzle and communicating the results. I hope that this book will have brought a measure of clarity to the mass of heretofore confusing evidence.

MICHAEL EDDOWES
New York
June 1977

PART 3:

APPENDICES

A

The Historic Diary

The following pages were handwritten in English presumably by 'Oswald,' and they are reproduced page by page as written. The left-hand numbers for some reason are out of sequence, although the right-hand numbers refer correctly to the order of the pages. According to the Warren Report that part of the diary relating to the first two months in Moscow was not written until the diarist had arrived in Minsk. The fact that the diary was found in 'Oswald's' rooming house in Dallas after the assassination indicates that the information therein is what was intended to be believed (disinformation) about the real Oswald and his activities. The Warren Commission treats its contents as the truth.

HISTORIC DIARY

30   From Oct. 16 1959 Arrival—   Leaveing

1959   1st Page

Oct. 16. Arrive from Helsinki by train; am met by Intourest Repre. and in car to Hotel "Berlin". Reges. as. "stedet" 5 day Lux. tourist. Ticket.) Meet my Intorist guied Rimma Sherikova I explain to her I wish to appli. for Rus. citizenship. She is flabbergassed, but aggrees to help. She checks with her boss, main office Intour; than helps me add. a letter to Sup. Sovit asking for citizenship, mean while boss telephons passport & Visa office and notifies them about me.

Oct. 17—Rimma meets me for Intourist sighseeing says we must contin. with this although I am too nevous she is "sure" I'll have an anserwer soon. Asks me about myself and my reasons for doing this. I explaine I am a communist, ect. She is politly sym. but uneasy now. She tries to be a friend to me, she feels sorry for me I am someth. new.

Sun Oct. 18. My 20th birthday, we visit exhib. in morning and in the afternoon The Lenin-Stalin tomb. She gives me a present Book "Ideot" by Dostoevski.

Oct. 19 Tourism. Am anxious since my visa is good for five days only and still no word from auth. about my reqest.

Oct. 20. Rimmer in the afternoon says Intourist was notified by the pass & visa dept. that they want to see me I am excited greatly by this news.

Oct. 21. (mor) Meeting with single offial. Balding stout, black suit fairly. good English, askes what do I want?, I say Sovite citizenship, he ask why I give vauge answers about "Great Soviet Union" He tells me "USSR only great in Literature wants me to go back home" I am stunned I reiterate, he says he shall check and let me know whether my visa will be (extended it exipiers today)

Eve. 6.00 Recive word from police official. I must leave country tonight at. 8.00 P.M. as visa expirs. I am shocked! My dreams! I retire to my room. I have $ 100. left. I have waited for 2 year to be accepted. My fondes dreams are shattered because of a petty offial; because of bad planning I planned to much!

7.00 P.M. I decide to end it. Soak rist in cold water to numb the pain. Then slash my left rist. Than plaug wrist into bathtub of hot water. I think "when Rimma comes at 8. to find me dead it will be a great shock. somewhere, a violin plays, as I

31
2nd page   DIARY

Oct 21. (con.): wacth my life whirl away. I think to myself. "how easy
to die" and "a sweet death, (to violins) about 8.00 Rimma finds me unconscious (bathtub water a rich red color) she screams (I remember
that) and runs for help. Amulance comes, am taken to hospital where
five stitches are put in my wrist. Poor Rimmea stays by my side an interrpator (my Russian is still very bad) far into the night, I tell her "go
home" (my mood is bad) but she stays, she is "my friend" She has a
strong will only at this moment I notice she is preety

Oct. 22. Hospital I am in a small room with about 12 others (sick persons.) 2 ordalies and a nurse the room is very drab as well as the
breakfast. Only after prolonged (2 hours) observation of the other pat.
do I relize I am in the Insanity ward. This relization disquits me.
Later in afternoon I am visited by Rimma, she comes in with two doctors, as interr she must ask me medical questions; Did you know what
you were doing? Ans. yes Did you blackout? No. ect. I than comp.
about poor food the doctors laugh app. this is a good sign Later they
leave, I am alone with Rimma (amonst the mentaly ill) she encourgest
me and scolds me she says she will help me get trasfered to another section of Hos. (not for insane) where food is good.

Oct. 23. Transfered to irdinary ward, (airy, good food.) but nurses
suspious of me.) they know).

Afternoon. I am visited by Rosa Agafonova of the hotel, tourist office
who askes about my health, very beauitiful, excelant Eng., very merry
and kind, she makes me very glad to be alive. Later Rimma vists

Oct. 24 Hospital routine, Rimma visits me in afternoon

Oct. 25 Hospital routine, Rimma visits me in afternoon

Oct. 26 An elderly American at the hospital grow suspious about me
for some reason. because at Embassy I told him I had not registered as
most tourist and I am in general evasive about my presence in Moscow
and at hospital.

Afternoon Rimma visits.

Oct. 27 Stiches are taken out by doctor with "dull" scisor

    Mo

Wed Oct. 28 Leave hospital in intorist car. with Rimma for Hotel
"Berlin" later I change hotels to "Metropole" all cloths packed, and

money from my room (to the last kopeek) returned as well as watch, ring. Ludmilla Dimitrova (Intorist office head) and Rosa invite me to come and sit and take with them any time. I get lonesome at new hotel. They feel sorry for me.

Oct. 28(con.) Rimma notifies me that, pass & registration office whshes
to see me about my future. Later Rimma and car pick me up and we
enter the officies to find four offials waiting for me (all unknown to me)
They ask How my arm is, I say O.K., They ask "Do you want to go to
your homeland. I say no I want Sovite citizen. I say I want to reside in
the Soviet Union. They say they will see about that. Than they ask me
about the lone offial with whom I spoke in the first place (appar. he
did not pass along my request at all but thought to simply get rid of me
by not extending my Soviet visa. At the time I requested it) I desqribe
him (they make notes) (what papers do you have to show who and
what you are? I give them my discharre papers from the Marine
Corps. They say wait for our ans. I ask how long? Not soon. Later
Rimma comes to check on me. I feel insulted and insult her.

Oct. 29. Hotel Room 214 Metropole Hotel. I wait. I worry I eat once,
stay next to phone worry I keep fully dressed

Oct. 31. I make my dision. Getting passport at 12"00 I meet and talk
with Rimma for a few minutes she says: stay in your room and eat
well, I don't tell her about what I intend to do since I know she would
not approve. After she leaves I wait a few minutes and then I catch a
taxi, "American Embassy" I say. 12"30, I arrive American Embassy, I
walk in and say to the receptionist 'I would like to see the Consular"
she points at a large lager and says "If you are a tourist please register". I take out my American passport and lay it in the desk, I have
come to dissolve my American citizenship. I saymatter-of-factly she
rises and enters the office of Richard Snyder American Head Consular
in Moscow at that time. He invites me to sit down. He finishes a letter
he is typing and then ask what he can do for me. I tell him I have
dicided to take Soviet citizenship and would like to leagly dissolve my
U.S. citizenship. His assistant (now *Head* Consular) McVickers looks
up from his work. Snyder takes down personall Information, ask questions

Sat. Oct 31 (con) warnes me not to take any steps before the soviets except me, say I am a "fool", and says the dissolution papers are along time in preparing (In other words refuses to allow me at that time to dissolve U.S. citiz. I state "my mind is make up" From this day forward I consider myself no citizen of the U.S.A. I spend 40 minutes at the Embassy before Snyder says 'now unless you wish to expound on your maxist belifes you can go." I wish to disolve U.S. citiz, not today he says in effect. I leave Embassy, elated at this showdown, returning to my hotel I feel now my enorgies are not spent in vain. I'm sure Russians will except me after this sign of my faith in them. 2:00 a knock, a reporter by the name of Goldstene wants an interview I'm flabbergassed "how did you find out? The Embassy called us" He said. I send him away I sit and relize this is one way to bring pressure on me. By notifying my relations in U.S. through the newspapers. Although they would say "ifs for the public record." A half hour later another reporter Miss Mosby comes. I answere a few quick questions after refusing an interviwe. I am surprised at the interest. I get phone calls from "Time" at night a phone call from the States I refuse all calles without finding out who's it from. I feel non-deplused because of the attention 10:00 I retire.

Nov. 1—more reporters, 3 phone calls from brother & mother, now I feel slightly axzillarated, not so lonly.

Nov-2-15 Days of utter loneliness I refuse all reports phone calls I remaine in my room, I am racked with dsyentary.

Nov 15—I decide to give an interview, I have Miss Mosbys card so I call her. She drives right over. I give my story, allow pictures, later story is distorted, sent without my perrmission, that is: before I ever saw and O.K.'ed her story. Again I feel slightly better because of the attention

Nov. 16. A Russian official comes to my room askes how I am. Notifies me I can remain in USSR till some solution in found with what to do with me, it is comforting news for me.

Nov 17—Dec. 30 I have bought myself two self-teaching Russian Lan. Books I force myself to study 8 hours a day I sit in my room and read and memorize words. All meals I take in my room. Rimmea arranged that. It is very cold on the streets so I rarley go outside at all for this month and a-half I see no one speak to no-one accept every-now-and-than Rimmea, who calls the ministry about me. Have they forgotten?, During December I paid no money to the hotel, but Rimmer told Hotel I was expecting alot of money from USA. I have $28 left. This month I was called to the passport office and met 3 new offials who asked me the same questions I ans. a month before. They appear not to know me at all.

Dec 31. New Yearseve, I spend in the company of Rosa Agafoneva at the Hotel Berlin, she has the duty. I sit with her until past mignight, she gives me a small 'Boratin', clown, for a New Years present She is very nice I found out only recently she is married, has small sone who was born crippled, that is why she is so strangely tender and compeling.

Jan 1-4 No change in routine

Jan 4. I am called to passport office and finilly given a Soviet document not the soviet citizenship as I so wanted, only a Residence document, not even for foringners but a paper called 'for those *without* citizenship.' Still I am happy. The offial says they are sending me to the city of 'Minsk' I ask 'is that in Siberia? He only laughes. he also tells me that they have arranged for me to recive some money through the Red Cross. to pay my hotel bills and expensis. I thank the gentelmen and leave later in the afternoon I see Rimma 'she asks are you happy' 'yes'

Jan. 5. I go to Red Cross in Moscow for money with Interrupter (a new one) I recive 5000. rubles a huge sum!! Later in Mink I am to earn 70 rubles a month at the factory.

Jan. 7. I leave Moscow by train for Minsk, Belorussia. My hotel bill was 2200, rubles and the train ticket to Minsk 150 rubles so I have alot of money & hope. I wrote my brother & mother letters in which I said 'I do not wish to every contact you again.' I am beginning anew life and I don't want *any part* of the old'.

Jan 7. Arrive in Minsk, met by 2 women Red Cross workers We go to Hotel "Minsk" I take room, and meet Rosa and Stellina two persons from intourist in hotel who speak English Stellina is in 40's nice married young child, Rosa about 23 blond attractive unmarried Excellant English, we attract each other at once.

Jan 8. I meet the city mayor, comrade Shrapof, who welcomes me to Minsk promisis a rent-free apartment "soon" and warns me about "uncultured persons" who somethimes insult foriengers. My interputer: Roman Detkof. Head For. Tech Instit. next door.

Jan. 10. The day to myself I walk through city, very nice.

Jan. 11 I vist Minsk radio factory where I shall work. There I meet Argentinian Immigrant Alexander Zeger Born a Polish Jew. Immi to Argen. in 1938 and back to Polish homeland (now part of Belo.) in 1955 speaks English with Amer. accent he worked for Amer. com. in Argen. He is Head of a Dept. a quialified Engenier, in late 40's mild mannered likable He seems to want to tell me somet. I show him my tempor. docum. and say soon I shall have Russ. citiz. Jan. 13-16 I work as a "checker" metal worker, pay: 700 rubles a month, work very easy, I am learning Russian quickly Now, Everyone is very freindly and kind. I meet many young Russian workers my own age they have varied personatities all wish to know about me even offer to hold a mass meeting so I can say. I refuse politly. At night I take Rosa to the thearter, movie or operor almost every day I'm living big and am very satisfied. I recive a check from the Red Cross every 5th of the month "to help." The check is 700 rubles. Therefore every month I make 1400. R. about the same as the Director of the factory! Zeger observes me during this time I don't like: picture of Lenin which watchs frome its place of honour and phy. training at 11.-11.10 each morning (complusery). for all. (shades of H.G. Wells!!)

March 16. I recive a small flat one-room kicten-bath near the factory (8 min. walk) with splendid view from 2 balconies of the river, almost rent free (60. rub. a mon.) it is a Russians dream.

March 17-April 31—work, I have lost contact with Rosa after my house moving. I meet Pavil Golovacha. A yonuge man my age friendly very intelligent a exalant radio techniction his father is Gen. Golovacha Commander of Northwestenr Siberia. Twice hero of USSR in W.W.2.

May 1—May Day came as my first holiday all factories Ect. closed after sptacular military parade all workers parad past reviewing star..l waving flags and picutres of Mr. K. ect. I follow the Amer. custom of marking a Holiday by sleeping in in the morning. At night I visit with the Zegers daughters at an party throw by them about 40 people came many of Argentine origen we dance and play around and drink until 2 am. when party breaks up. Leonara Zeger oldest dau. 26 formally married, now divorced, a talented singer. Anita Zeger 20 very gay, not so attractive but we hit it off. Her Boy-friend Alferd is a Hungarian chap, silent and brooding, not at all like Anita. Zeber advised me to go back to U. S. A. its the first voice of oppossition I have heard. I respect Zeger, he has seen the world. He says many things, and relats many things I do not know about the U. S. S. R. I begin to feel uneasy inside, its true! June-July Summer months of green beauty, pine forest very deep. I enjoy many Sundays in the enviorments of Minsk. with the Zegers who have a car "mos.vick" Alfred always goes along with Anita, Leonara seems to have no permanet Boy-friend, but many admirirs. She has a beautiful Spanish figure, long black hair, like Anita. I never pay much atten. to her shes too old for me she seemes to dislike my lack of attention for some reason. She is high strung. I have become habituatated to a small cafe which is where I dine in the evening the food is generally poor and always eactly the same, menue in any cafe, at any point in the city. The food is cheap and I dont really care about quiality after three years in the U.S.M.C.

Aug-Sept As my Russian improves I become increasingly conscious of just what sort of a sociaty I live in. Mass gymnastics, compulsary after work meeting, usually political information meeting. Complusary attendance at lectures and the sending of the entire shop colletive (except me) to pick potatoes on a Sunday, at a State collective farm. A "patroict duty" to bring in the harvest. The opions of the workers (unvoiced) are that its a great pain in the neck. They don't seem to be esspicialy enthusiastic about any of the "collective" duties a natural feeling. I am increasingly aware of the presence, in all thing, of Lebizen, shop party secretary, fat, fortyish, and jovial on the outside. He is a no-nonsense party regular.

Oct. The coming of Fall, my dread of a new Russian winter, are mellowed in splendid golds and reds of fall in Belorussia plums peachs appricots and cherrys abound for these last fall weeks I am a healthy brown color and stuffed with fresh fruit. (at other times of the year unobtainable)

Oct. 18 my 21st birthday see's Rosa, Pavil, Ella at a small party at my place Ella very attractive Russian Jew I have been going walking with lately, works at the radio factory also. Rosa and Ella are jelous of each other it brings a warm feeling to me. Both are at my place for the first time. Ella and Pavil both give ask-tray's (I don't smoke) we have a laugh.

Nov. Finds the approach of winter now. A growing lonliness overtakes me in spite of my conquest of Ennatachina a girl from Riga, studying at the music conservorie in Minsk. After an affair which last a few weeks we part.

Nov. 15 in Nov. I make the acquaintaces of four girls rooming at the For. Ian. domitory in room 212. Nell is very interesting, so is Tomka, Tomis and Alla. I usually go to the institute domatory with a friend of mine who speaks english very well. Eraich Titov is in the forth year at the medical institute. Very bright fellow At the domatory we 6 sit and talk for hours in english

Dec

1 I am having a light affair with Nell Korobka.

Jan 1

New Years I spend at home of Ella Germain I think I'm in love with her. She has refused my more dishonourable advanis, we drink and eat in the presenec of her family in a very hospitable atmosfere. Later I go home drunk and happy. Passing the river homeward, I decide to propose to Ella.

Jan. 2. After a pleasant handin-hand walk to the local cinima we come home, standing on the doorstep I propose's She hesitates than refuses, my love is real but she has none for me. Her reason besides lack of love; I am american and someday might be arrested simply because of that example Polish Inlervention in the 20's. led to arrest of all people in the Soviet Union of polish oregen "you understand the world situation there is too much against you and you don't even know it" I am stunned she snickers at my awkarness in turning to go (I am too stunned too think!) I realize she was never serious with me but only exploited my being an american, in order to get the envy of the other girls who consider me different from the Russian Boys. I am misarable!

Jan 3. I am miserable about Ella. I love her but what can I do? It is the state of fear which was alway in the Soviet Union.

Jan. 4. On year after I recived the residence document I am called in to the passport office and asked if I want citizenship (Russian) I say no simply extend my residental passport to agree and my document is extended until Jan 4. 1962

Jan-4-31 I am stating to reconsider my disire about staying. The work is drab the money I get has nowhere to be spent. No nightclubs or bowling allys no places of recreation accept the trade union dances I have have had enough.

Feb. 1st Make my first request to American Embassy, Moscow for re-considering my position, I stated "I would like to go back to U.S."

Feb. 28th I recive letter from Embassy. Richard E. Sneyder stated "I could come in for an interview anytime I wanted."

March 1-16 I now live in a state of expectation about going back to the U.S. I confided with Zeger he supports my judgment but warnes me not to tell any Russians about my desire to reture. I understade now why.

March 17—I and Erich went to trade union dance. Boring but at the last hour I am introduced to a girl with a French hair-do and red-dress with white slipper I dance with her. than ask to show her home I do, along with 5 other admirares. Her name is Marina. We like each other right away she gives me her phone number and departs home with an not-so-new freiend in a taxi, I walk home.

March-18-31-We walk I talk a little about myself she talks alot about herself. her name is Marina N. Prosakoba

Apr: 1st-30 We are going steady and I decide I must have her, she puts me off so on April 14 I propose, she accepts.

April 3', after a 7 day delay at the marraige beaure because of my unusual passport they allow us to registra as man & wife two of Marinas girl friends act as bridesmaids. We are married at her aunts home we have a dinner reception for about 20 friends and neboribor who wish us happiness (in spite of my origin and accept) which was in general rather disquiting to any Russian since for. are very rare in the soviet union even tourist. after an evening of eating and drinking in which uncle Wooser started a fright and the fuse blow on an overloaded circite We take our leave and walk the 15 minutes to our home. We lived near each other. at midnight we were home.

1st

May Day 1961. Found us thinking about our future. Inspite of fact I married Marina to hurt Ella I found myself in love with Marina.

May — The trasistion of changing full love from Ella to Marina was very painfull esp. as I saw Ella almost every day at the factory but as the days and weeks went by I adjusted more and more my wife mentaly. I still hadn't told my wife of my desire to return to US. She is maddly in love with me from the very start, boat rides on Lake Minsk walks throught the parks evening at home or at Aunt Valia's place mark May.

June — A continuence of May, except. that; we draw closer and closer, and I think very little now of Ella. in the last days of this month I revele my longing to return to America. My wife is slightly startled. But than encourages me to do what I wish to do.

July — I decived to take my two week vacation and travel to Moscow (without police permission) to the American Embassy to see about getting my U.S. passport back and make arrangements for my wife to enter the U.S. with me.

July 8 — I fly by plane to Minsk on a i1-20, 2 hrs 20m later after taking a tearful and anxiou parting from my wife I arrive in Moscow departing by bus. From the airfield I arrive in the center of the city. Making my way through heavy traffic I don't come in sight of the embassy until 3:00 in the afternoon. Its Saturday what if they are closed? Entering I find the offices empty but mange to contact Snyder on the phone (since all embassy personal live in the same building) he comes down to greet me shake my hand after interview he advised he to come in first thing mon.

(see—July 8-13)

July 8. Interview July 9 recive passport; call Marina to Moscow also.

July 14. I and Marina returen to Minsk.

July 15. Marina at work, is shocked to find out ther everyone knows she entered the U. S. embassy. They were called at her place of work from some officials in Moscow." The boses hold a meeting and give her a strong browbeating. The first of many indocrinations.

July 15 Aug 20. we have found out which blanks and certifikates are necessceary to apply—for a exit visa they number about 20 papers; Birth certificates affidavite photos ect. On Aug 20th we give the papers out they say it will be 3 ½ months before we know wheather they'll let us go or not. In the meantime Marina has had to stade 4 different meeting at the place of work held by her Boss's at the direction of "someone" by phone. The young comm. leauge headquthers also called about her and she had to go see them for 1 ½ hrs. The purpose (expressed) is to disaude her from going to the U.S.A., Net effect: Make her more stubborn about wanting to go Marina is pregnet, we only hope that the visas come through soon.

Aug 21-Sept 1 — I make expected trips to the passport & visa office also to ministry of for. affairs in Minsk, also Min. of Interal affairs, all of which have a say in the granting of a visa. I extracked promises of quick attention to US.

Sept-Oct 18. No word from Min. (They'll call us.") Marina leaves Minsk by train on vaction to the city of Khkov in the Urals to vist an aunt for 4 weeks. During this time I am lonely but I and Erich got to the dances and public places for enitanment. I havent done this in quite a few months now. I spend my birthday alone at the opera watching my favoriot "Queen of Spades." I am 22 years old.

Nov-2 Marina arrives back, radient, with several jars of preserses for me from her aunt in Khkov.

Nov-Dec. Now we are becoming anoid about the delay Marina is beginning to waiver about going to the US. Probably from the strain and her being pregrate, still we quarrel and so things are not to bright esp. with the approach of the hard Russian winter.

Dec 25th Xmas Day Tues. Marina is called to the passport & visa office. She is told we have been granted Soviet exit visa's. She fills out the completing blank and then comes home with the news. Its great (I think!) New Years, we spend at the Zeger's at a dinner party at midnight. attended by 6 other persons.

Jan.4. I am called to the passport office since my Residenceal passport expires today, since I now have a US. passport in my possition I am given a totly new resid. pass. called, "Pass for Forin," and since they have given US permission to leave, and know we shall, good to July 5, 1962.

Jan 15.

Feb. 15. Days of cold Russian winter. But we feel fine. Marina is supposed to have baby on March 1st.

Feb 15 — Dawn. Marina wakes me. Its her time. At 9:00 we arrive at
the hospital I leave her in care of nurses and leave to go to work. 10:00
Marina has a baby girl. when I vist the hospital at 500 after work, I
am given news. We both wanted a boy. Marina feels well, baby girl,
OK.

Feb 23 Maria leaves hospital I see June for first time.

Feb. 28 I go to registra (as prespibed by law) the baby. I want her
name to be June Marina Oswald. But those Beaurcrats say her middle
name must be the same as my first. A Russian custom support by a
law. I refuse to have her name written as "June Lee". They promise to
call the city ministry (city hall) and find out in this case since I do have
an U.S. passport. Feb. 29. I am told that nobody knows what to do exactly, but everyone agrees "Go ahead and do it, "Po-Russki." Name:
June Lee

March. The last commiques are exchanged between myself and Embassy. letters are always arriving from my mother and brother in the
U.S. I have still not told Erich who is my oldest existing aquaintance,
that we are going to the State, he's o.k. but I'm afriad he is too good a
young communist leage member so I'll wait till last min.

March 24—Marina quits her job in the formal fashion.

March 26 — I recive a letter from Immigration & Natur. service at
San Antonio, Texas, that Marina has had her visa petition to the U.S.
(Approved!!) The last document. Now we only have to wait for the
U.S. Embassy to recive their copy of the approval so they can officially
give the go ahead.

March 27 I recive a letter from a Mr. Philles (a employ. of my mother,
pleging to support my wife in case of need.

April—

B

Time Line:
Oswald and 'Oswald'

1956	24 Oct.	Enlisted in Marines.
1959	4 Mar.	Applied for entrance to Swiss college.
	3 Sept.	Marine medical examination.
	4 Sept.	Applied for passport.
	10 Sept.	Passport issued.
	11 Sept.	Discharged from Marines.
	14 Sept.	Arrived mother's home, Fort Worth.
	17 Sept.	Arrived New Orleans.
	20 Sept.	Sailed for Soviet Union.
	16 Oct.	Arrived Moscow.
	21 Oct.	Attempted suicide? Admitted Botkin Hospital?
	28 Oct.	'Oswald' released from hospital.
	31 Oct.	Visited U.S. Embassy, Moscow, to renounce U.S. citizenship.
1960	4 Jan.	Issued Soviet identity document.
	7 Jan.	Sent to Minsk to work in radio factory.
	3 June	Hoover's memo; warning against imposture.
1961	13 Feb.	Wrote Embassy in Moscow asking for return of passport.
	17 Mar.	Met Marina at dance; Minsk.
	31 Mar.	Hickey's memo; evidence of imposture and

		warning against return of passport to wrong man.
	30 Apr.	Married Marina
	10 July	'Oswald' given Oswald's passport at U.S. Embassy.
	11 July	Rusk's memo to U.S. Embassy in Moscow; warning against dealing with the wrong man.
1962	4 June	Departed for U.S. with wife and baby June.
	14 June	Arrived Fort Worth, Texas.
	26 June	Interviewed by FBI, Fort Worth.
	17 July	Employed at Leslie Welding.
	Aug.	'Oswald' and Marina met George & Jeanne De Mohrenschildt.
	14 Aug.	Interviewed by FBI, Fort Worth. 'Oswald's' file given "closed status."
	8/9 Oct.	Departed Fort Worth for Dallas. Opened P.O. Box.
	12 Oct.	Employed Jaggars-Chiles-Stovall.
	16 Oct.	Kennedy received first hard information on missile sites in Cuba.
	16 Oct.	'Oswald' executed work for Army Map Service.
1963	22 Feb.	'Oswald' and Marina met Ruth Paine.
	20 Mar.	Rifle & revolver dispatched to Hidell at 'Oswald's' P.O. Box, Dallas.
	6 Apr.	Dismissed, Jaggars-Chiles-Stovall.
	10 Apr.	Shot at General Walker.
	24 Apr.	Vice President Johnson announced Kennedy's visit to Dallas in fall. 'Oswald' departed Dallas alone for New Orleans.
	11 May	Ruth drove Marina and June to New Orleans.
	26 May to 5 June	'Oswald' printed literature for New Orleans chapter FPCC in name of Osborne.
	23 June	'Oswald' obtained passport in name of Oswald.
	9 Aug.	Arrested by New Orleans police.

10 Aug.	Interviewed by FBI. Omitted residency in Soviet Union.
13 Sept.	Dallas papers announced Kennedy's one-day Texas visit on 21 or 22 November. Frazier obtained work at Depository.
17 Sept.	Obtained in-transit tourist card for Mexico.
23 Sept.	Ruth, Marina, and June to Irving.
24 Sept.	'Oswald' disappeared for night.
25 Sept.	Departed New Orleans for Houston.
26 Sept.	Dallas press announced Kennedy's two-day Texas visit.
	'Oswald' departed Houston for Nuevo Laredo. Departed Nuevo Laredo with Albert Osborne for Mexico City.
27 Sept. to 2 Oct.	Arrived Mexico City. Visited Soviet Embassy.
3 Oct.	'Oswald' arrived Dallas from Mexico City.
4 Oct.	Applied for employment on Industrial Blvd., one of three possible motorcade routes.
14 Oct.	Mrs. Robert's coffee klatch; Ruth called Depository on behalf of 'Oswald.' 'Oswald' applied for employment on Inwood Road, on return motorcade route.
15 Oct.	Took employment at Texas School Book Depository, covering two of three possible motorcade routes.
1 Nov.	Rented P.O. Box. Dallas
	FBI agent interviewed Marina & Ruth; asked for 'Oswald's' address.
5 Nov.	Agent interviewed Marina & Ruth; asked again for 'Oswald's' address.
9 Nov.	'Oswald' reported in by letter to Soviet Consulate in Washington, D.C.
22 Nov.	Killed President Kennedy and Patrolman Tippit.
24 Nov.	Killed by Jack Ruby.
	Autopsy on 'Oswald's' body performed.
25 Nov.	A.M. FBI inspected body in funeral parlor.
	P.M. 'Oswald's' body buried.

C

Soviets Involved
in the Assassination

Because of the number of possibly confusing Russian names appearing in this book, this list has been compiled. The dates shown are times of direct or indirect involvement of Soviet personnel in the plot to assassinate the President.

LAST NAME UNKNOWN, Alek,
Soviet citizen and member of Department 13. Moscow and Minsk, Russia, and the United States. 1959-1963. The assassin.

PRUSAKOVA, Marina Nichilayeva,
Niece of Colonel Prusakov, member of Komsomol, and wife of the assassin. 1959-1963.

PRUSAKOV, Ilya,
Colonel in the Soviet Secret Police (MVD). Stationed in Minsk, Russia. 1959-1962.

AKSENOV, Nicolay,
Colonel in the Soviet Secret Police (MVD). Stationed in Minsk, Russia. 1959-1962.

NOSENKO, Yuri Ivanovich,
KGB officer stationed at the KGB Center in Moscow, Russia. 1959-1964.

SHITOV, Aleksander I.,
Veteran clandestine KGB officer stationed at the Soviet Embassy in Havana, Cuba, under the alias of Aleksandr I. ALEKSEEV, 1959-1962. In the same alias, Ambassador to Cuba. 1962-1968.

KOSTIN, Valeri Dmitrevich,
Clandestine KGB officer possibly stationed at the Soviet embassies in Havana or Mexico City, Mexico. September and October 1963.

KOSTIKOV, Valeri Vladimirovich,
Clandestine KGB officer stationed at the Soviet Embassy and Consulate in Mexico City. Veteran member of Department 13, the sabotage and assassination squad of the KGB. September and October 1963.

YATSKOV, Paul Antonovich,
Clandestine KGB officer stationed at the Soviet Embassy and Consulate in Mexico City. September and October 1963.

REZNICHENKO, N.,
Senior Consul at the Soviet Consulate in Washington, D.C., U.S.A. June 1962-November 1963.

SHAPKIN, Georgiy Mikhaylovich,
Third Secretary to Soviet Consulate, Washington, D.C. Appointed October 1959. Withdrawn December 1963.

D

An Analysis of Heights

Below are the details of Oswald's and 'Oswald's' heights from 24 October 1956 to 24 November 1963. Entries marked with an asterisk indicate occasions when he was measured. The two occasions when the Warren Commission made available photographs of the height measured *against a scale* are marked with a double asterisk.

*1. 24 October 1956. When just 17 years of age, Oswald enlisted in the Marine Corps and his height was measured as 5'8" (XIX.615).

**2. 28 December 1956. On completion of initial Marine training Oswald was measured against a scale and recorded as 5'9" (XIX.717).

3. 4 March 1959. Oswald applied for admission to the Albert Schweitzer College in Switzerland to attend the spring term in 1960, and on the application form he gave his height as 5'11" (XVI.622).

*4. 3 September 1959. At Santa Ana, California, Oswald underwent a full medical examination prior to his release from the Marines and transfer to the inactive reserve. His height was measured by Marine doctor Vincent as 71" (XIX.584.XXIII.744).

5. 4 September 1959. Oswald applied for a passport and gave his height as 5'11" (XXII.77).

6. 10 September 1959. Oswald was issued a passport recording his height as 5'11" (XVIII.161).

*7. 11 September 1959. At Santa Ana, Oswald was issued a Department of Defense Identification card by Marine officer Ayers, who measured his height as 71" (WR.616).

8. 14 September 1959. At the Fort Worth, Texas, Local Board, Oswald was issued a Marine Selective Service System Registration card on which his height was recorded by Marine official Burger as 5'11" (XXIII.743.WR.615).

9. 12 October 1959. At the Fort Worth Local Board, Oswald's height was recorded as (approx.) 5'11" on an Armed Forces registration card by Marine Registrar Sheridan (XXIII.744).

In June 1962, 'Oswald' entered the United States using Oswald's original passport showing the bearer's height to be 5'11". Thereafter, 'Oswald' always gave his actual height of 5'9" except when he wanted to deceive the FBI agents in Fort Worth in June 1962, and to obtain a new passport in New Orleans in June 1963, and when it was clear he would not be measured.

10. 26 June 1962. 'Oswald' was interviewed by Special Agents Carter and Fain of the FBI in Fort Worth, Texas. The written report on this interview under the heading, "From observation and interrogation," is a physical description of "Lee Harvey Oswald" giving his height as 5'11" (XVII.730). In reply to their question about the height of his wife, 'Oswald' also added two inches to her height, saying that she was 5'5" (XVII.730). Her height as shown in her Russian passport issued on 11 January 1962 was 160cm (5'3") (XVI.138).

11. 13 July 1962. 'Oswald' completed an application form for employment at Leslie Welding Company, Fort Worth, stating his height as 5'9" (XXIV.885).

12. 14 August 1962. 'Oswald' was reinterviewed in Fort Worth by FBI agents Fain and Brown. He did not correct the false heights that he had given at the first interview, and his file was then given a "closed status."

13. 9 October 1962. 'Oswald' registered with the Texas Employment Commission, stating his height as 5'9" (XIX.399).

14. 12 October 1962. 'Oswald' completed an employment questionnaire at Jaggars-Chiles-Stovall, Dallas, stating his height as 5'9" (XVII.156).

15. April 1963. 'Oswald' registered with the local Department of Labor, New Orleans, stating his height as 5'9" (XXI.282).

16. 9 May 1963. 'Oswald' completed an application for employment at William B. Reily Company, New Orleans, stating his height as 5'9" (XXIV.902).

17. 10 May 1963. 'Oswald's' employee's Withholding Exemption

Certificate recorded ex-Marine Oswald's height as 5'9" (XXIV.905).

18. 24 June 1963. 'Oswald' applied in New Orleans for a new passport in the name of Lee Harvey Oswald and on the application form stated his height as 5'11" (XVII.666). (The application had to tally with the original passport issued to Lee Harvey Oswald to avoid complications and perhaps suspicion at the Passport Office in Washington.)

19. 25 June 1963. 'Oswald' was issued a new passport in the name of Lee Harvey Oswald, stating his height as 5'11" (XXIII.819).

**20. 9 August 1963. 'Oswald' was arrested by the New Orleans police for causing a minor disturbance on the street, and the Police Identification Bureau measured him against a scale and recorded his height as 5'9" (XXII.820.828).

21. 10 August 1963. 'Oswald' was interviewed by FBI Agent Quigley at the New Orleans police station. Under "Physical description obtained by observation and interrogation," Quigley recorded the height as 5'9" (XVII.762).

22. 4 October 1963. 'Oswald' completed an application form for Padgett Printing Company, Dallas, stating his height as 5'9"(XX.3).

23. 14 October 1963. 'Oswald' completed an application form for Weiner Lumber Company, Dallas, stating his height as 5'9" (omitted from the Warren Exhibits).

24. 15 October 1963. 'Oswald' completed an application form at the Texas School Book Depository, Dallas, stating his height as 5'9" (XVII.210).

25. 9 November 1963. 'Oswald' partially filled in an application for a driver's license, stating his height as 5'9" (XVI.483).

*26. 22 November 1963. 'Oswald' was arrested by the Dallas police and measured. His height was recorded as 5'9½" (XVII.285). The police found in his wallet a 1959 Marine Selective Service System Registration card, which recorded the height of Marine Oswald as 5'11" (WR.615), together with a Department of Defense Identification card recording his height as 5'11" (WR.616). Also in his wallet they found a counterfeit Selective Service System Registration card in the fictitious name of "Alek James Hidell" on which the height of Hidell was recorded as 5'9" (XVII.682-683. WR.615).

27. 22 November 1963. At the Dallas police station FBI Agent
Clements interviewed 'Oswald' for the purpose of obtaining "descriptive and biographical" data. Clements recorded the height of
"Lee Harvey Oswald" as 5'9" (WR.614). Clements also observed
and recorded the contents of the three cards mentioned in No. 26
above.

*28. 24 November 1963. An autopsy was performed on the body of
'Oswald' by two doctors at Parkland Hospital, Dallas. The report
of the autopsy recorded the length of the corpse as 5'9"
(XXVI.521).

The Warren Report states correctly that Lee Harvey Oswald was
just 17 years old and 5'8" when he enlisted in the Marines in October
1956 and was 5'9" when he was arrested (WR.681.144) but says *nothing* about his height of 5'11" when released from the Marines in September 1959 (WR.688-689).

The Exhibits do not include a photographic record of the height of
5'11" recorded by Vincent and Ayers in September 1959, although a
Marine photograph of his height was taken on 28 December 1956 with
the usual readable scale at the back of his head showing 5'9". This appears prominently *twice* in the Exhibits (XIX.656.717).

A student of the Warren Report and the Exhibits would certainly be
misled by the omission of any mention of 5'11" in the Warren Report,
by the statement in the Warren Report that the assassin was Marine Oswald—5'9" in height, and by the two photographs in the Exhibits of
the 5'9" Marine Oswald which were taken in 1956. Students would
certainly assume that when Oswald was released from the Marines in
1959 he was 5'9".

Height is the most important item of physical data, and it takes
pride of place at top left on the first page of the Marine medical
records. It is not unreasonable to suppose that the 1959 photographic
recordings of the height 5'11" were made against a scale and that these
were removed from the Marine records before the records appeared in
the Exhibits.

The significant documents are reproduced in the following pages.

Oswald's height on entering the Marine Corps on 24 October 1956.

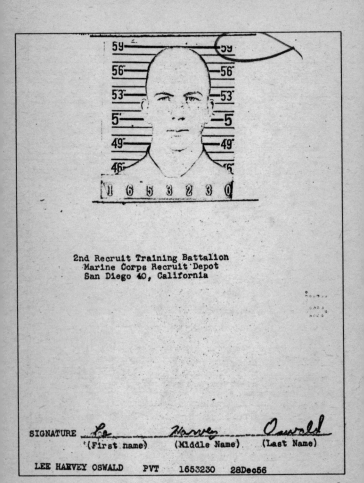

2nd Recruit Training Battalion
Marine Corps Recruit Depot
San Diego 40, California

SIGNATURE   *Lee*   *Harvey*   *Oswald*
    '(First name)   (Middle Name)   (Last Name)

LEE HARVEY OSWALD   PVT   1653230   28Dec56

Oswald's height ten weeks later on 28 December 1956.

Oswald's height on separating from the Marine Corps on 3 September 1959.

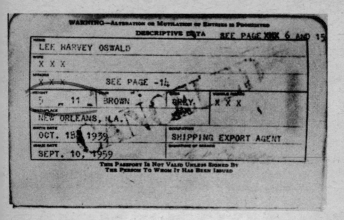

Marine Oswald's passport dated 10 September 1959.

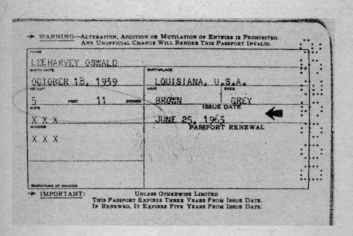

'Oswald's' passport dated 25 June 1963.

OSWALD furnished the following description of his wife:

Name	MARINA NICHILYENA OSWALD
Race	White
Sex	Female
Age	20
Birth Data	July 17, 1941, at Arxangles (city near the White Sea)
Height	5' 5"
Weight	105 lbs.
Eyes	Blue
Hair	Brown
Children	JUNE LEE OSWALD, age four months

The following description of OSWALD was obtained through observation and interrogation:

Name	LEE HARVEY OSWALD
Race	White
Sex	Male
Age	22
Birth Data	October 18, 1939, at New Orleans, Louisiana
Height	5' 11"
Weight	150 lbs.

From observation and questioning, OSWALD is described as follows:

Race	White
Sex	Male
Age	23
Date of birth	October 18, 1939
Place of birth	New Orleans, Louisiana (at time of arrest claimed from Cuba)
Height	5'9"
Weight	140 pounds
Build	Slender
Hair	Light brown
Eyes	Blue-hazel
Teeth	Good
Marital Status	Married, wife, MARINA OSWALD nee Prossa
Occupation	Mechanic
Military record	U. S. Marine Corps, October 24, 1956, to September 11, 1959, MSN 1653230, honorable discharge
Criminal record	Denies any
Residence	4907 Magazine Street, New Orleans, La.

OSWALD was advised questions were intended to obtain his complete physical description and background. Upon repetition of the question as to his present employment, he furnished same without further discussion.

Race	White
Sex	Male
Date of Birth	October 18, 1939
Place of Birth	New Orleans, Louisiana
Height	5'9"
Weight	140
Hair	Medium brown, worn medium length, needs haircut
Eyes	Blue-gray
Scars	No tattoos or permanent scars
Relatives	Mother - MARGUERITE OSWALD, unknown address, Arlington, Texas, practical nurse (has not seen for about one year)

FBI recordings of height. *Top:* By Agents Carter and Fain, 26 June 1963. *Middle:* By Agent Quigley, 10 August 1963. *Bottom:* By Agent Clements, 22 November 1963.

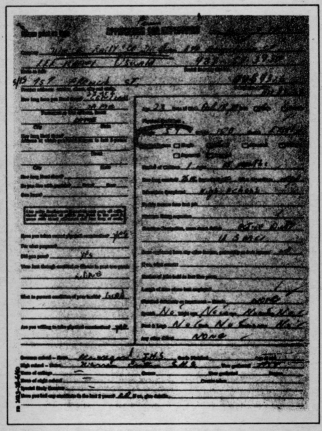

Job application for Wm. B. Reily & Co., Inc., 9 May 1963, New Orleans.

Job application for Padgett Printing Co., 4 October 1963, on Industrial Blvd., a location from which 'Oswald' could have shot the President had the motorcade used the alternate route. On reverse of application 'Oswald' gave his height as 5'9".

Job application for Wiener Lumber Co., 14 October 1963, on Inwood Rd., a location from which 'Oswald' could have shot the President.

E

The Warren Commission on Mexico City

The events occurring in Mexico City in September and October 1963 were deliberately obscured by the Warren Report in order to cover up conspiracy in the following ways.

The Warren Report almost completely obliterates the existance of 'Oswald's' bus companion, Albert Osborne *alias* John Howard Bowen, although the FBI with their unlimited resources conducted an interstate, intercountry, and intercontinental investigation into his activities.

The CIA could not satisfactorily answer the questions put to them by the Commission on the "American male" and 'Oswald,' and, in fact, glossed over the Commission's query about Kostin. On 17 September 1964, one week before the Report of the Commission was presented to President Johnson, the CIA wrote to Rankin (XXVI.149):

CENTRAL INTELLIGENCE AGENCY
WASHINGTON 25 D.C.

17 September 1964

MEMORANDUM FOR:

    Mr. J. Lee Rankin
    General Counsel
    President's Commission on the
    Assassination of President Kennedy

SUBJECT: Valeriy Vladimirovich KOSTIKOV

1. In reply to your request, I am forwarding information on Valeriy Vladimirovich KOSTIKOV, one of the Soviet officials

with whom Lee Harvey Oswald is believed to have dealt during his visit to Mexico City on 28 September-3 October 1963.

2. In his letter of 9 November to the Soviet Consulate in Washington, OSWALD wrote about his ". . . meetings with comrade Kostin in the Embassy of the Soviet Union, Mexico City, Mexico." There was no officer with that name listed as being a member of the Soviet representation in Mexico City during September and October 1963. "KOSTIN" is probably identical with Attaché KOSTIKOV, who was serving in the Consular Section of the Soviet Embassy in Mexico City at that time. KOSTIKOV is one of several Consular representatives who deal with visas and related matters. Pavel Antonovich YATSKOV, Second Secretary of Embassy, was in charge of the Consular Section at the time of Oswald's visit. Oswald may also have discussed his visa problems with YATSKOV and other members of the Consular Section.

3. KOSTIKOV and YATSKOV are known officers of the Soviet State Security Service (KGB). The State Security Service is the principal Soviet intelligence service, and is charged with espionage, counterintelligence and related matters.

4. It should be noted that Soviet intelligence and security officers such as KOSTIKOV and YATSKOV, when placed under official cover, are required to perform the routine and legitimate functions demanded by their cover positions in an embassy or consulate.

5. I hope that the information given above is responsive to the Commission's needs.

Richard Helms
Deputy Director for Plans

The CIA stated that Kostikov was one of the Soviet officials "with whom Lee Harvey Oswald is believed to have dealt during his visit," yet they knew from their own informant and photographs that the man who had dealt with Kostikov was not Lee Harvey Oswald but an approximately 35-year-old "American male" using the name "Lee Oswald." The CIA also succeeded in telescoping Kostin and Kostikov into one person. Accepting this view, the Warren Report states that 'Oswald,' when he referred to Kostin, was "undoubtedly" referring to Kostikov (WR.734). The CIA also telescoped the "American male" and 'Oswald' into one person, the Warren Report also accepting this convenient view. The CIA did not tell Rankin that Kostikov was suspected of being a veteran member of the assassination squad (Department 13) of the KGB.

The Warren Report maintains that Lee Harvey Oswald did not intend to use the false name, Lee, when traveling to, residing in, and returning from Mexico City. It says that the inserted comma on the Mexican intransit tourist card was possibly a clerical error, and that although Lee Harvey Oswald sometimes used the last name of "Lee" in Mexico, he also used the name of Lee Harvey Oswald. This is untrue. In the letter of 9 November 1963, the impostor himself wrote that unless he used his "real name" he could not stay longer in Mexico City. The only time the last name, Oswald, was used in Mexico was when it was used by 'Oswald's' confederate, the approximately 35-year-old "American male" at the Soviet Consulate in Mexico City. It is possible, of course, that 'Oswald' used the name Lee Harvey Oswald when having his secret meetings with Kostin.

No attempt was made by the Warren Commission, the FBI, or any agency to discover the identity of the "American male," although through their informant and surveillance cameras, the CIA knew his physical appearance and the dates on which he had been in Mexico City. All the photographs except one of the "American male" were committed to the National Archives and do not appear in the Exhibits to the Warren Report.

On two dates in mid-October, the CIA warned the FBI of the presence of the "American male" at the Soviet Consulate in Mexico City, giving the name Lee Oswald; the FBI did nothing about it, although the CIA memoranda gave his physical description which in no way resembled either of the two Lee Harvey Oswalds in the FBI file. The Warren Report does not mention the CIA warnings, which were committed to the National Archives.

The CIA rushed the photograph of the "American male" wearing a "dark jacket" to Hoover shortly after the assassination, believing it to be of the assassin. This photograph was shown to Marguerite Oswald, who later said it was Ruby. The Warren Report mentions this photograph and includes it in the Exhibits to illustrate that the photograph she believed to be of Ruby was in fact the unidentified "American male." After Hoover had received the photograph, there was no further mention of the existence of the "American male" and his activities.

Perhaps there was no need for Hoover to institute inquiries; the identity of the "American male" may have been known, although it has never been admitted. In any case, no apparent attempt was made to find him.

The Warren Commission had received from Richard Helms an affidavit that the photograph was "taken in Mexico City on October 4, 1963." Yet the Warren Report states that, according to a CIA affidavit of 7 August 1964 supplied to the Commission, the "dark jacket" photograph "was taken outside of the Continental United States during the period July 1, 1963 to November 23, 1963." This second affidavit giving the blanket period of five months—on any day of which the photograph might have been taken anywhere in the world—was the one included in the volumes of Testimony (VI.470), and obliterates from the record the earlier affidavit stating the precise place and date of the photograph, Mexico City and 4 October 1963. The first affidavit, also excluded from the Exhibits, was placed in the National Archives and only recently released.

On 23 or 24 November 1963, the CIA supplied to the Secret Service, who should have supplied them to the FBI, at least two further photographs of the "American male." These two photographs are larger and clearer than the first photograph reproduced in the Exhibits. They show a man of between 35 and 45 years of age with curly and apparently darkish hair, of powerful build, with no glasses, clean-shaven but this time attired in a white short-sleeved shirt. Under his left forearm and clasped to his side is a small bag or pouch, in his left hand he is holding what appears to be a wallet, and in his right hand he is holding what appears to be a passport-size booklet. The first of the two photographs shows him intently studying the "wallet" and the "passport," and the second shows him replacing one of the objects in the pouch. It was known to the Warren Commission that on the bus journey to Mexico City the assassin had an "overnight bag or pouch" on the rack above his head in which he carried the real Oswald's passport. The authorities also knew that the word POUCH appeared on an aide-mémoire taken from 'Oswald's' wallet by the New Orleans police after his arrest in connection with the street distribution of FPCC literature.

Neither the Warren Report nor the CIA have disclosed on what date these two "white shirt" photographs were taken. No pouch was found among the assassin's possessions after the assassination, and neither of the two "white shirt" photographs is referred to in the Warren Report or shown in the Exhibits; in 1975 the photographs were released from the National Archives.

As a result of the above obfuscation, the Warren Report states that only the real Lee Harvey Oswald visited the Soviet Embassy Consulate and spoke with either Kostikov or Yatskov, and only to ask about a visa for the Soviet Union.

2. EXPRESSIONS OF SORROW AND SYMPATHY RECEIVED FROM TOP COMMAND
~~THE BRITISH GOVERNMENT~~ AS WELL AS WORKING LEVEL. EFFECT IN U.K.
IS ONE OF PROFOUND SHOCK AND PUBLIC REACTION HERE SIMILAR TO DEATH
FRANKLIN ROOSEVELT.

3. DUE TO BACKGROUND MAN CHARGED WITH ASSASSINATION, _BRITISH_
REPORTED MORNING 23 NOV FOLLOWING DUE SOME SIMILAR PHONE CALLS OF
STRANGELY COINCIDENTAL NATURE PERSONS RECEIVED IN THIS COUNTRY OVER
PAST YEAR, PARTICULARLY IN CONNECTION WITH DR WARD CASE. _BRITISH_
REPORTED THAT AT 1805 GMT 22 NOV AN ANONYMOUS CALL WAS MADE IN
CAMBRIDGE, ENGLAND TO THE SENIOR REPORTER OF THE CAMBRIDGE NEWS
RPT CAMBRIDGE NEWS. THE CALLER SAID ONLY THAT THE REPORTER SHOULD
CALL THE AMERICAN EMBASSY IN LONDON FOR SOME BIG NEWS AND THEN
RANG OFF. LAST NIGHT AFTER WORD OF THE PRESIDENT'S DEATH WAS
RECEIVED THE REPORTER INFORMED THE CAMBRIDGE POLICE OF THE ABOVE
CALL AND THE POLICE INFORMED _BRITISH_ IMPORTANT THING IS THAT CALL
WAS MADE, ACCORDING _BRITISH_ CALCULATIONS, ABOUT TWENTY FIVE MINUTES
23 NOV 63
BEFORE PRESIDENT WAS SHOT. CAMBRIDGE REPORTER HAD NEVER RECEIVED
CALL OF THIS KIND BEFORE A J _BRITISH_ SAY HE IS KNOWN   THEM AS SOUND
AND LOYAL PERSON WITH NO SECURITY RECORD. _BRITISH_ WANTED ABOVE
REPORTED PARTICULARLY IN VIEW REPORTED SOV BACKGROUND OSWALD.
DEPENDING ON CIRCUMSTANCES, HQS MAY WISH PASS ABOVE TO _FBI_ AS
BRITISH COULD NOT REACH _FBI_ REP THIS MORNING. _BRITISH_ STAND READY
ASSIST IN ANY WAY POSSIBLE ON INVESTIGATIONS HERE.

23 November 1963. CIA telegram, London to Washington. Reproduced
here as released by CIA with security omissions and insertions. Note
reference to Dr. (Stephen) Ward who had committed suicide four
months earlier.

'Oswald's' letter to the Soviet Embassy in Washington.

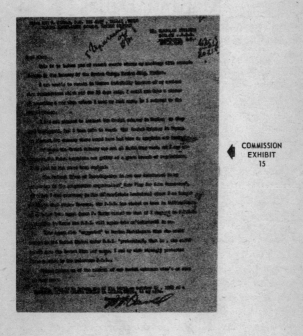

COMMISSION
EXHIBIT
15

Letter making reference to " 'Oswald's' plans" is reproduced legibly
in the Warren Exhibits measuring 7.3" x 5.2" (XVI.33). In the Report
itself the letter is reduced as above to 3.1" x 2.2" (R.311) making it
difficult to decipher.

F

Maps of Dallas

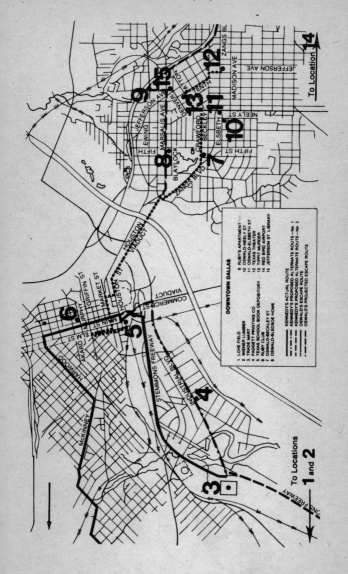

DOWNTOWN DALLAS

1. LOVE FIELD
2. WIENER LUMBER
3. TRADE MART
4. JOBBETT PRINTING CO.
5. TEXAS SCHOOL BOOK DEPOSITORY
6. RUBY CLUB
7. OSWALD-BECKLEY ST
8. OSWALD-BLEDSOE HOME
9. RUBY'S APARTMENT
10. OSWALD-NEELY ST
11. OSWALD-ELSBETH ST
12. TEXAS THEATER
13. TIPPIT MURDER
14. RED BIRD AIRPORT
15. JEFFERSON ST LIBRARY

KENNEDY'S ACTUAL ROUTE
KENNEDY'S PROPOSED ALTERNATE ROUTE—No 1
KENNEDY'S PROPOSED ALTERNATE ROUTE—No 2
OSWALD'S ESCAPE ROUTE
OSWALD'S PROJECTED ESCAPE ROUTE

To Locations 1 and 2

To Location 14

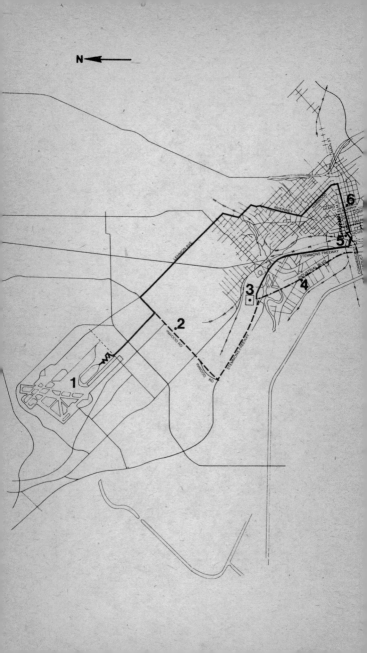

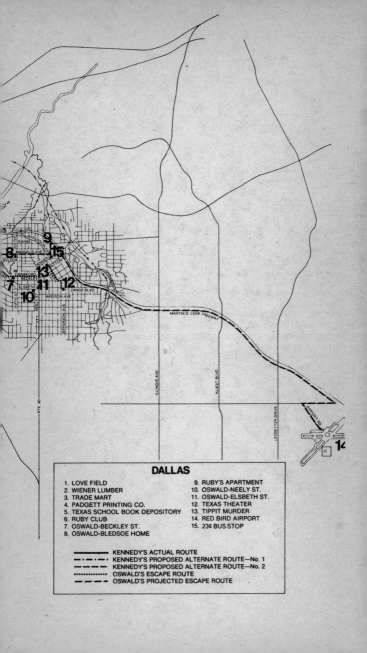

DALLAS

1. LOVE FIELD
2. WIENER LUMBER
3. TRADE MART
4. PADGETT PRINTING CO.
5. TEXAS SCHOOL BOOK DEPOSITORY
6. RUBY CLUB
7. OSWALD-BECKLEY ST.
8. OSWALD-BLEDSOE HOME
9. RUBY'S APARTMENT
10. OSWALD-NEELY ST.
11. OSWALD-ELSBETH ST.
12. TEXAS THEATER
13. TIPPIT MURDER
14. RED BIRD AIRPORT
15. 23¢ BUS STOP

——————— KENNEDY'S ACTUAL ROUTE
—·—·—·— KENNEDY'S PROPOSED ALTERNATE ROUTE—No. 1
— — — — KENNEDY'S PROPOSED ALTERNATE ROUTE—No. 2
·············· OSWALD'S ESCAPE ROUTE
– – – – OSWALD'S PROJECTED ESCAPE ROUTE

Albert Schweitzer College (Switzerland), 16, 17, 154

Alek, 28, 68

Alekseevna, Natalie, 68

Alexander (Dallas assistant district attorney), 114

"American male," 68, 69, 112

Amos, Ada, 66, 67

Army Map Service, 'Oswald' works for, 49, 50, 51, 107

Askenov, Nicholay, 31

Autopsy of 'Oswald'
scars and mastoidectomy, 132-133
discrepancies, 134-135

Ayers, Lt., 17

Baker, Lt., 106

Baker, Marrion, 90, 93

Barnes (Dallas police officer), 104, 143

Bates, Pauline, 38, 39, 81

Bay of Pigs invasion, 179, 180

Belmont, Alan H., 153, 157-158
testimony of, regarding connection of Oswald and Ruby, 157-158

Beria, Lavrenti, 3

Berlin crisis of 1961, 4-5

Bledsoe, Mary, 41-42, 73, 75
on bus ride with Oswald after assassination, 92-93, 94

Bogard, Albert, 78

Boggs, H., 9

Bowen, Jack Leslie (alias for John Caesar Grossi), 52, 67

Bowen, John Howard (alias for Albert Osborne), 64-65, 67

Brennan, Howard, 89-90

Brown, Arnold, 43

Bulganin, N. A., 3

Carr, Waggoner, 103, 109-110, 114

Carter, Tom, 40, 134, 150, 155
in June 1962 Ft. Worth interview with 'Oswald,' 40-41

Castro, Fidel, 3, 8, 57, 60, 62, 64
plan to implicate Castro in Kennedy assassination, 54
question of involvement in the assassination, 160
Rusk denies motive for assassination, 167-169

Castro, Raúl, 5

Cheek, Bertha, 84, 124

CIA (Central Intelligence Agency), 4
information of Soviet emigration, 33
'Oswald's' contact with Soviets and Cubans in Mexico City and, 151-153, 155, 164-165

Cieplinski, Michel, 32

Clements, Manning, 100, 134

Comacho, Maximo, 178

Connally, John, 87-88

Cooper, John Sherman, 9

Cover-up of the assassination
CIA denial of conspiracy, 163-165
FBI handling of investigation and, 146-163
first steps in, 99
pressure to conceal Russian conspiracy, 102-103, 112-114
Rusk denial of conspiracy, 166-169

Crafard, Larry, 123-124, 126-128

Cuba, 181
    attempt to implicate in Kennedy assassination, 54, 56-62
    'Oswald's' contact with Cuban officials in Mexico City, 68
    Ruby's activities in, 122-123
Cuban Missile Crisis, 5-7
Cuban Student Directorate, 60
Cunningham, Helen, 48, 49, 50
Curry (Dallas police chief), 100, 107, 110-111
    testimony regarding assassination, 110-111

"Dallas Triangle" conspiracy involved in assassination, 186-187
Davis, Benjamin, 118
Delgado, Nelson, 17, 18, 67
De Mohrenschildt, George, 11, 52-53
    acquaintance of 'Oswald,' 44-47
    as agent involved in conspiracy, 173, 186
    depression and apparent suicide of, 184-185
    'Oswald's' political views and, 183
    personality of, 173-174
    possible espionage activities of, 172-173, 175-180
    relationship of, with 'Oswald,' 173, 174, 182-184, 185-187
    talks with journalist Oltmans, 184-186
    testimony of, 177-184
De Mohrenschildt, Jeanne (LeGon), 52, 172, 179
    acquaintance of 'Oswald,' 44-45
    involved in "Dallas Triangle," 186
    testimony of, 178, 181-182
Dillon, C. Douglas, 146, 165-166
Dockery, Karl, 132-133
Dulles, Allen W., 9, 51

Fain, John, 150, 155
    in August 1962 FBI interview with 'Oswald,' 43-44
    in June 1962 FBI interview with 'Oswald,' 40-41
Fair Play for Cuba Committee (FPCC), 64, 76, 80, 81, 85
    FBI concern about, 149
    'Oswald's' association with, 57-62
FBI (Federal Bureau of Investigation)
    acceptance of 'Oswald's' identity upon his return from Russia, 36-38
    Dallas office information on 'Oswald,' 77-78, 80
    disciplining of employees involved in assassination investigation, 147
    Ft. Worth interview with 'Oswald' in August 1962, 43-44
    Ft. Worth interview with 'Oswald' in June 1962, 40-41
    handling of assassination investigation, questions concerning cover-up activities, 146-165
    identity of two 'Oswalds' and, 62
    involvement with Ruby, 121-122
    list of contents of 'Oswald's' wallet, 100-102
    New Orleans interview with 'Oswald,' 61, 150-153
    'Oswald' directs attention to FPCC, 60-61
    'Oswald' fingerprint records switched by KGB, 140-145
    questions regarding 'Oswald' autopsy, 135, 136
Featherstone, Emily, 67, 83
Fehrenbach, George, 130-131
Fingerprint question, 137-145
    FBI records possibly switched, 140-142
    list of existing Oswald fingerprints, 138
Fonzi, Gaeton, 185
Ford, Gerald R., 9
Frazier, Wesley, 74, 85, 86
Fritz (Dallas police captain), 99, 104, 106, 107-108, 110, 115
    interrogation of Oswald, 112-113, 117
    interrogation of Ruby, 113

Goldberg, Abraham, 23-24
Golitsin, Anatoli, 4
Graef, John, 48-50, 52
Gregory, Paul, 39, 40, 43
Gregory, Peter, 39-40
Grossi, John Caesar (used alias Jack Leslie Bowen), 52, 67, 101, 112, 150
GRU (Soviet military intelligence), 3, 5, 7, 9
Guevara, Ernesto "Che," 5

Hall, Gus, 118
Heindel (marine), 57-58
Helms, Richard M., testimony concerning 'Oswald's' Soviet connections, 146, 163-165
Hickey, Edward J., 30, 139, 169
Hicks, J. B., 104
Hidell, Alek James (alias used by 'Oswald') 53, 57, 58, 61, 85, 92, 100, 101, 112, 116, 118

Hoover, J. Edgar, 80, 103, 106, 135, 139
  comments on "unimportant" role of Ruby, 161
  conspiracy denied by, 158-165
  file on Oswald, 102
  role of, in investigation and cover-up of the conspiracy, 146-165
  testimony of, on Oswald in Russia, 26-27
  warning of impostor 'Oswald' in 1960, 28
Hosty, James P., 76-80, 81, 85
  'Oswald' letter destroyed by, 163

Immigration and Naturalization Service, 'Oswald's' return to U.S. and, 31-32
Ivanov, Yevgenni, ix

Jaffe, Sam, 131
Jaggars-Chiles-Stovall, 46, 53, 61, 76, 106
  'Oswald' employed at, 48-52, 67, 173
John Birch Society, 130
Johnson, Lyndon Baines, 1, 54, 82, 83, 99
  on day of assassination, 95, 102, 103
  problem of dealing with Soviet Union after assassination, 2
  Warren Commission and, 9-10
Johnson, Priscilla, interview with 'Oswald' in Moscow, 24-25, 139

Kaack, Milton R., 150, 151, 156
Kaganovich, C. M., 3
Kennedy, Jacqueline, 109
Kennedy, John F.
  Cuban Missile Crisis and, 6, 7
  death of, 95
  policy of, toward Soviet Union, 4-5
  visit to Dallas, November 1963
  assassination during motorcade, 88-89
KBG (Soviet state security apparatus), 3, 4, 8, 22, 38, 81, 139, 186
  agents of, in Mexico City, 68, 69
  Department 13 of, 2
  Oswald fingerprint files in FBI switched by, 140-144
  Oswald's "diary" and, 20-21
  possible connection of, with Ruby, 130
  responsibility for emigration from Soviet Union, 33
Khrushchev, Nikita, 3, 4, 45, 167
  Cuban Missile Crisis and, 7
  deposed in 1964, 3

intention to launch missile attack against U.S., 5
  rise to power of, 3
Knight (Dallas police officer), 106
Komsomol, 131
Kostikov, Valeri Vladimirovich, 68-69, 152, 156
Kostin, Valeri Dmitrevich, 69, 79, 156-157

Latham, Louise, 48, 49, 50
Latona, Sebastian, testimony regarding Oswald fingerprints, 140-144
Lee, Harvey Oswald (alias used by 'Oswald'), 63, 67
Lee, O. H. (alias used by 'Oswald'), 75
Lee, Vincent T., 118
LeGon, Jeanne. See Jeanne De Mohrenschildt
LeGon, Robert, 179
Leslie Welding Co., 43, 46, 61
Lonsdale, Gordon, 9
Lyalin, Oleg, 69

McCloy, John J., 9
McCone, John A., 146
  testimony concerning 'Oswald's' Soviet connections, 163-165
McFarland, Mr. and Mrs. John, 64
McFarland, Georgi, 3
Malenkov, Georgi, 3
Martello (New Orleans police officer), 165
Meller, Anna, 48
Melody, Koron, 7, 8
Mexico City, 'Oswald's' 1963 trip to
  applies for visa to visit Cuba, 67-68
  arrival, 67
  bus trip en route, 63-66
  FBI and CIA investigations concerning 'Oswald's' contacts with Soviet officials in, 151-157, 160-161, 164-167
  letter concerning, 82
  purpose of trip, 68
  return to U.S., 70
  Rusk denies importance of 'Oswald' contacts in, 168
  surrogate visits Soviet Embassy, 68-69
Molotov, V. M., 3
Mosby, Aline, interview with 'Oswald' in Moscow, 24, 36, 139
Mumford, Pamela, 64
Murret, Gene, 58
Murret, Lillian, 56
MVD (Soviet secret police), 1, 3, 8

New Orleans, 'Oswald' lives in, in 1963
  applies for new passport, 58
  arrested in "scuffle," 60
  arrival, 56
  contact and activity with Fair Play for Cuba
    Committee, 57, 59, 60-62
  post office box established, 57
  radio broadcast defending Cuba, 62
Nixon, Richard, 8
  Soviet plan to assassinate, 3-4
Nosenko, Yuri, 20, 160

Oltmans, Willem, interviews with De
  Mohrenschildt, 184-186
Osborne, Albert (used alias John Howard
  Bowen), 57, 150
  accompanying 'Oswald' on Mexico City
    trip, 64-67
  after Mexico City trip, 70
  background of, 67-68
  trip to Britain in November 1963, 69
Osborne, Lee (alias of 'Oswald'), 57
Oswald, Audrey Marina Rachel (daughter of
  'Oswald'), 76, 80, 82
Oswald, June Lee (daughter of 'Oswald'), 34
Oswald, Lee Harvey
  defects to Soviet Union, 18
  dependency discharge from Marines, 17
  "diary" not written by Oswald, 20
  disciplinary problems in Marines, 16
  enlistment in Marines, 15
  interest of, in Soviet Union, 15
  in Moscow, exchanged for impostor, 21-22
  psychology and motives of, 10-11
  reading habits of, 15
  skill as a rifleman, 15
  support for his mother, 19
  talks of going to Cuba, 18-19
  Warren Report conclusions about, 10
  writes to Socialist Party at age 17, 15
'Oswald' (designation for the impostor substituted for Lee Harvey Oswald in the Soviet
  Union)
  accepted by Marguerite and Robert upon his
    return from Soviet Union, 37-38
  activities paralleling Ruby, 121-123
  apparent assassination attempt on Gen.
    Walker, 53-54
  arrives in U.S. in 1962, 35
  burial of, 135-136
  choice of Texas School Book Depository
    site by, 89

in Dallas
  contact with FBI, 78
  days just prior to assassination, 84-85
  incident at car lot, 78-79
  in rooming house, 73-74, 76
on day of assassination, 58-95
  arrest, 94
  escape from scene of crime, 90-92
  killing of officer Tippit, 93, 112
dual identity problem, 62, 117-118
employed at Jaggars-Chiles-Stovall, 48-52
employed at Leslie Welding, 44, 48
employed at Texas School Book Depository,
  74
espionage activities in 1962, 51-52
interviewed by FBI in Ft. Worth in 1962,
  40-44
letter to Soviet Embassy in November
  1963, 79-83
marital relationship strained, 46-47
Mexico City trip in 1963
  application for visa to visit Cuba, 68
  arrival, 67
  bus trip enroute, 63-67
  FBI and CIA investigations concerning
    contacts with Soviet officials in Mexico
    City, 151-157, 160, 161, 164-167
  letter concerning, 82-83
  purpose of trip, 68
  return to U.S., 70
  Rusk denies importance of Soviet contacts,
    167-168
  surrogate visits Soviet Embassy, 68-69
in New Orleans in 1963, establishing the
  "Cuban connection"
  applies for new passport, 58
  arrested in "scuffle," 60
  arrival, 56
  contact and activity with Fair Play for
    Cuba Committee, 57-58, 59-62
  FBI interview, 61, 149-151
  radio broadcasting defending Cuba, 62
"photographs" of, charged as montages,
  117-119
in police custody after assassination
  fingerprinting, 104-106
  interrogation, 99, 107-108, 112-113
  line up, 112
  murder of, 108-109
  transfer attempted, 107-108
prepares story on activities in Soviet Union,
  38-39

question of height of, 43-44, 56, 154-155
in the Soviet Union
  attempted suicide, 21
  at Botkin Hospital, 21-22
  contact of, with American journalists in
    Moscow, 23-25, 139
  impostor replaces the real Oswald, 22
  marriage to Marina Prusakova, 30
  meets Marina Prusakova, 28-29
  in Minsk Clinical Hospital, 29
  not granted Soviet citizenship, 26
  renounces U.S. citizenship, 22-23
  requests permission to leave Soviet Union,
    28
  sources for information about, 20
Oswald, Marguerite S. (mother), 17, 18, 19,
  27-28, 34, 37, 38, 100, 107, 117, 118
accepts 'Oswald' upon his return, 36
correspondence with 'Oswald' after his marriage, 30
in custody of Secret Service after assassination, 119
Hoover's comments on, 161-162
interviewed by FBI in 1960, 27
Oswald, Marina Prusakova (wife of 'Oswald'),
  20
activities of, in 1959 to 1961 paralleling Oswald, 28-30
arrives in U.S. in 1962, 35-36
character of, according to De Mohrenschildt,
  45-46
corresponds with Soviet officials in U.S. in
  1963, 59-60
in custody of Secret Service after assassination, 118-119
in days just prior to assassination, 83-86
first daughter born to, 34
goes to New Orleans, 56
Hoover's comments about, 161-163
living with Ruth Paine, 74-80, 84-86
marital problems with 'Oswald,' 46-47
marriage to 'Oswald,' 30
meets 'Oswald' in Minsk, 28
obtains entry to the U.S., 31-33, 34
photographs of 'Oswald' taken by, 117-118
second child born to, 63, 76
testimony concerning 'Oswald's' attempted
  assassination of Gen. Walker, 53-54
Oswald, Robert (brother), 23, 40, 42, 107,
  117, 118
accepts 'Oswald' upon his return to U.S.,
  35-38

on the burial of 'Oswald,' 136
correspondence with 'Oswald' after his marriage, 30
interviewed by FBI in 1960, 27

Paine, Ruth
friendship of, with Marina Oswald, 53, 54-
  55, 56, 59, 60, 63, 72, 73, 79, 82
helps 'Oswald' obtain employment at Texas
  School Book Depository, 74-75
Marina Oswald lives with, in 1963, 75, 76-
  78, 84, 85
Pardo, Lilia, 177
Penkovsky, Oleg, 5-6, 7
Pic, John, 37-38
Profumo, John, x
Prusakov, Colonel, 29, 31, 34

Quigley, John, New Orleans FBI interview
  with Oswald, 61, 62, 150, 151

Rackmann, Perec (alias Peter Rackman), x
Randle, Linnie, 74
Randle, J. Lee, 74
Rankin, J. Lee, 9, 148, 153
  questions about FBI investigation, 150-156
Reznichenko (Soviet consul), 59, 60, 79, 81-82,
  112
Roberts, Dorothy, 74-75
Roberts, Earlene, 85, 124
Robinson, Robert H., 32
Rose, Earl Forrest, autopsy of 'Oswald' and,
  132-136
Rose, Guy, 116
Rossi (friend of Jack Ruby), 125
Ruby, Jack, 1, 75, 76, 77, 84, 93, 104, 105,
  106
activities paralleling 'Oswald,' 121-122
activities prior to killing 'Oswald,' 108-109,
  125-127
circumstantial evidence linking to assassination, 123-127
connection with 'Oswald' denied by FBI,
  157, 159-160
on day of Kennedy assassination, 94
interrogation of, 113
involved in "Dallas Triangle" conspiracy,
  186-187
involvement of, with FBI, 121-122
murder of 'Oswald' by, 108-109
possible involvement of, with KGB, 130-131

role of, in escape plan for Kennedy assassin, 128-129
underworld connections of, 109, 130
Warren Report conclusions concerning, 10-11
Rusk, Dean, 30-31, 139, 146
conspiracy in assassination denied by, 166-169
Russell, Richard B., 9

Secret Service
conspiracy in assassination denied by, 165-166
treatment of 'Oswald's' family by, 118-119
Senator, George, 123-126, 127-128, 130
Serov, Ivan, 7
Shapkin, G. M., 59-60
Shepilov, D. T., 3
Shitov, Aleksandr I. (alias Aleksandr I. Alekseev), 67-68
SIS (British intelligence service), 5
Soviet Union
basic plot for assassination, 8-9
contact by 'Oswald' with Soviet officials in Mexico City, 68-70, 151-157, 160, 164-166
letter from 'Oswald' to Soviet Embassy in November 1963, 79-83
motive for assassination, 2, 7
'Oswald's' activities in
attempted suicide, 21-22
at Botkin Hospital, 21-22
contact of 'Oswald' with American journalists, 23-25, 139
impostor replaces real Oswald, 22
marriage of 'Oswald' to Marina Prusakova, 30
meets Marina Prusakova, 28
in Minsk Clinical Hospital, 29
not granted Soviet citizenship, 26
renounces U.S. citizenship, 22-23
requests permission to leave Soviet Union, 28
sources for information about, 20
political events leading to assassination plot, 3-4
pressure in U.S. to conceal Soviet involvement in conspiracy, 102, 111-115
tension of, with Kennedy and Cuban Missile Crisis, 6-7
Stalin, Iosip, 3

State Department, Marina Oswald's entry into U.S. and, 32-33
Stewart, Sidney, 132, 135, 136
Stovall, Robert, 49
Stuckey, William, 62, 132, 135, 136, 183

Taylor, Gary, 46
testimony on De Mohrenschildts, 173-176
Texas School Book Depository building, 60, 76, 88
chosen by 'Oswald,' 89
'Oswald' obtains employment at, 72-75
Texas Employment Commission, 50, 74
aid in obtaining employment for 'Oswald,' 48-49
Tippit, J. D., 'Oswald' kills, 93, 94, 99, 102, 107, 110, 112
Travelers Aid Society in New York, 35
Truly, Roy, 75
Turku, University of (Finland), 16, 17

U-2, 5, 50

Wade, Henry, 37, 103, 105-106
on arrest of 'Oswald,' 113-115
Jack Ruby talks with, 110, 126
Walker, Edwin, attempted assassination of, 53-55, 86, 116
Ward, Stephen, ix, 12
Warren, Earl, 9, 10, 109-110, 166
Warren, Sgt., 106
Warren Commission and Report
Belmont testimony to, 157-158
conclusions on Ruby, 10-11
De Mohrenschildts' testimony to, 177-184
fingerprint issue investigated by, 140-145
Hoover's testimony and communications to, 148-163
importance of first FBI interview with 'Oswald,' 41
Latona testimony to, 140-142
letter from 'Oswald' to Soviet Embassy and, 82
McCone and Helms testimony to, 163-165
Marina Oswald's testimony to, 51
omissions from, 146, 147
on Osborne, 65-67
postmortem report not mentioned in, 136
report issued by, 10-11
Rusk testimony to, 166-169
staff and basic operation of, 9-10

Taylor testimony to, 173-176
Weissman, Bernard, 125, 126
Whittam (British surgeon), 133
Wiener Lumber Co., 75
William B. Reily Co., 56
Wilson, Eugene, 78

Winston, Patricia, 64
Wynne, Greville, 5, 7, 9

Yatskov, Paul Antonovich, 68, 69, 157

Zhukov, G. V., 3

About the Author

The eminent British solicitor Michael Eddowes, born to a family of lawyers, has had a lifelong fascination with the workings of the law and the administration of justice. An investigator of unparalleled persistence, he has devoted his talents and attention over the past twenty-five years exclusively to two cases.

The first is the case of the young laborer Timothy Evans, who, although pleading innocence, was charged with the murder of his wife and infant daughter and hanged in 1950. After the mass murderer Reginald Christie confessed to one of these murders, Eddowes began his long study and found that the "esoteric art of omission" had falsified the government report. He wrote *The Man on Your Conscience*, setting forth the facts, this resulting in public pressure for review. The government transcript of the trial was made public and a new investigation was called. Timothy Evans was subsequently exonerated and posthumously pardoned by the Queen, an event without precedence in English history. The outcry over the Evans case was one of the major factors leading to the abolition of capital punishment.

In concluding this work, Michael Eddowes' help was sought in connection with other cases, but he was unwilling to undertake another long legal battle unless it was a matter he considered to be of supreme importance. Such a matter tragically presented itself in November 1963 with the assassination of President Kennedy. Eddowes' investigation has taken fourteen years, and, as in the Evans case, when studying government records, he has encountered "the esoteric art of omission." Throughout, he has steadfastly followed the evidence wherever it has led. Time after time, events that his research has led him to anticipate have in fact occurred, the most recent of which is the suicide of George De Mohrenschildt. Michael Eddowes's extraordinary knowledge of the facts surrounding the assassination make him one of the world's experts on the subject.

There are a lot more
where this one came from!

ORDER your FREE catalog of ACE paperbacks here. We have hundreds of inexpensive
books where this one came from priced from
75¢ to $2.50. Now you can read all the books
you have always wanted to at tremendous
savings. Order your *free* catalog of ACE
paperbacks now.

ACE BOOKS ● Box 576, Times Square Station ● New York, N.Y. 10036